W9-BWI-846

THE BARRISTERS OF TOULOUSE

THE JOHNS HOPKINS UNIVERSITY STUDIES IN HISTORICAL AND POLITICAL SCIENCE

NINETY-THIRD SERIES (1975)

1. The Barristers of Toulouse in the Eighteenth
Century (1740-1793)
BY LENARD R. BERLANSTEIN

2. Western River Transportation:
The Era of Early Internal Development, 1810-1860
BY ERIK F. HAITES,
JAMES MAK, AND GARY M. WALTON

LENARD R. BERLANSTEIN

THE BARRISTERS
OF TOULOUSE
IN THE
EIGHTEENTH CENTURY
(1740–1793)

THE JOHNS HOPKINS UNIVERSITY PRESS
BALTIMORE AND LONDON

This book has been brought to publication
with the generous assistance of the
Andrew W. Mellon Foundation.

Manufactured in the United States of America.

The Johns Hopkins University Press, Baltimore, Maryland 21218
The Johns Hopkins University Press Ltd., London

Library of Congress Catalog Card Number 75-9784
ISBN 0-8018-1582-7

Library of Congress Cataloging in Publication data
will be found on the last printed page of this book.

1-19-79

TO MY PARENTS

CONTENTS

TABLES

FIGURES

ABBREVIATIONS

A.D.   Archives Départementales de la Haute-Garonne
A.M.   Archives Municipales, Toulouse
B.M.T.   Bibliothèque Municipale, Toulouse
D.E.S.   Diplôme des études supérieures

PREFACE

The outstanding achievement of recent French historiography has been the vast extension of our knowledge about the popular social groups, both urban and rural. The methods developed to accomplish this—case study, quantification, and interdisciplinary analysis—have been applied fruitfully to the study of the aristocracy as well. However, the careful examination of the middling social categories, which Professor Labrousse proposed over twenty years ago, has yet to materialize. To be sure, historians like Alfred Cobban and George V. Taylor have advanced important and challenging theses about the values, goals, and interests of propertied commoners in 1789; but their stimulating ideas demand further research and amplification.

A case study of eighteenth-century barristers (*avocats*) seemed particularly appropriate in this regard. The barristers were strategically positioned to express both the aspirations and the discontents of their milieu. Moreover, they were incumbents of many significant social roles: lawyer, commoner, landlord, social climber, social critic, local notable, and revolutionary officer, to name but a few. I have endeavored to explore the major social, cultural, and political movements of the century as they impinged on the nearly 300 Toulousan barristers. All too frequently, lack of documents or of personal knowledge restricted the examination of certain areas. I was especially troubled by the absence of documents relating to the advocates' professional lives; and to claim that the Toulousan barristers were necessarily "typical" of their entire profession or social stratum would involve more speculation than fact at this point (though there is no prima facie reason to consider them an aberrant case). My hope, despite these limitations, is that the reader might gain some useful insights into the structure and functioning of Old Regime society by examining it from the vantage point of the Toulousan bar.

This study has benefited from the kindness and expertise of many people. In Toulouse, professors Jacques Godechot and Jean Sentou were most generous with their time and advice; I am accordingly grateful to them. So, too, do I thank numerous friends and colleagues for reading parts of the manuscript: Josef Barton, Cissie Fairchilds,

Richard Kagan, H. C. Erik Midelfort, and Hans Schmitt. Jack R. Censer and James Hoopes were constant sources of encouragement and advice. The editorial staff of The Johns Hopkins University Press deserves a special acknowledgment for making innumerable improvements in the text. I wish to express my deep gratitude to Orest Ranum and George V. Taylor for reading the entire work and offering many insightful suggestions. Above all, I thank Robert Forster for his untiring and unerring guidance in all stages of this work.

Charlottesville, Virginia
October 1974

I

THE PROFESSIONAL LIFE
OF THE BARRISTERS

TOULOUSE—THE LEGAL CITY

L egal institutions determined the pace and tone of life in eighteenth-century Toulouse, so the city assumed a new sense of animation each year after November 12, Saint Martin's Day. This date marked the annual convocation of the Parlement, after which the city was busy handling the legal affairs of the huge province of Languedoc whose capital it was. Litigants came to Toulouse in very large numbers, on foot, by coach, or by sedan. Everyone, from the sharecropper to "Monsieur," the king's brother,[1] brought cases to the bar of Toulouse. The courts in this proud capital were numerous, and anyone who contested a will, attempted to collect a debt, or defended himself against criminal accusations might well have found himself called before a Toulousan magistrate.

This renewed flow of litigants was supplemented by the arrival of nearly 400 law students.[2] Toulouse was the home of the most important law faculty in the Midi. Some revered legal scholars, Cujas in particular, had lectured there and endowed it with much prestige. That academic standards had become scandalously low by the late eighteenth century did not diminish the éclat of a degree from the Law Faculty of Toulouse.[3] On the contrary, low standards probably encouraged more students to matriculate.

[1]Toward the end of the Old Regime, the barrister Jamme defended some property belonging to the count of Artois at the Parlement. Tragans, "Eloge de M. Jamme," *Recueil de l'Académie des Jeux Floraux*, 1819, p. 36.

[2]Animé Rodière, "L'enseignement du droit à la Faculté de droit de Toulouse," *Recueil de législation* 15 (1866): 223.

[3]On the poor quality of legal education, see Charles Jourdain, "L'Université de Toulouse au dix-septième siècle," *Revue des sociétés savantes des départements* 8 (1862): 314-35, 406-35; Jean Donat, "L'Université de Toulouse et les Etats Généraux," *Annales du midi* 49 (1937): 294. For legal education in general, see Baron Francis Delbèke, *L'action politique et sociale des avocats au XVIIIe siècle* (Paris and Louvain, 1927), chap. 2.

With its tribunals and law school, Toulouse was the legal city par excellence. In one corner of the city stood the Palace of the august Parlement. This was the second Sovereign Court of the kingdom in age and extent of jurisdiction, the court of last resort for an immense area encompassing fourteen present-day departments. The Parlement received cases on appeal from fifteen seneschal-*présidial* courts, ten seneschal courts, and thirty-one royal jurisdictions.[4] Near another end of Toulouse stood the University, whose heart was the Law Faculty. Between the Parlement and the University were the numerous tribunals which, though far humbler than the Parlement, were nonetheless active. These included the Seneschal-*Présidial* Court of Toulouse, the Mastery of Waters and Forests, the Salt-Tax Court (*Grenier à sel*), the Court of Coinage (*Cour des Monnaies*), the Municipal Tribunal, the Merchants' Court (*Bourse des Marchands*), the Bureau of Finances, and numerous others. The judicial institutions of Languedoc were heavily concentrated in Toulouse;[5] they gave the city its profound sense of being a capital.

No great commercial center, Toulouse depended on its courts and university to animate its economic life. Litigants traveling to the city required lodging, food, drink, paper, pens, and innumerable other items. So did the students who, by the end of the Old Regime, were coming in such large numbers. It was thus understandable that in 1789 the aldermen (*capitouls*) of Toulouse viewed the possible suppression of the Parlement with apprehension, claiming that the city's "principal resources, its unique means of work and existence, were founded on the great current of strangers whom the pursuit of cases and studies attracted here."[6] Revolutionary administrators would seek unsuccessfully to create a textile industry in order to generate revenue formerly provided by the Parlement.[7]

If these secondary and incidental expenditures of the litigants were important to the Toulousan economy, so too were the sums spent directly upon the legal procedure. A myriad of people were attached to the courts by profession. There were over 140 magistrates in Toulouse, including the 100 at the Parlement. Nearly 300 barristers and 120 attorneys (*procureurs*) handled the cases of the parties. Many barristers had secretaries, and almost all attorneys had one or two clerks.[8] To

---

[4]Eugène Lapierre, *Le Parlement de Toulouse, son ressort, ses attributions, et ses archives* (Toulouse, 1869), pp. 8–9.

[5]The *Cour des aides* in Montauban and the *Cour des comptes* in Montpellier were exceptions, but both lacked the éclat of the Parlement.

[6]*A.M.*, AA–95, "Délibérations prises par le Conseil . . . le 26 novembre 1789," p. 10.

[7]Henri Causse, "Un industriel toulousain au temps de la Révolution et de l'Empire," *Annales du midi* 69 (1957): 121–33.

[8]For a study of these clerks and secretaries, see Maurice Gresset, "Les practiciens à Besançon au dernier siècle de l'ancien régime," *Annales de démographie historique*, 1970, pp. 231–36.

these must be added a substantial number of minor clerical officers working directly for the courts (*huissiers* and *greffiers*). The total number of functionaries attached to the courts may have approached 1,000 or more. When the wives, children, and servants of these men are considered, it is easy to imagine that nearly a tenth of the population of Toulouse was tied by function or family to the various tribunals.[9]

These legal functionaries constituted the dominant social groups of the city. The most outstanding commoners in terms of number, influence, and prestige were the judges, barristers, attorneys, and lesser court officials. The barristers alone were nearly as numerous as the important merchants, those of the *Grande Bourse*.[10] Court personnel heavily outnumbered merchants on all governing councils and administrative bodies of the city.

At the very pinnacle of Toulousan society were the magistrates of the Parlement. Indisputably the richest men in the city—more than ten times wealthier than the average commoner[11]—they served also as the cultural and political elite. These *parlementaires* were the "fathers of the people," from whom the populace expected paternalistic guidance.[12] When the Garonne River inundated the city, when a bad harvest raised bread prices, Toulousans looked to the parlementaires to deal with public disaster. The stern justice issuing from the Parlement was thought to be the bulwark of religion, morality, and order.[13] The magistrates of Toulouse, more than judges of other sovereign courts, enjoyed the reputation of being austere, learned, and upright.[14] It was a commonplace encouraged by the provincial resentment of the capital to compare the stern virtue of the Toulousan magistrates to the foppishness and immorality of Parisian aristocrats.

Since the Law Faculty and the courts had such a profound influence upon the economic and social structure of Toulouse, it is not surprising that the cultural life of the city had a strong legal foundation. Before the educated Toulousan read Voltaire he studied the *Digest*. The aristocratic salons buzzed with discussion of the most interesting cases; the man who could not talk of their legal implications with insight

[9]The population of Toulouse was about 52,000 in 1750 and 58,000 by 1790. See Jean Rives, "L'évolution démographique de Toulouse au XVIIIe siècle," *Bulletin d'histoire économique et sociale de la Révolution française* 10 (1968): 85–95.

[10]G. Marinière, "Les marchands d'étoffes de Toulouse à la fin du XVIIIe siècle," *Annales du midi* 70 (1958): 251.

[11]Jean Sentou, *Fortunes et groupes sociaux à Toulouse sous la Révolution* (Toulouse, 1969), p. 146.

[12]Edmond Lamouzèle, *Toulouse au XVIIIe siècle, d'après les 'Heures perdues' de Pierre Barthès* (Toulouse, 1914), p. 14. Even criminals spoke respectfully of the parlementaires. See Yves Castan, "Mentalitiés rurales et urbaines à la fin de l'ancien régime . . ." (Ph.D. diss., University of Toulouse, 1961), p. 42.

[13]See the manuscript diaries of Pierre Barthès, a minor legal clerk, *B.M.T.*, MSS. 704-6.

[14]Vicomte de Bastard d'Estang, *Du Parlement de Toulouse et de ses jurisconsultes* (Paris, 1854), p. 5.

was considered uncultivated.[15] Toulouse was the home of the oldest literary society in the world, the Academy of Floral Games, and the muse most honored by its poets was Themis.[16] The educated of Toulouse admired, above all else, the eloquence and the rhetorical skill displayed at the bar. They read Cicero with zeal as a model of eloquence and hoped to find a new Cicero at the bar of Toulouse. The appearance of a new talent was a source of pleasure to the magistrates.

The éclat of the magistrature, the reverence for legal knowledge, and the pomp of the court ceremony dazzled the minds of Toulousans and heightened the prestige of legal careers. Young men were avid for the respectability of a career in one of the courts, especially the Parlement, and their fathers shared their enthusiasm. Toulousans themselves claimed that the centuries of cultural domination by the Parlement and the university had turned the "genius" of the residents from commerce to law.[17] There was a general awareness that the legal institutions virtually determined the way of life in the city. It was probably of a provincial capital like Toulouse that the municipal officers of Lyon were thinking when they denounced all plans to establish a superior court or university in their city; they feared that this would undermine its commercial mentality.[18] In Toulouse these Lyonnais had an example of complete social domination by legal professions.

PROFESSIONAL FUNCTIONS OF BARRISTERS

There was much pride and satisfaction in being associated by profession with a court in Toulouse, but this honor was divided unequally among the various courts and occupational groups. The magistrates of the Parlement, so respected by the populace, enjoyed the greatest portion of this honor. Just below them, superior even to the judges of nonsovereign courts, were the *avocats* or barristers of Toulouse. These were the legal experts who pleaded and offered their university training and juridical knowledge to clients in need of counsel. All that Toulousans admired—profound legal learning, impressive displays of eloquence, honorable participation in the ceremonies of the Parlement, the trust and regard of important people —was attainable by barristers. Their opinions were sought by men at

[15]The local newspaper carried information about the latest cases, and the court personnel were requested to contribute articles about interesting cases. See *Affiches, annonces, et avis divers, ou Feuille hebdomadaire de Toulouse,* 4 janvier 1775.

[16]See the collection of prize-winning poems in the *Recueil de l'Académie des Jeux Floraux* (1750–1789).

[17]*Lettre des avocats au Parlement de Toulouse à Monseigneur le garde des sceaux* . . . (n.p., n.d.), p. 16.

[18]Louis Trénard, *Lyon, de l'Encyclopédie au préromantisme,* 2 vols. (Grenoble, 1958), 1: 59, 92.

all social levels, from magistrates to miserable criminals in need of defense. The most important barristers became well-known and highly respected figures.[19] After the successful defense of a widow, an orphan, or a pauper, the barrister's humanitarian concern might be celebrated in verse,[20] and when he handled a case involving socially prominent people, he could become the center of public attention.[21] The barrister was, without question, a key figure in the legal and social structure of Toulouse.

These barristers were a product of three years at a law faculty, where they acquired at least the *licence*. In Toulouse these years were occupied with lectures in civil law (the *Institutes*, the *Digest*) and French law (the royal ordinances and decrees).[22] Upon receiving their degrees, the prospective barristers could present themselves to the magistrates of a court and take the oath of their profession. After the oath, the young men had the right to entitle themselves "advocates at the court" in which they took the oath. Professionally, however, they were not yet fully advocates and were not considered ready to practice. A career as a practicing barrister required two years of attendance at court sessions and lectures given by leading advocates. During this period of apprenticeship, the young men were known as "listening barristers" and were expected to learn from their more experienced colleagues.[23] Whether every aspirant to the bar was more conscientious as a "listener" than he had been as a law student is debatable, but those who hoped for serious careers learned the basics of their vocation during these years. Their full admission to the profession came when their names were inscribed on the tables of their professional association, the Order of Barristers.

With this background, the barrister was the most highly trained and esteemed legal professional, but he did not handle a litigant's case alone, nor did the law define him as the "master" of the case. At all times the barrister was associated with a *procureur* or attorney, who was an officer of the court and his professional inferior. The attorney was not required to attend university but learned his work through apprenticeship. His role was to guide the case through all the proce-

---

[19]The local journal proclaimed that barrister Jerome Taverne died "with the esteem of the Court, the praise of the bar, and the confidence of the public." *Affiches, annonces, et avis* (17 mai 1775), p. 85.

[20]The poem "Epitre à M. le Cauchois," *Recueil de l'Académie des Jeux Floraux*, 1787, celebrates the defense of a poor girl by the barrister Jamme.

[21]When Jean Mascart pleaded a case involving the partition of the fortune of President d'Aspe, even the Intendant in Montpellier heard of it. *A.D.*, C–278, letter from Subdelegate Raynal to Intendant, 26 July 1766.

[22]Rodière, "L'enseignement du droit," p. 248.

[23]Alain Madrange, "Les avocats au Parlement de Toulouse de 1610 à 1715" (D.E.S., Faculty of Law of Toulouse, 1966), pp. 28–29. This work is based almost entirely on published materials and deals only with the barristers' professional life.

dural details, from inscribing it on the court dockets to accepting the final sentence.[24] The attorney was, by convention, the procedural expert, whereas the barrister was the legal expert. The barrister performed the most learned and intellectually demanding activities: pleading, instructing, consulting, and arbitrating. In practice, however, this segregation of activities broke down. Attorneys and all sorts of practitioners performed these four functions, too. But the barrister felt that they were distinctively and most properly his own. They embodied his professional ideals of erudition, eloquence, and independence. The barrister had a finely developed sense of the professional activities suitable to his status, and he left the "mechanical" ones to his inferiors.[25]

Because the barrister confined his interests to the learned, purely legal elements in a case, his services were sometimes superfluous. All parties had to engage an attorney whenever the court had one,[26] and the *procureur* was the first person to whom a litigant went with his case. For many suits, especially those in which facts rather than points of law were in dispute, his counsel alone sufficed. And, since the Parlement of Languedoc permitted the attorney to plead and instruct, the services of a barrister were necessary even less often.[27] Indeed, the court dockets indicate that many cases were heard without the presence of a barrister.[28] However, litigation involving sophisticated legal arguments did require the ministry of a barrister.

The barrister did not enter a case until these arguments were needed. The attorney instituted a civil suit before the Parlement by having it inscribed on the dockets.[29] He then procured from his client all documents bearing on the case and the papers from the lower courts if it was on appeal. The attorney deposited these papers with the office (*greffe*) of the court, and within the next three days he decided whether the arguments would be presented in oral or written form. Both procedures were practiced in the Parlement, with the choice depending on the nature of the case.[30] By this time, the attorney and client would

[24]Pierre Paquin, *Essai sur la profession d'avocat dans les duchés de Lorraine et de Bar au XVIIIe siècle* (Paris, 1961), pp. 105-09.

[25]See the memoirs of the Parisian barrister Pierre-Nicolas Berryer, *Souvenirs de M. Berryer*, 2 vols. (Paris, 1839), 1: 80. He refused to handle certain details even if there were no attorney conveniently near.

[26]Marc-Antoine Rodier, *Questions sur l'Ordonnance de Louis XIV relative aux usages des cours de Parlement et principalement celui de Toulouse* (Toulouse, 1769), p. 32.

[27]*A.D.*, E-1181, fol. 248, deliberations of Community of Attorneys.

[28]*A.D.*, B-registers of *audiences* for all chambers of the Parlement.

[29]For a more detailed description of civil procedure, see Paquin, *La profession d'avocat*, pp. 97-126; Madrange, "Les avocats," pp. 61-80.

[30]Jacques Gauret, *Stile universel de toutes les cours et jurisdictions du royaume pour l'instruction des matières civiles* (Paris, 1716), p. 171; Bastard-d'Estang, *Les Parlements de France. Essai historique*, 2 vols. (Paris, 1857), 1: 211-12.

have determined whether a barrister was necessary and which one would argue the case.

If the written procedure was selected, the barrister's work took the form of a brief, known as an *instruction*. He prepared it by studying the documents, meeting with the client, if possible, and searching for the laws that supported his argument.[31] In important disputes, many instructions, replies, and counter-replies were penned for each party before the termination of the case.[32] Once the opposing barristers had agreed to end the instruction, the case was out of their hands. A magistrate, called the reporter (*rapporteur*) studied the documents and briefs (together known as the *production*) and wrote an abstract of the arguments for his colleagues. The judges met, voted on the case, and the reporter wrote the decision.

In the written procedure, only the barrister's erudition was on display. The oral procedure, however, provided him an occasion to display his eloquence in pleading and to take part in the intricate pageantry of the court. On the day of the trial, the barrister rose early, for he had to attend six o'clock mass at the Parlement. The judicial sessions (*audiences*) began at seven, but only the minor cases were heard so early.[33] The barrister with more consequential matters to argue waited on the porch of the Great Chamber and consulted with his client and his attorney. The conscientious barrister, of course, prepared his plea in advance, though the less diligent ones might have had to compose it on the spot.

From the moment the barrister and attorney entered the chambers, their demeanor was precisely regulated by etiquette designed to maintain the dignity of their respective professions.[34] The barrister wore a black cloth robe with a black, square hat and hood (*chaperon*), and sat on a specially-designated bench behind the benches reserved for noblemen. As the time for pleading neared, he stepped to the bar with his head bared. The advocate waited for several invitations from the presiding judge to put on his hat, as a matter of courtesy, and then began his argument. He usually spoke from memory, though he might have notes and other necessary papers. The form of his plea was traditionally divided into several parts, proceeding from the *exordium*, in which basic legal questions were raised, to the refutation of the

---

[31]Armand-Gaston Camus, *Lettres sur la profession d'avocat, sur les études relatives à cette profession et sur la manière de l'exercer* (Paris, 1777), pp. 145–58.

[32]See the instructions by Jacob Londois, *Observations pour Dame Perimon . . . contre M. Benzech . . .* (Toulouse, n.d.), and *Réplique pour Dame Perimon* (Toulouse, n.d.). These were the last of six instructions.

[33]Madrange, "Les avocats," pp. 70–71. The barristers pleading the minor cases were called "advocates of seven o'clock."

[34]For the details of this ceremony, see Antoine-Gaspard Boucher d'Argis, *Règles pour former un avocat . . .* (Paris, 1778), pp. 134–42.

opponents' case. When the barrister read a document, he was careful to remove his hat, for this was the "mechanical" work that an attorney could do. But when he cited a law or ordinance, the barrister wore his hat, for he alone was the master of the law.

The attorney, in the meantime, stood behind the barrister and furnished him with the necessary documents and papers. Overall, the professional stature of the attorney had improved during the eighteenth century. Until 1697, attorneys at certain sovereign courts were required to kneel while the barrister pleaded and to speak only to the barrister, who then addressed the court.[35] The Parlement of Toulouse may never have relegated the attorneys to such a humiliating position, and in the eighteenth century the attorneys claimed to be the near equals to the barristers.[36] Undoubtedly, the barristers resented this claim, but there was little they could do about it.

At the end of his plea, the barrister returned to his seat and listened to his opponent's case. If the pleas had been informative enough, the magistrates would vote on the case at once. If not, the judges would request both parties to produce instructions solely for the elaboration of arguments already presented in the plea.[37] From this point on, the case followed the lines of the written procedure.

Of all the professional functions of the barrister, pleading was the most admired. It was at the bar that the advocate, expounding his legal insights and citing his authorities, gained the esteem of both magistrates and public.[38] The skillful pleader embellished his legal points with appropriate classical allusions and rhetorical devices to capture the interest of the judges. In a criminal case, the barrister often hoped to move the court to tears of sympathy for his innocent client. Erudition and eloquence at the bar could bring the barrister a fine reputation.

Not all barristers could plead, for many lacked the good memory, sonorous, powerful voice, and fecund imagination necessary for success. But even lacking these, a barrister could defend clients through the written procedure, and the "instructing barristers" devoted their careers completely to writing briefs. If the pleader withheld learned references for the sake of total rhetorical effect, the instructing advocate was expected to display the depths of his erudition through numerous citations of laws, canons, and authorities. In almost all important cases, briefs called *mémoires* were printed and circulated with the hope

[35]Bastard-d'Estang, *Parlements de France*, 1: 40; Jean Fournel, *Histoire des avocats au Parlement et du barreau de Paris*, 2 vols. (Paris, 1813), 2: 27.

[36]*A.D.*, E-1181, deliberations of Community of Attorneys (28 December 1754). ". . . Que lesdits procureurs sont confondus avec les avocats dans le barreau sans qu'il y ait aucun rang qui les distingue . . . ."

[37]Madrange, "Les avocats," pp. 79–81. This was called *assignation en droit*.

[38]The pleading was supposed to be addressed to the audience in the court chamber as much as to the judge.

of arousing public opinion in the client's favor.[39] These printed briefs brought the advocate to the attention of a circle much wider than the officers of the court. The most learned mémoires were collected in the libraries of advocates and magistrates.

If the barrister used his expertise to defend private interests through pleading and instructing, a third important function, arbitration, was a sort of public service. Parties who wished to avoid an open airing of their differences often sought a private, amicable settlement through arbitration.[40] This was a practice especially common in family quarrels. Disputing parties were not compelled by law to select barristers as arbiters,[41] but the fact that they almost always did so indicates the high level of public confidence that barristers enjoyed.[42] Only with a reputation for insight and impartiality could they have imposed a settlement as arbiters.

Consultation may have been the professional function barristers performed most frequently, and at its highest level, it was another public service of considerable importance and prestige. Barristers had no monopoly over the mundane matters of consultation: the proper way to compose a will, foreclose a mortgage, and so on. Toulousans could seek such advice from notaries, attorneys and a host of minor practitioners. But for the more abstruse legal problems, barristers were the final resort. In important cases, several barristers were consulted jointly, and their opinion had authoritative weight in a suit.[43] A few especially learned and scholarly barristers specialized in consultation, and distinguished pleaders often retired to this activity after a long and successful career in the court chambers. These "consulting barristers" were recognized as the leading legal minds of the city and region, and they were honored as such. Colleagues customarily called upon these revered colleagues for advice when working on a difficult case. Magistrates, too, sought their help for solutions to intricate legal questions. The Parlement rewarded them with special honorific privileges, and if a chamber ever lacked the required number of magistrates, a consulting barrister would temporarily sit on the *fleur-de-lys* bench.[44]

Consulting barristers served not only clients and colleagues but also the law itself, by helping the magistrates to preserve and interpret it. In this age before legal journals systematically collected judicial decisions, much of the jurisprudence of the Parlement would have been

[39]Camus, *Lettres*, pp. 150-51; Madrange, "Les avocats," p. 80.
[40]Camus, *Lettres*, pp. 157-59.
[41]Rodier, *Questions*, p. 425.
[42]See the arbitration reports for the second half of the century: *A.D.*, 3E 12731-12736.
[43]Carrière cited a consultation by his colleage Jouve in his mémoire, *Réflections pour le sieur Joseph Chapoulie* . . . (n.p., n.d.), p. 3. An example of a joint consultation is Jean Laviguerie et al., *Consultation pour Me Poirson* . . . . (n.p., n.d.).
[44]Boucher d'Argis, *Règles*, pp. 169-76. For Toulousan consultants with national reputations, see Animé Rodière, *Les grands jurisconsultes* (Toulouse, 1874), p. 379.

lost without the work of consulting barristers.[45] Their notes, printed opinions, and mémoires, informally collected and circulated, were an important supplement to the few major published collections of decisions.[46] Furthermore, barristers of the late eighteenth century began to serve the law in a new way, by editing and publishing the jurisprudence of the court.[47] They thus continued the work of the seventeenth-century *arrêtistes*, all of whom had been magistrates. Finally, consulting barristers exerted an important influence on the decisions themselves through their advice to the magistrates. Thorny legal questions were often put before them, so their opinions were incorporated into the jurisprudence of the Sovereign Court itself.

In performing his professional activities of pleading, instructing, arbitrating, and consulting, the barrister assumed a position of independence vis-à-vis the client, and he had no personal identity with the case. It was the attorney who directed the action step by step and who was defined by law as the "master of the case."[48] The attorney, not the barrister, signed all relevant papers presented to the courts, including the barrister's briefs.[49] Even in pleading, the barrister retained his independence: he spoke for the litigant but he did not *represent* the client symbolically or legally. If the attorney and his party were not present when the case was before the judges, the barrister was under no obligation to plead. The barrister took an oath to defend only just causes, and he could withdraw from a case at any time. Moreover, when the decision was finally rendered, the barrister returned all papers and documents concerning the affair to the attorney. This independence was a mark of the high status of the barrister's profession: he was an intermediary between the law and the public.

Conscientious barristers hoped to perform all of their honorable functions or to specialize in one of them. The extent to which they

[45]Raymond Benech, *De l'enseignement du droit français dans . . . l'ancienne Université de Toulouse* (Toulouse, 1847), p. 97.

[46]The major collections of the jurisprudence of the Parlement were by La Roche-Flavin, Cambolas, d'Olive, de Catellan, de Maynard, de Lestang, Vedal, and de Juin. Florentin Astre, *Les arrêtistes du Parlement de Toulouse* (Toulouse, 1856), p. 6. For a collection of briefs and memoirs that were eventually published in the nineteenth century, see Jean Laviguerie, *Arrêts inédits du Parlement de Toulouse*, 2 vols., (Toulouse, 1831). Laviguerie was a leading consultant.

[47]Jean-Antoine Soulatges issued a revised edition of the *Observations sur les questions notables du droit décidées par divers arrêts du Parlement de Toulouse* (Toulouse, 1784). The original was the work of Simon d'Olive, counselor in 1638. Another collection by a barrister was Aguier, *Recueil d'arrêts notables, ou Supplément au Journal du Palais de Toulouse*, 2 vols. (Nîmes, 1782).

[48]Rodier, *Questions*, p. 150.

[49]The Departmental Archives of the Haute-Garonne possesses about 80,000 *sacs à procès* from the Parlement. I have examined fifty of them from the last years of the Old Regime.

could do so depended not only on their talents but also on practical matters and opportunities. It is necessary to examine these, too, in order to understand the nature of the barristers' professional life.

STRUCTURE OF THE TOULOUSAN BAR

The presence of a Parlement and a university in Toulouse ensured the existence of a large population of barristers within the city. Each year during the eighteenth century, an average of fifty-six holders of the *licence* took the professional oath in the Sovereign Court and became *avocats au Parlement*.[50] The great majority of these new barristers had no intention of remaining in Toulouse to exercise their professional skills. Most judges in royal courts were required to be barristers, so among the oath-takers were several who went almost immediately to the bench of a court. Each year about three oath-takers became parlementaires and about eight became officers in one of the many inferior courts within the jurisdiction of the Parlement.[51] Other oath-takers left Toulouse to become barristers at one of these tribunals. A certain number were attorneys or notaries who wanted a law degree to help them in their own careers. A few would occupy financial offices or would become estate agents. Still others, perhaps the majority, wanted the title of *avocat* for reasons of prestige but did not enter specifically legal careers. They lived "nobly" without a profession or entered financial, administrative, or even ecclesiastical positions. Only about one out of ten oath-takers remained in the city of Toulouse to practice the law. Nevertheless, this influx was sufficient to make the advocates in Toulouse very numerous—indeed, excessively so.

The absence of the official tables of the Order of Barristers, listing all practicing men at the bar, renders the task of enumeration somewhat precarious. Fortunately, the almanacs of the period provide copies of the tables and seem fairly reliable.[52] In 1789, there were 276 practicing barristers in Toulouse. The great majority, 215 of them, were attached to the Parlement. Forty-two were at the bar of the Merchants' Court. The Seneschal Court had only 14 advocates, and

[50]*A.D.*, B-registers of *audiences* of the *Grand'Chambre*. The names of the oath-takers were supposed to be inscribed in a special register known as the *matricule*; there is no trace of such a register in Toulouse. But the dockets of the *Grand'Chambre* of the Parlement recorded the names of the oath-takers.

[51]See the letters for provision of offices in B. Faucher and T. Gerard, *Inventaire sommaire des archives . . . Série B, Tome V: Enregistrement des actes du pouvoir royal* (Toulouse, 1965).

[52]Unfortunately, the almanac that covers the longest period, *Calendrier de Toulouse* (1732-1790) did not usually contain a list of barristers. The most useful almanacs include the *Almanach historique de la ville de Toulouse* (Toulouse, 1780-1783); the *Calendrier de la cour de Parlement de Toulouse* for 1740, 1767, 1775, and 1778; and the *Almanach historique de la province de Languedoc* (Toulouse, 1785-1790).

the Municipal Court had 5.[53] The other courts of the city did not seem to have a distinct body of advocates at their bars.

Never before had the number of advocates been so great. This figure of 276 was reached after a dramatic expansion which started at mid-century. In 1740, there were only 87 barristers at the Parlement; twelve years later there were 119; and on the eve of the Revolution, 215.[54] This was a 140 percent increase in a period of fifty years. Similarly, the number of barristers at the Seneschal Court doubled in this period (from 7 to 14). The expansion began slowly in the early 1750s, when the number of university graduates taking the oath first rose above the seventeenth-century average of 42 a year.[55] The increase in number of oath-takers became dramatic by the mid-1760s, when their annual average rose from 50.5 to 74.1. The number of new barristers reached its peak in 1779, with 123 graduates taking the professional oath.[56] It is not possible to follow the trend after 1780 because the registers of the Great Chamber have been lost, but it certainly remained at a high level. In 1789, for example, 72 barristers took their professional oath. The proportion of *avocats au Parlement* who took their two-year apprenticeship and had their names inscribed on the tables of the Order of Barristers remained fairly constant at about 10 percent throughout this period. From the incomplete almanac lists, it seems that the average number of barristers to begin practice in Toulouse each year rose from 3.8 in the first half of the century to 7.5 during the last twenty-five years of the Old Regime.[57]

Unfortunately, tracing these trends is much easier than explaining them. It would be tempting to attribute the growth of the bar to the national economic prosperity from 1760 to 1778, since the timing of the legal expansion coincided with this economic upswing.[58] However, Toulouse and its region were not commercial centers, so the manifestations of the prosperity must have been minimal. Perhaps, indirectly, the upswing created both an atmosphere of optimism and a new pattern of vocational aspirations for men who would not have entered

[53]Jean Baour, ed., *Almanach historique de la province de Languedoc* (Toulouse, 1789).

[54]*Calendrier de la cour de Parlement de Toulouse* (Toulouse, 1740); *Almanach historique et chronologique de Languedoc* (Toulouse, 1752); *Almanach historique de la province de Languedoc* (Toulouse, 1789).

[55]Alain Madrange has listed all the oath-takers received by the *Grand'Chambre* in the seventeenth century: "Avocats inscrits au Parlement de Toulouse, 1610 à 1715" (*A.D.*, MS. 88).

[56]*A.D.*, B–registers of *audiences* of the *Grand'Chambre*, 1750–82, 1788–1790. The number of oath-takers was about 70 percent of the number of students who received the *licence*, but the percentages varied somewhat from year to year.

[57]The almanacs cited above list the year in which each barrister took his oath. From this information, one can calculate the number of barristers who entered the Order each year.

[58]Camille-Ernest Labrousse, *La crise de l'économie française à la fin de l'ancien régime* (Paris, 1943), pp. xxii–xxiii.

the bar earlier. A more certain cause of the expansion was the declining mortality rate, which was especially pronounced among young people (ages fifteen to thirty-nine) in the social strata from which barristers were recruited.[59] Whatever the proper combination of economic and demographic factors, the dramatic rise in the number of Toulousan barristers was part of a larger movement that was bringing men in greater numbers than ever before to law faculties and bars all over France.[60]

There was no minimum age qualification for practicing barristers, but a royal decree of 1690 restricted the law faculties to youths of at least sixteen years.[61] This made nineteen or twenty the lowest practical age for entering the bar. In Toulouse, the actual age for becoming a fully inscribed barrister varied from as young as twenty to as old as thirty-three, with the mean at 24.1 years.[62] The modal age of entry was twenty, the minimum, indicating that many youths prepared directly and without interruption for this profession. The limited biographical material available indicates that a few barristers had tried careers in the army, teaching, or literature before entering the bar. But the youthfulness of most new barristers suggests that this was their first and only profession.

These law graduates entered a bar that was populated by relatively youthful men. At mid-century, more than 40 percent of the barristers were under forty years of age. By 1789, the proportion of barristers under forty had risen to 54 percent.[63] A full third were in their twenties and early thirties. This reflected the influx of young graduates evident since the 1770s and was significant in a profession that had valued maturity and experience. But at the Toulousan bar, at least, relative youth did not preclude professional success, as we shall see.

Access to the bar could not have been especially difficult or restricted. But was it as easy to acquire clients and a substantial practice? Was the rapid growth of the bar a response to increased demand for legal service, or was it an autonomous movement that occurred

[59]Rives, "L'évolution démographique," pp. 115–30; Gérard Engelman, "Etude démographique d'un village de la commune de Toulouse: Pourvourville (1756–1798)," *Annales du midi* 77 (1965): 432.

[60]Professor Richard Kagan is currently investigating enrollment in law schools. I am grateful to him both for information on this subject and for data on matriculations in Toulouse.

[61]Charles de Fouchier, *Règles de la profession d'avocat . . . dans l'ancienne législation française* (Paris, 1895), pp. 225–26.

[62]The barristers' ages are difficult to obtain. I found the ages of fifty-four in the documents of Toulousan Freemasonry at the *Bibliothèque Nationale* and the dossiers of revolutionary "suspects," *A.D.*, L–283–344.

[63]These are approximate figures. To arrive at the age structure for a given year, I used the average age (twenty-four) and the date at which each barrister took his oath as points of calculation. For example, if a barrister took his oath in 1776, I assumed he was born in 1752 and was thirty-seven years old in 1789. This method may err on the side of age.

without much relation to the volume of legal affairs? To answer these important questions, we need to study the barristers' career patterns and the size of their practices. Unfortunately, documents that provide careful and conclusive answers are lacking. It is not possible to count the number of cases heard in the courts of Toulouse,[64] nor are professional papers available to illuminate the day-to-day activity of consulting. The printed briefs collected in the library and archives indicate the identity of only a few instructing barristers. The only useful sources are the registers of the various courts, in whose margins were recorded the names of the barristers pleading each case. To be sure, pleading was only one of a barrister's professional functions and cannot be taken as a complete measure of his practice. But it was the most glorified of the barristers' services and a key to success in all other legal functions. The leading pleaders wrote briefs for the clients they defended orally and established a reputation that made them frequently-sought consultants and arbiters. Indeed, whenever royal officials discussed the competence of a barrister, it was always in terms of his pleading.[65] Though far from fully adequate, these registers of pleaders do provide important insights into professional conditions and opportunities at the Toulousan bar.

The registers demonstrate that at the Parlement, where the expansion was most pronounced, even a limited amount of pleading was rare. From 1760 to 1790, there were about 300 different advocates inscribed on the tables of the Order of Barristers, and only 140 of them pleaded during this period.[66] In any one year, far fewer than half the barristers at the Parlement appeared at the bar of any chamber. In 1777, for example, only 35 of 173 barristers argued cases, and in 1788, when there were 215 advocates attached to the Parlement, only 42 of them pleaded.

Not only did the majority of barristers fail to argue cases in the Parlement, but those who pleaded did so very unequally. The career structure at the bar of the Sovereign Court might be likened to a pyramid with an extremely narrow pinnacle and a very wide base. At the top of the profession were twelve to fifteen advocates who nearly monopolized the bar. The registers of the Parlement record their names with monotonous regularity, and they were undoubtedly as familiar at the court as any of its officers. The names of these leading barristers are worth listing here, for they will appear repeatedly throughout this study. In the 1760s and 1770s, the masters of the bar of Toulouse were

[64]The thousands of sacs à procès have not yet been cataloged or indexed. It is not possible to determine the number of cases from court dockets because suits often appeared more than once and the parties to the suit were not identified by name.

[65]See especially the correspondence of the subdelegate, A.D., C-268-278.

[66]A.D., B-registers of audiences of all chambers of the Parlement.

Jean Baptiste Jouve, Guillaume Chabanettes, Jean Pierre Carbonel, Jean Mascart, Alexandre Augustin Jamme, Jean Forent Monyer, Jean Baptiste Viguier, Jean Antoine Joly, Jean Carrière, Jean Desirat, Pierre Alexandre Gary, and Joseph Marie Duroux. Many of these men (Viguier, Mascart, Jamme, Gary, Duroux) retained their predominance at the bar until the very end of the Old Regime. With the death or retirement of some (Carbonel, Joly, Jouve, Carrière, and Chabanettes), new pleaders entered this elite group of barristers: Jean Douyou, Joseph Dominique Monyer *fils*, Claude Castor Bragouse, Pierre Roucoule, and Jean Raymond Marc Bastoulh. Such was the narrow elite of barristers at the end of the Old Regime.

The next echelon of the professional pyramid was considerably below the group just described. Its members appeared in the court dockets only a half to a third as often as the masters of the bar, yet it was still a small, select group. At most, twenty-five barristers might have been included, among them Hughes Nully, Professe Detté, Michel Malpel, Jean Baptiste Lafage, Jacques Marie Rouzet, Jacob Londois, and Jean Joseph Gez. Within this category were several younger barristers who seemed to be on the verge of even more distinguished careers by 1789: Bernard Etienne Arbanere, Jean Baptiste Mailhe, Jean Joseph Janole, Pierre Roques, and Bertrand Barère.

Below this second echelon, the career pyramid broadened rapidly. The barristers who pleaded infrequently or at long intervals numbered between forty and fifty. Jean Ignace Vidal de Lacoste, for example, pleaded once in 1762, 1763, 1767, and 1768. In the next year he appeared at the bar three times, but rarely after that. Antoine Cahusac addressed the judges twice in 1766 and once again in 1768. Some of the barristers in this group may well have been more frequently employed as instructing advocates then as pleaders; this would explain the long intervals between their appearances at the bar. Others may simply have lacked cases.

Near the bottom of the professional pyramid was a group of thirty to forty advocates who appeared at the bar only once or twice in their careers.[67] How many of these had learned from their limited experience as pleaders that instructing or consulting was more suitable to them cannot be ascertained. Such was the case of Jean Baptiste de Laviguerie, who pleaded only once but became one of the most respected consulting barristers in Toulouse.[68] At any rate, below this group was the majority of the bar, which did not plead at all.

Thus, it seems that even a moderate degree of success was the exception rather than the rule. Although the number of barristers

[67]It is particularly difficult to assess the size of this group because of the large portion of new men at the bar in 1789.

[68]Auguste Albert, *Eloge de Laviguerie* (Toulouse, 1882), pp. 9–14.

specializing in instructing might possibly have been large, there was clearly a superfluity of barristers at the Parlement. This was true even for the attorneys, who numbered only 120 in 1765 and whose employment on every case before the Parlement was obligatory. A royal edict of 1768 recognized this and reduced the number of attorneys' positions to 60.[69] There was no similar way to reduce the number of barristers with marginal practices. As a result of the expansion of the bar, they existed in unprecedented numbers.

In assessing the final impact of the legal expansion at the Parlement, several points must be made about the barristers' vocational expectations and motivations. Overcrowding and severe competition for cases was nothing new at the bar. As far back as one may look in the court dockets, the number of active pleaders was always a small minority of the total inscribed on the table of the Order. The mid-century growth of the bar only exacerbated a long-standing situation, and young barristers entered a profession that was well-known as a highly competitive one, offering absolutely no assurances of success.

A large practice, however, was not the goal of all barristers. In this preeminently legal city, where the advocate was a highly respected figure, many men sought the barrister's status without intending to practice. It has been noted that the number of *bourgeois* (in the sense of *rentier*) in Toulouse was quite low.[70] The reason seems to have been that men who wished to "live nobly" sought the status of an advocate, so those who might have been *bourgeois* elsewhere became titular barristers in Toulouse. We cannot ascertain just how many such men there were at the bar. In Paris, perhaps half of the 600 inscribed pleaders at the Parlement did not practice.[71] The portion at the Toulousan bar was probably considerable, too. A third would not be an unreasonable guess.

Finally, it is important to note that the level of professional ambition at the Toulousan bar does not seem to have been very high.[72] Though the number of barristers at the Parlement more than doubled within fifty years, there were no signs of crisis and few recognizable

[69]Florentin Astre, *Les procureurs près le Parlement de Toulouse* (Toulouse, 1858), pp. 31–32.

[70]Sentou, *Fortunes et groupes sociaux*, p. 185. Of 2102 acts of succession, he found only 19 belonging to *bourgeois*. Michel Vovelle estimated that 7 to 15 percent of the Parisian population were *bourgeois*, and 8.3 percent of the households at Chartres were headed by *bourgeois*. See his "Bourgeois, rentiers, propriétaires: éléments pour la définition d'une catégorie sociale à la fin du XVIIIe siècle," *Actes du 84e congrès des sociétés savantes* (Dijon, 1954), pp. 421, 428.

[71]Berryer, *Souvenirs*, 1: 19.

[72]Studies of "middle-class" groups usually attribute to their subjects an energy and ambition that may not have existed. Serious work on "ambition" as a social attitude and practice would be most useful. For an interesting start, see Theodore Zeldin, *France, 1848–1945*, vol. 1, *Ambition, Love, and Politics* (Oxford, 1973).

responses to the entirely new professional conditions. Caseless barristers did not violate professional taboos in search of clients; as we shall soon see, they certainly did not avail themselves of all opportunities to use their legal expertise. In this sense, the titular barrister was more typical of his colleagues than was the young Robespierre, who wrote with flaming ambition: "Of all the qualities necessary to distinguish oneself in this profession, I bring to it at least . . . an extreme desire to succeed."[73] If this had been the spirit in which many young barristers entered their profession, the bar of the Parlement would have been seething with discontent, frustrated ambitions, and disregard for traditional norms—and it was not.

Thus, the expansion of the bar was not quite the financial and psychological catastrophe it might have seemed. It undoubtedly created some hardship, but most barristers were able to face the limited professional opportunities with equanimity, because their ambitions had never been those of the young Robespierre.

Thus far, we have concentrated on the bar of the Parlement, for it merited special attention by virtue of its size and prominence. But the barristers did not compose a unified profession; rather, they were divided along corporate lines, and the advocates of each court had their distinctive status, interests, and career perspectives. The fourteen barristers at the second tribunal of Toulouse, the Seneschal-*Présidial* Court, faced a vocational situation that was more favorable than that of their colleagues at the Parlement. Their numbers had doubled since 1750, but in this case, the expansion might have reflected enhanced opportunities. An edict of 1774 greatly enlarged the competence of the Seneschal Court by permitting its magistrates to judge cases up to 2,000 livres in value; their previous limit had been only 250 livres.[74] Even though the Parlement constantly fought this edict and whittled away some gains, the Seneschal Court surely had more legal business than before. Its registers show that the number of barristers inscribed at the bar was not excessively large; in fact, twelve of the fourteen pleaded with some frequency.[75] But if career prospects were brighter at this tribunal, the improvement was achieved at the expense of status. Being at the bar of the Parlement entitled a barrister to much more prestige, and the advocates at the Sovereign Court were very sensitive

[73]Georges Michon, ed., *Correspondance de Maximilien et Augustin Robespierre* (Paris, 1926), p. 22. Robespierre wrote this, while still a student, to the well-known parlementaire and criminal law reform proponent Dupaty.
[74]Philip Dawson, *Provincial Magistrates and Revolutionary Politics in France, 1789-1795* (Cambridge, Mass., 1972), pp. 63-65.
[75]Still, there were some barristers who pleaded more than others: Jean-Antoine Romiguières, Guillaume Bordes, and Michel Martin. *A.D.*, B-registers of *audiences* of the Seneschal-*Présidial* Court.

to this difference. They refused to admit Seneschal Court barristers to full participation in their Order, and they would never have pleaded in the inferior court. Moreover, the Seneschal Court barristers had more modest origins than their colleagues at the Parlement;[76] they could not so easily afford the possibility of unemployment which being at the Parlement entailed. Their place at the Seneschal Court reflected different financial needs and, perhaps, a different set of professional motivations and expectations.

The two other courts regularly receiving barristers were the Merchants' Court and the Municipal Tribunal. The advocates at these courts differed from those of the Parlement not only in status but also in function. Since these courts lacked the attorney's office, the barristers must have handled the procedural details which were usually the responsibility of the *procureurs*. This placed these barristers in an inferior branch of the profession. The very nature of the actions at these tribunals did not usually require pleading or instructing, so procedure might have been the core of their work. Summary matters formed the bulk of affairs at the Hôtel de Ville; as the alderman (*capitoul*) Desirat stated: "We see daily twenty to thirty people, one demanding his wages of two or three days, another a payment of small value, a domestic who cries against his master who refuses him some wages."[77] In the Merchants' Court, too, disputes concerned mainly questions of fact and did not usually require the legal skills of the barrister. This tribunal was said to have heard a hundred summary cases a day,[78] and for a long time the presence of barristers had been prohibited for fear that they would complicate simple questions of fact.[79] The advocates at the bar of the *Bourse* were, thus, professionally more akin to attorneys than to the pleaders at the Parlement and Seneschal Court.

Structurally, the Municipal and Merchants' Courts were similar to the numerous courts of exceptional or special jurisdiction in Toulouse. Most of them did not have a separate body of attorneys, and the cases in most did not warrant pleading.[80] The Mastery of Waters and Forests, the Bureau of Finances, the Court of Coinage, the Salt-Tax Court, and the Court of the Canal du Midi heard mostly criminal actions, and the Ordinance of 1667 prohibited the counsel of barristers in criminal cases

---

[76]For further discussion of this point, see chapter 2.

[77]*A.D.*, C-63, "Discours de M. Desirat, chef de consistoire." The barrister Esperonnier wrote in a brief, "Mais toutes matières qui exigent une connaissance sérieuse . . . et ministère d'avocat ne sont pas de compétence des capitouls." See his *Mémoire sur partages* (n.p., n.d.), p. 4, n. 4.

[78]*Almanach de la province de Languedoc* (1783), p. 164.

[79]*Almanach historique de la ville de Toulouse* (1780), part 2, p. 29; Florentin Astre, *Essai sur l'histoire et les attributions de l'ancienne Bourse de Toulouse* (Toulouse, n.d.). In addition to barristers, there were legal counsels, called *postulans*, who were not law school graduates.

[80]One exception was the *bureau des finances*, which had its own attorneys.

of the first instance. The advocates at the numerous courts of exceptional jurisdiction must have functioned more as *procureurs* than as *avocats*, too.

It is unfortunate that the records of these minor courts are so often missing or lacking in information about the court personnel. Only the papers of the *Officialité diocésaine*, an ecclesiastical tribunal,[81] and the Court of Coinage (*Cour des Monnaies*) provide some insight into the identity of the pleaders. They indicate that the legal personnel of the lower courts accumulated positions at several tribunals simultaneously. Vincens, Wizer, and Sepierre, who belonged to the bar at the Municipal Court, also served in the *Officialité*.[82] Penaveyre, an attorney at the Seneschal Court, was also a barrister at this ecclesiastical court, and the notaries Richard and Mirepoix were advocates at the Bureau of Finances and Merchants' Court respectively.[83] Accumulating legal positions was beneath the dignity of the Sovereign Court barristers, even the caseless ones. The image of the poor barrister seeking clients where he could find them does not fit the caseless men of the Parlement, many of whom lived in honorable indolence, but it was an accurate picture of their professional and social inferiors, the advocates of the minor courts in Toulouse.

The separation between the upper, respectable branch of the profession and the lower one seemed fairly complete. The barristers at the Parlement would never have served at the bar of the inferior tribunals: the status of the courts and the procedural details handled in them were beneath their dignity. Only as special or temporary magistrates (*assesseurs* or *opinants*) did they enter the courts of exceptional jurisdiction, and such positions were usually held by the more distinguished pleaders of the Parlement.[84] Thus, because of functional and status gradations within the profession, Toulouse presented the paradoxical situation of a city filled with courts and, at the same time, with briefless barristers.

How did barristers, especially those at the Parlement, obtain cases? The well-known pleaders, of course, did not search for clients; litigants came to them and were fortunate to engage these very busy legal

---

[81]This tribunal heard cases concerned largely with disputes over the administration of the sacraments. See Marcel Marion, *Dictionnaire des institutions de la France aux XVIIᵉ et XVIIIᵉ siècles* (Paris, 1923), p. 407.

[82]*A.D.*, B-registers of *audiences* of *Officialité*; *A.D.*, 3E-10875, Testament of Vincens. Vincens may also have been an attorney at the Bureau of Finances. Wizer may have been secretary to the barrister Albaret; see *A.D.*, E-12733.

[83]*A.D.*, 3E-5971, fol. 437; *Almanach historique de la province de Languedoc* (1789), p. 116.

[84]*A.D.*, B/2-11, registers of *Cour des monnaies*. The Parlement barristers Jean Ozun and Jean Soulatges were assessors. Jamme and Duroux were *opinants*.

experts. The new or less respected barristers must have employed a variety of methods to gain clients if they were at all interested in doing so, but only the most important methods can be discussed here. The best source of cases was the attorney: litigants first engaged an attorney, who then directed his client to a suitable barrister. For this reason, the president of the Parlement wrote a letter to the Community of Attorneys, requesting its members to "give cases to plead to young barristers because the older ones are too occupied and lack the time to prepare all the affairs they are given."[85] The barrister had to be on good terms with the attorneys and, perhaps, supplicate them for cases. Some barristers, however, strongly conscious of their superior status, bitterly resented this dependence upon their inferiors. The advocate Gélibert recorded this resentment in his "Epistle to My Pleading Robe":

Mais à propos des Procureurs, ma chère
Pour s'illustrer il faut, dit-on, leur plaire.
Aussi voit-on des avocats du jour
De notre état obliant la noblesse,
A ces messieurs faire une indigne cour
Et devant eux plier avec supplesse.[86]

For Gélibert, the idea of humbling himself before an attorney was unthinkable:

Qui moi, que j'aille en lache adulation
Brûler sans honte un encens mercenaire!
Non . . . je sens trop les devoirs de l'honneur.[87]

Gélibert's overweening attitude toward attorneys may explain why he never pleaded in the Parlement. A second important method of winning clients was through contact with older, more successful barristers. A young advocate would enter the office of an established pleader and handle the more routine work until ready to establish his own practice. The Parisian barrister Linguet complained about the subordination and dependence in which this placed the newcomer to the bar,[88] and some Toulousans may have shared his view. But many successful pleaders must have begun their careers in this manner nonetheless.

Building a large practice required uncommon talent. That law was a profession in which individual ability determined success was considered one of the long-standing glories of the bar. This ideal had

[85]*A.D.*, E–1190, deliberations of attorneys (session of 30 January 1773).
[86]*Recueil de l'Académie des Jeux Floraux*, 1783, p. 4.
[87]*Ibid.*
[88]*Nécessité d'une réforme dans l'administration de la justice et dans les loix civiles en France* (Amsterdam, 1764), pp. 93–94.

been enunciated in the late seventeenth century by the chancellor d'Aguesseau in an oft-quoted apotheosis of the profession:

Men are esteemed, not for what their fathers did, but for what they do themselves. When a barrister enters his Order, he leaves behind the rank given to him by prejudices that dominate in the world and assumes the rank that reason gives in an order of nature and truth.[89]

This was not merely a glorified description of the legal profession; at the Toulousan bar it had some basis in reality. Men of humble birth became important barristers entrusted with consequential cases, and in some instances their colleagues made them heads (or *batonniers*) of the Order.[90] Clients seemed to weigh talent more heavily than any personal consideration in selecting a barrister. Even a bishop and a parlementaire allowed the Protestant barrister Lavaysse to handle their cases.[91]

Good "connections" were insufficient to assure success at the bar. Barristers who were sons or nephews of attorneys had a familial claim upon the clients of their relatives and an initial advantage over others, but such advocates were often professionally obscure. Likewise, the sons of leading pleaders were not able to benefit from their fathers' clients and reputations unless they, too, were professionally competent. The children of Jean Baptiste Jouve, Jean Chipoulet, or Alexandre Jamme were pleaders of moderate or little stature though their fathers had been masters of the bar.[92] In this aristocratic society, where achieved status was not the rule, the barristers' profession was probably the most distinguished one to reward personal merit in so unqualified a manner.

The few barristers who did attain professional success had deep knowledge of the law, superior rhetorical skills, quick, penetrating minds, and an authoritative air, all of which gave confidence to their clients. A perfect familiarity with the corpus of French law—a formidably large body of material—was expected of leading advocates. One of them, Jean Desirat, was criticized for having "the instinct rather than the science of law," for he was often unable to cite a text though he could affirm its existence.[93] The leading pleaders were old enough to have acquired profound legal knowledge and experience but were not

[89]"L'indépendance de l'avocat," appendix to William Forsyth, *An Historical Essay on the Office and Duties of an Advocate* (London, 1879). D'Aguesseau delivered this discourse in 1693.

[90]The careers of these barristers will receive more attention in chapter 3.

[91]Aguier, *Recueil d'arrêts notables ou Supplément au journal du Palais de Toulouse,* 2 vols. (Nîmes, 1782), 2: 272; Defos, *Mémoire pour Messire de Cassagnaur . . .* (n.p., n.d.), p. 2. In theory, of course, Protestants were not permitted to be barristers; tacit tolerance was practiced in a few cases.

[92]Sons of the leading pleaders Gary, Laviguerie, Taverne, and Duroux were successful barristers, however.

[93]Benech, *De l'enseignement du droit,* p. 100.

so old that they had lost the forcefulness of their voices and minds. It was a very significant feature of the profession that younger barristers of talent were able to rise quickly to a place of preeminence. At the very top of the legal profession in 1785, there were seven pleaders in their early or mid-fifties, two in their forties, and four in their thirties. Claude Castor Bragouse was only thirty-nine years old. Pierre Bruno Roucoule attained the height of his profession at the age of thirty-two, and Jean Raymond Marc Bastoulh was only thirty-five years old. Barristers like Giles François Astre, Joseph Etienne Pouderoux, and Bernard Etienne Arbanere had pleaded many times in the Parlement by the time they were thirty years old and were probably on their way to becoming masters of the bar.[94]

Barristers attained their professional status early and remained at this level for most of their careers. If an advocate did not receive cases while he was young, he was unlikely to do so later in his career, and almost all successful barristers made early appearances at the bar. Jean Baptiste Viguier took his oath in 1758 and first pleaded in January of 1761. From then on, he pleaded regularly, and by 1776 he had attained the pinnacle of the professional pyramid.[95] The career of Pierre Roucoule advanced even more rapidly. He was received as a barrister on 13 January 1777 and first addressed the magistrates of the Chamber of Inquests in April of 1778. After 1784, he was certainly among the top twelve pleaders at the bar. Most remarkable of all was the career of Joseph Marie Duroux. An attorney from 1754 to 1766,[96] he then became a barrister. From the moment that he entered the profession, he was one of the leading pleaders. The early attainment of success explains the professional longevity of the leading barristers. Viguier, Duroux, Gary, and Mascart were able to dominate the bar for the last thirty to forty years of the Old Regime because they had achieved their ascendancy at the start of their careers. The tendency of practices to flourish or wither at an early stage was a result of the considerable ability required by legal work, the severe competition for cases, and the conservatism of the clients. Not all barristers had the opportunity to make a reputation, and still fewer had the talent to do so, even when an opportunity presented itself. Then clients, encouraged by their attorneys, continued to bring all their cases to the few select barristers who had proven their ability. The circle of pleading barristers was thereby restricted to the successful few.

[94]This might be compared to the dismal picture of young barristers at the *bailliage* court of Bayeux. See Olwen Hufton, *Bayeux in the Late Eighteenth Century* (Oxford, 1967), p. 62.

[95]*A.D.*, B-registers of *audiences* of Parlement chambers.

[96]*A.D.*, B-1950, fol. 314-16. This is the only example I have found of professional migration from the attorney's office to the bar, but attorneys did obtain law degrees frequently.

Young advocates who received few or no clients in the first several years of their careers could presume they would never build a solid practice. Many became resigned to this, while others left the profession, living as rentiers or acquiring a civil office. Defection from the bar may have been assuming considerable dimensions by the end of the Old Regime, and at least one successful barrister lamented it.[97] Of twenty-eight advocates received from 1775 to 1780, nine were not inscribed on the tables of the Order in 1789; there were at least twenty young barristers on the table of 1784 who were not on that of 1789.[98] This large-scale professional migration was the clearest—perhaps the only —response which young barristers made to the overcrowded conditions that existed at the bar of the Parlement in the second half of the eighteenth century.

BARRISTERS AND SEIGNEURIAL COURTS

The city walls did not encompass all the tribunals in the immediate region of Toulouse. Outside were the numerous seigneurial courts, whose benches had to be filled by graduates of a law faculty.[99] Theoretically, these courts provided opportunities for the Toulousan barristers, especially the caseless ones, to find honorable employment; in practice, however, the courts did not do so. The judges on seigneurial benches were all "avocats au Parlement," but few were in the Order of Barristers and had practices in Toulouse.[100] Apparently, they had taken their oath at the Parlement but had never intended to practice there. Their function as seigneurial judge was a substitute for a career at the bar, not a supplement to it. The typical seigneurial officer served at several courts at once, since the bench was not particularly lucrative.[101] Jean Desclaux, for example, was judge of Vacquins, Capet, and St. Sauveur, lieutenant judge of Castelnau and St. Jory, and, finally, assessor of Bouloc. Raymond Entraigues was judge of St. Géniès, St. Loup, Pechbonnieur, Montbrun, Labastide, Gaignac, and Mondonville, and lieutenant judge of Fenouillet.[102] Neither practiced law at the bar

[97] Jean Joseph Gez, *Discours adressé à une société d'avocats au Parlement de Toulouse . . .* (n.p., 1783). This interesting speech can be found only in the library of the departmental Archives.

[98] Of course, death may have removed some of these men from the tables.

[99] Most aspects of the seigneurial regime are covered in an excellent study by Jean Bastier, "La féodalité au siècle des lumières dans la région de Toulouse," 2 vols. (Doctoral thesis, Faculty of Law of Toulouse, 1970). M. Bastier has been most generous in giving me advice and assistance.

[100] *A.D.*, B–seigneurial justice records. See also Félix Pasquier and François Galabert, eds., *Cahiers paroissiaux des sénéchaussées de Toulouse et de Commenges en 1789* (Toulouse, 1928), and Daniel Ligou, ed., *Cahiers de doléances du tiers état du pays et jugerie du Rivière-Verdun* (Paris, 1961).

[101] Bastier, *Féodalité*, 1: 120.

[102] *A.D.*, B–seigneurial court records for these communities.

of a court in Toulouse itself. Even when barristers were owners (or co-
owners) of seigneurial rights, they did not appoint themselves to the
benches of their courts. The rich barrister Jean Prévost was lord of
Fenouillet, but the seigneurial judge was the *feudiste* Tremolières.
Jean Raymond Bastoulh, an important pleader at the Parlement and
seigneur of Nogaret, appointed his uncle Raymond to his court.[103]

The available (and incomplete) evidence suggests that no more than
10 percent of the barristers who practiced at the Parlement were also
seigneurial justices. Interestingly enough, those who took these positions were not the obscure, caseless advocates at the Parlement; rather,
the younger barristers who were already beginning to have successful
careers at the Sovereign Court were the ones who supplemented their
practices with magisterial service in the countryside. Thus, Jean
Baptiste Mailhe was judge at Rouffiac, Jean Joseph Janole served at
Auzeville, and Jean Boubée presided at Bonrepas.[104] Each of these was
a promising young pleader at the Parlement in the 1780s. This suggests
that service as seigneurial judge was a practical matter, undertaken by
the younger, more ambitious barristers, often those from relatively
modest backgrounds.[105] Most of the caseless barristers at the Parlement
apparently had no interest in exploiting this opportunity for legal
employment.

The Seneschal Court barristers, generally men of a more practical
temperament than their colleagues at the Parlement, presided over
seigneurial courts fairly frequently. Half or more of them seem to have
been seigneurial judges. Paul Guion, for example, was judge at
Blagnac; Guillaume Bordes and François Passeron were officers at
Castelnau d'Estrefonds and Fronton respectively. Serving in seigneurial courts placed these barristers in a strategic position to encourage
villagers to appeal cases to the Seneschal Court—where they could
plead the suit as barristers. Some *cahiers* of 1789 complained of this
practice,[106] and it is possible that barristers of the Seneschal Court were
guilty of taking advantage of their seigneurial offices in this manner.

If the benches of the seigneurial courts were not a source of
employment for many practicing advocates of Toulouse, neither were
the bars. The seigneurial courts had their own barristers, who were
usually not university graduates. Very often, they were notaries or law
clerks who lived in villages and market towns. The table of barristers

---

[103]*A.D.*, B-seigneurial justice of Fenouillet and Nogaret.

[104]*A.D.*, B-seigneurial justice, and L-223, list of deputies of Third Estate Assembly for
these communities. One exception was the important older barrister Joseph Bonaventure
Dutour, judge at Rebigue. Attorneys also served as seigneurial officers.

[105]For a good example of this type of young barrister, see Geneviève Thoumas, "La
jeunesse de Mailhe," *Annales historiques de la Révolution française* 43 (1971): 221–47.

[106]Raoul Aubin, *L'organisation judiciaire d'après les cahiers de 1789* (Paris, 1928), p.
75.

(or *postulans*) of Castelnau in 1784, for example, contained six names: three notaries, from St. Jory, Castelnau, and Grenade respectively, a *greffier* of the Estates of Foix, and two villagers from Castelnau and Bouloc.[107] Like the seigneurial justices, these barristers served at several courts at once. A barrister at the Parlement would never have inscribed himself on the table of a seigneurial court nor pleaded at its bar—not even if he were a party to the dispute.[108] Toulousan barristers had a role in cases before seigneurial courts only occasionally. When seigneurial advocates wanted a sophisticated legal argument or an outside opinion to embellish a case, they could call upon a Toulousan barrister to prepare a brief.[109] But such briefs were rarely a part of litigation before seigneurial tribunals.[110]

Outside the small group of Toulousan pleaders who served as seigneurial officers, the barristers' main role in the rural courts was an honorific one. Noted barristers at the Parlement and Seneschal Court were consulting judges (*opinants*) who assisted the regular court officer in rendering a decision. The distinguished pleaders Alexandre Jammes and Louis Doazan appeared in this capacity at the court of Rebigue in 1787, and the leading barristers of the Seneschal Court, Bordes and Martin, were frequently *opinants*. Thus, the practicing barristers of Toulouse were a repository of advice and expertise for the seigneurial courts on the specific occasions such outside authority was required. By and large, the Toulousan barristers—especially those at the Parlement —were not attached by profession or financial interest to the seigneurial regime.

PROFESSIONAL FEES

The barrister could trace his proud history back to a stage in which pleaders did not accept payment from clients. The professional ideal was—and remained—that of the barrister as an economically self-sufficient gentleman who defended clients for the sake of justice, not for gain.[111] While the advocate did not, in theory, solicit remuneration, he was free to accept what the client offered out of gratitude. This was why the client's payment was an "honorarium" instead of a "fee." The barrister always endeavored to present a public image of unconcern

[107]*A.D.*, B-seigneurial justice of Castelnau.

[108]Barrister Joseph Cluzet was involved in a suit in Fenouillet, but he engaged a seigneurial barrister to handle it. See *A.D.*, B-seigneurial justice of Fenouillet (case of 1783).

[109]One such brief was prepared by barrister Marie Joseph Gratian in 1768. He received twenty-one livres for it. See *A.D.*, B-seigneurial justice of Pompignan.

[110]Bastier, *Féodalité*, 1: 145. Among the papers of the seigneurial courts preserved in the archives, there are very few such briefs.

[111]Boucher d'Argis, *Règles*, p. 176.

about pecuniary matters and, at least in part, he was successful. Although the *cahiers* of 1789 very frequently contained complaints about the high costs of justice, the grievances were usually directed against the attorney, not the barrister, for his exorbitant charges.[112]

Here we are concerned less with the barristers' total revenue, the subject of a later chapter, than with the arrangements by which he received individual fees. A few barristers, known as *pensionnaires*, were retained as permanent counsels, primarily by religious and corporate bodies, and paid on a yearly basis.[113] Sometimes, barristers followed the traditional standards and allowed the client to pay what he thought appropriate. This was the method by which one barrister at the Merchants' Court received his honorarium when he defended the interests of the municipality of Toulouse.[114] In general, the barristers set their own charges for each plea, brief, or consultation. They vigorously resisted all attempts by the Parlement to regulate their fees, as it had done to those of the attorneys. This resistance cost them the right to sue clients for nonpayment of fees.[115]

Since the barristers set their own compensation, it would be useful to know on what basis they did so and what effect this had on the general cost of justice. Did they compete for the none-too-numerous clients by lowering fees? Did well-known barristers charge more than their obscure colleagues? Were the charges adjusted to suit the importance of either the client or the property being defended? Unfortunately, a dearth of documents permits only tentative answers to these questions and no insights at all into other important matters. It seems fairly certain, though, that the fees for the most common professional activity, consulting, were set by custom or convention at about six livres per session. This did not change during the last fifty years of the Old Regime[116] (as far as we can tell from existing documents), nor did it seem to vary with the stature of the consultant. The minor Seneschal Court advocate, Resplendy, charged six livres for a consultation,[117] as did the most distinguished legal experts at the Parlement for both consultation and arbitration.[118] Even the attorneys, notaries, and *feudistes* expected the same compensation for a consultation.[119] The

[112]Aubin, *L'organisation judiciaire*, pp. 166–69.

[113]Madrange, "Les Avocats," p. 33.

[114]*A.M.*, BB-123, fol. 66–67, register of municipal council deliberations.

[115]Bastard-d'Estang, *Parlements de France*, 1: 95; Astre, *Procureurs*, pp. 80–83.

[116]See *A.D.*, 3E-12731-12736, arbitration papers, 1740–1793. The consultation fee remained constant at six livres per session.

[117]*A.D.*, 3E-10854, fol. 219, marriage contract of Jeanne Soulié.

[118]*A.D.*, B-*sac à procès civil*, no. 3, 1780. Six consultations with each of seven leading barristers (Delort, Courdurier, etc.), plus three more sessions with each of three others cost the litigant 306 livres. This was six livres per session.

[119]*A.D.*, E-1190, letter of syndic of attorneys, 3 January 1771.

charges for pleas and instructions, however, could vary widely. We have examined the instructions contained in fifty *sacs à procès* (burlap sacks in which were stored all papers relating to the case), twenty-two of which indicated the compensation demanded by the barrister. The amounts varied from twenty-five to eighty livres.[120] But for what was the client paying? Professional ethics permitted the advocate to increase his fee in proportion to the value of the property he was defending,[121] and barristers undoubtedly did so when they had the opportunity. But for the instructions we have examined, the honorarium varied only with the length of the brief. That is, barristers usually conceived of their fees as compensation for the amount of work done rather than as a payment for property defended.

Evidently, it would have required many instructions or hundreds of consultations to yield a very substantial revenue. But in relation to the general distribution of fortunes and income in eighteenth-century Toulouse, barristers' fees were very high—prohibitively so for much of the population. In 1789 the value of a day's labor was assessed at one livre, a figure which may have been too high.[122] Laborers could not afford even a simple consultation, which would have cost a full week of work. Moreover, the practice of charging in proportion to the length of the brief made legal fees proportionately more expensive for the small property-owners, whose litigation would presumably involve only small sums. Cases that required a plea or instruction and several consultations could easily cost 100 livres or more. It is quite possible that many litigants tried to avoid engaging a barrister whenever possible, since the inevitable fees of the attorney were high enough.[123]

Though already expensive, legal charges seemed to be increasing. A protest from the Community of Attorneys provides indirect evidence of a sizeable rise in barristers' charges. The group was disturbed by the rapid increase in the fees paid to the barristers' secretaries, who customarily received a fifth of the advocates' honorarium.[124] One must suppose, then, that the barristers' compensation was rising proportionately. Moreover, the attorneys complained that secretaries were receiving as much as barristers had thirty years ago. No doubt this claim was exaggerated, but it does suggest a very substantial increase, probably

---

[120]The charge was written in the margin of the last page of the instruction. It included the fee for copying the document and was called the "solvit."

[121]Boucher d'Argis, *Règles*, pp. 176–89.

[122]Jean Sentou, "Impôts et citoyens actifs à Toulouse au début de la Révolution," *Annales du midi* 61 (1948): 62.

[123]The *cahiers* may have criticized the high fees of attorneys much more than barristers because the populace in general had little contact with barristers. Studies of the type of legal counsel accessible to different social groups would be useful to scholars in the field.

[124]*A.D.*, E-1881, fol. 223, deliberations of attorneys, 23 March 1754.

enough to keep pace with the general inflationary trend of the period. In 1772, the Parlement granted attorneys a new schedule of fees that was about 25 percent above the one in effect since 1754.[125] Surely, the barristers raised their fees for pleas and instructions by at least this much. These higher charges by both barristers and attorneys set the stage for the ubiquitous complaints about legal costs that filled the *cahiers* of 1789.

But not all barristers were able to raise their fees with equal facility. As we have seen, consultation fees seemed to have been almost invariable. This meant that the older consulting barristers, who had retired from pleading, and the less important barristers, whose practices consisted largely of consultations, were not beneficiaries of the general rise in legal costs. Only those who pleaded and instructed regularly could increase the compensation for their services. But receiving fees was only one aspect of a profession that was, for most of its practitioners, much more than a livelihood.

FUNCTION AND PROFESSION

The extent to which Toulousan barristers exercised their traditional professional functions varied enormously, especially at the Parlement. A few pleaded very frequently and must have worked incredibly hard to prepare the cases they argued. Many others practiced little or not at all. What did being a barrister mean to those 215 Toulousans who wrote "avocat au Parlement" after their names from the day they took their oath to the end of their lives? It seems that the barristers' professional self-conception was much more general than present-day vocational identifications. For them, being a barrister was as much a social status as a career, a way of life more than a function. Their profession—or "state" (*état*) as they often referred to it in family documents—determined where they would live, with whom they would associate, and how others would regard them. The uniting factor among barristers was not a common type of work but rather a participation in the honor of the profession.

The barristers took great pride in their "state." They gloried in the fact that nobles could and did become barristers, and the claim was often made that being a barrister conferred a sort of personal nobility.[126] The barristers of the Parlement experienced a special pride in being associated with that august court and with its magistrates, the most prominent men in Toulouse. Their sense of identify with the Parlement was very strong; as the barrister Courdurier proclaimed in

[125]*A.D.*, B-1729, fol. 491–498; B-1605, fol. 109–119.
[126]Boucher d'Argis, *Règles*, pp. 190–93.

1775, "The glory of the magistrates belongs to us in a way. Our honor is bound to yours."[127]

Residential patterns and habits of social interaction reinforced this identification with the court and with the profession as a way of life. Virtually all barristers of the Parlement, titular or practicing, lived in the parishes of Dalbade or Saint-Etienne (the quarters or *capitoulats* of Saint-Etienne, Dalbade, La Pierre, Saint-Barthélemy).[128] No less than eighteen of them lived along the extended street called, at various points, Rue des Coutelliers, du Temple, de l'Inquisition, Sainte-Claire, and de la Dalbade (see figure I-1). Ten lived in the Petite Rue Montgaillard. The other personnel of the courts lived here, too—magistrates, attorneys, *hussiers*, *greffiers*, clerks of all kinds, and even law students. On the Rue Nazareth, in 1789, there were twelve barristers, seven magistrates of the Parlement, and three attorneys. Vieux-Raisin had five magistrates, five advocates, and two attorneys, and Rue Verlane was similar. The functionaries of the same court—from the highest to the lowest—were also fellow-parishioners and neighbors. To be sure, living so near the court was convenient for the pleaders, who had to arrive at an early hour, but non-practicing barristers lived in the area too. It seems clear that residence in this section was a way of identifying with the professional group—a part of its definition.

The spirit of the Parlement totally permeated this section of the city and wove it into a community—not of equals, certainly, but of people with shared interests, loyalties, and outlooks. What transpired at the court was, of course, of central interest to the entire community. In this sense the Parlement was more than a tribunal; it was a total environment that offered the barristers a place in the community, the city, and the world.

The young barrister entered this community not only by moving to the environs of the *Palais de Justice* but also through a process of acculturation. This process began at the Law Faculty and intensified, after he began his practice in Toulouse. Through lectures and instruction offered by experienced colleagues, the new barrister learned jurisprudence and a veneration for Roman law as the embodiment of "reason." At the same time, he was inculcated with professional standards and outlooks. Constant contact with colleagues and other court personnel reinforced these lessons.

The professional functions that barristers performed composed only one dimension of their professional self-conception, albeit an important one. These activities were part of the barristers' total social role and

---

[127]*Journal de ce qui s'est passé à l'occasion du rétablissement du Parlement de Toulouse dans ses fonctions* (n.p., n.d.), p. 8.

[128]The streets of residents were listed in the *Almanach historique de la province de Languedoc* (Toulouse, 1789).

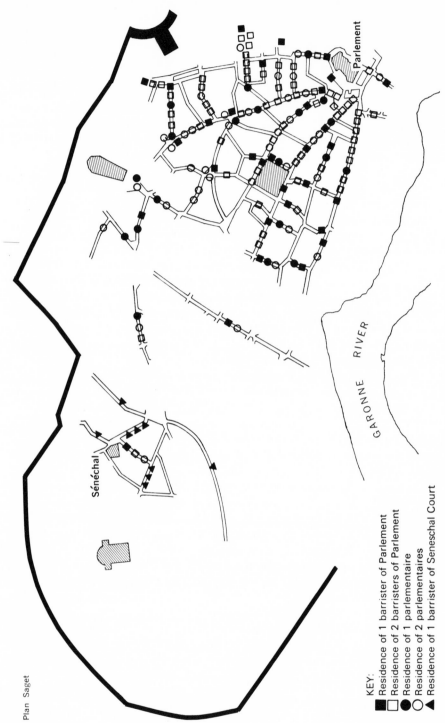

Plan Saget

KEY:

Residence of 1 barrister of Parlement ■

Residence of 2 barristers of Parlement □

Residence of 1 parlementaire ●

Residence of 2 parlementaires ○

Residence of 1 barrister of Seneschal Court ◀

FIGURE I-1. Residences of Toulousan Barristers (1789).

were subject to the standards and values shaping that role. Consistent with this was the opinion, expressed by Gélibert, that actively seeking cases from an attorney was "mercenary" and dishonorable. Better not to plead than to do so at the cost of independence and professional pride. And, certainly, a busy barrister at the Parlement felt a greater sense of affinity with a caseless colleague at the Sovereign Court than with an equally busy advocate at a minor court.

Pleading, instructing, and consulting were more than "work"; they were part of the barristers' social role. Like the magistrates, who were not economically dependent on their offices but, nonetheless, were tied to these charges by pride and identity, so the barristers received dignity and meaning from their functions. Hence, the very wealthy and prominent barrister Savy de Brassalières, possessing a fortune of perhaps 180,000 livres,[129] defended the interests of a small shopkeeper against the claims of the merchant's brother for a share in the shop.[130] Surely, he received only a pittance for this defense, but it allowed him to fulfill his honorable social role. For the same reason, the rich and ennobled advocate Pierre Arexi pleaded for a *greffier* of the Seneschal Court at Béziers.[131] These so-called *petites-affaires* were the typical ones, and all important barristers argued them, not just for financial reasons, but as part of their social function.

It is clear that this solidarity and this consensus on professional values did not persist undiminished during the entire eighteenth century. The economic, demographic, and social forces which expanded the bar also forced the legal community to assimilate men at an unprecedented rate. As we shall see, too, the Enlightenment and changing attitudes opened the legal world more than ever before to outside influence and interests. The fact that barristers no longer pursued their legal studies through to the doctorate, as they had done in the seventeenth century,[132] may have denoted a weakening of that intense identification with the law and with the legal community. But just as dramatic as the changes was the persistence of these solidarities and sources of collective identification. Individuals became, often unconsciously, less submerged in the framework of values and loyalties imposed by the profession, but the legal community itself endured. And despite the rapid influx of new men, the bar was able, if not to employ them all, at least to impose its standards and expectations upon them.

[129]*A.M.*, CC-1008, *capitation* roll of Dalbade, 1788. Savy paid the very high head-tax of ninety livres.

[130]*Instruction contenante réponse pour le sieur Antoine Talansier, marchand de Maruejoles . . .* (Toulouse, n.d.), in *B.M.T.*

[131]*Mémoire pour Me Brès . . . contre les maires, lieutenant de maire . . .* (n.p., n.d.), in B.M.T.

[132]Madrange, "Les avocats," p. 22.

II

SOCIAL AND ECONOMIC STATUS

In court, the barrister won esteem and respect through his erudition and eloquence. Social origins, fortune, and even religion were easily forgotten when the sonorous voice of a barrister, booming over the incessant hubbub in the court chambers, wittily refuted an opponent's claims or artfully applied an obscure passage in Cujas to his client's arguments. Then the raised eyebrows of the magistrates and the nodding heads of the barrister's colleagues signaled approval of his performance. Outside the court, however, the advocate did not inhabit that "order of reason and truth" in which, according to d'Aguesseau, people were judged on the basis of merit alone. Wealth and family determined his social status, which found expression in his life style and social aspirations. Each of these factors must be examined in turn to determine the social position of the Toulousan barristers.

Social Origins and Recruitment

"Whoever feels he has the talent can compete"—this is how the author of one professional manual announced the bar's accessibility to merit.[1] In reality, economic and social barriers of varying proportions ensured that the man who entered the competition for cases would come from a respectable background. The educational costs were not unreasonable though they certainly placed this profession beyond the capacity of most Toulousan families. Attendance at a *collège* was free or moderately priced if a student did not have to board there; the cost for boarding might be 400 livres or more a year.[2] Tuition at the university, however, was not costly.[3] What made the educational

---

[1]Armand-Gaston Camus, *Lettres sur la profession d'avocat, sur les études relatives à cette profession et sur la manière de l'exercer* (Paris, 1777), pp. 17-18.

[2]Baron Francis Delbèke, *L'action politique et sociale des avocats au XVIIIe siècle* (Paris and Louvain, 1927), pp. 40-41.

[3]Charles Jourdain, "L'Université de Toulouse au dix-septième siècle," *Revue des sociétés savantes des départements* 8 (1862): 327.

prerequisites of the profession financially prohibitive for most were the years of successive fee-paying and the delayed-earning period, which might last until the barrister was about twenty-two.[4] And, then, the small chance for success might have hardly seemed worth this large sacrifice.

There were also social restrictions on entry, the most important of which were undoubtedly self-imposed. For most people outside the legal professions, the abstruse laws and pageantry of the court were foreign, if not intimidating. Sons of artisans and small merchants often lacked the cultural horizons and aspirations for a legal career even when they had some wealth. The dread of being snubbed by their better-born colleagues discouraged young men of the lower strata from entering the bar.[5] Moreover, the Order of Barristers exercised some control over the accessibility to the bar. Inscription on the table of the Order carried certain minimum material and moral requirements. The material prerequisites were of a practical nature: all barristers were supposed to possess certain basic legal books and a separate room in their homes in which to receive clients. These, in themselves, assumed a certain level of prosperity, and the moral requirements could, at some bars, tend even more in the direction of a socially exclusive policy. The Parisian Order apparently judged not only a candidate's moral recti- tude but also his wealth and family. Numerous exclusions were made, especially of artisans' sons. This policy engendered complaints, most notably from the future revolutionary Brissot de Warville, the son of an innkeeper.[6] In Rennes, the Order of Barristers excluded all candidates whose fathers performed manual work of any kind.[7] In subtle and not- so-subtle ways, the position of the advocate was reserved for "respec- table" families.

For Toulouse, there exists no direct evidence of a deliberate policy to exclude prospective barristers on the basis of birth. Of course, a candidate from a respectable legal background did not have to meet even minimal moral standards. Thus, the successful attorney Jean Esparbié had a son whose "dissipations" made him unfit to continue his father's profession.[8] This scandalous behavior, however, did not

---

[4]This included the two-year period of "apprenticeship," known as the *stage*, during which the young graduate attended lectures and court sessions. Technically, the young barristers could accept some cases during this period.

[5]In 1772, students at the Law Faculty of Besançon refused to attend classes because the son of a master wigmaker was admitted. See Delbèke, *L'action politique*, p. 112.

[6]Brissot de Warville, *Un indépendant à l'Ordre des avocats, sur la décadence du barreau en France* (Berlin, 1781), pp. 18–30.

[7]Frédéric Saulnier, "Le barreau du Parlement de Bretagne au XVIIIe siècle," *Revue des provinces de l'ouest*, 1856, p. 484.

[8]The father forbade his son to become an attorney. See Esparbié's testament, *A.D.*, 3E–11834, no. 3571.

prevent his inscription on the rolls of the bar (though it is questionable that he actually practiced law). Would a shopkeeper's son have been so easily admitted? Probably not.

In fact, the recruitment pattern at the Toulousan bar was one that would become common for high-status professions over the next century.[9] The barrister's profession was an "open" one—but it was accessible, in practice, chiefly to a narrow stratum of propertied, cultivated families, noble and common alike. The bar was open only in the sense that it was not self-recruiting. It did not involve venal offices which remained within the same family generation after generation,[10] and fathers did not endeavor to exclude outsiders for the benefit of their sons. In fact, only about a fourth of the barristers were sons of Toulousan advocates. The dramatic expansion of the bar after 1750 was symptomatic of the entry of "new men" at an unprecedented rate.

These new men had "respectable" backgrounds and, usually, some family contact with the law (see table II-1). Less than 2 percent were sons of master artisans, and in these cases the fathers had been uncommonly prosperous artisans and the sons, exceptionally talented and ambitious.[11] The barrister's profession was most attainable to men whose families were already in legal occupations in Toulouse or elsewhere. Two-thirds of the barristers were sons of legal men ranging from court clerks (*greffiers*) to magistrates in nonsovereign tribunals. It is easy to understand the attraction the bar had for them. They were familiar with law and judicial ceremony, and if they were natives of Toulouse, they had undoubtedly lived in the "legal" parishes of Dalbade or Saint Etienne, where the great barrister was a venerated figure. It was with good reason, then, that the offspring of Toulousan legal professionals were so disproportionately represented at the bar.

Families that did not already engage in legal activities were not excessively eager to place sons at the bar. It is hardly surprising that the sons of even the wealthiest cultivators did not aspire to the bar.[12] Yet, the fears of Jacques Savary (and other proponents of commerce) that

[9]See Edmond Goblot, *La barrière et le niveau, étude sociologique sur la bourgeoisie française moderne* (Paris, 1967).

[10]In his study of royal magistrates, Philip Dawson found that even venal offices did not necessarily create a closed profession. See his *Provincial Magistrates and Revolutionary Politics in France, 1789-1795* (Cambridge, Mass., 1972), pp. 100-109. The legal professions in general were apparently open to "new men."

[11]The marriage contracts demonstrate the unusually large fortunes of their fathers; see *A.D.*, 3E-15256, fol. 105; 3E-73994, fol. 174; 3E-26487, fol. 184. The father of Louis Labat entitled himself "tailor" in some documents and "bourgeois" in others (see *A.D.*, 2C-2997, entry of 17 July 1780). More will be said about the talent and success of these barristers.

[12]The father of one barrister, Etienne Fabre, called himself a "négociant" from Valurenque, a village near Castres. He may well have been a grain and animal merchant with a hand in the production side of the business, an enterprising *laboureur*. See *A.D.*, 3E-26528, fol. 8.

TABLE II-1.   Social Origins of Barristers and Attorneys, 1750-1789

Father's Occupation	Barristers No.	%	Attorneys No.	%
Barrister	50	31.6	0	0
Bourgeois	25	15.8	10	24.5
Merchant[a]	19	12.0	7	17.1
Attorney	17	10.8	12	30.0
Civil officer	15	9.6	2	4.5
Notary	14	9.0	8	19.5
Greffier	6	3.8	1	2.2
Seigneur, écuyer	7	4.4	0	0
Master artisan	3	1.9	1	2.2
Doctor	2	1.1	0	0
Total	158	100.0	41	100.0

Source: A.D., 3E. This table is based on a study of marriage contracts of advocates and attorneys.

[a]"Merchant" includes *marchand* and *négociant*, usually the latter.

merchants' sons were all too eager to desert trade for law were also unfounded, even in this legally-minded city.[13] In aggregate, merchants of all kinds supplied a substantial portion of barristers (12 percent), but this was not large in relation to their importance in the general population. There were over 2,000 merchants in Toulouse alone, constituting nearly 5 percent of the male population.[14] The large-scale traders of the *Grande Bourse* were certainly as numerous as barristers, but only about 5 percent of the pleaders (as compared to 25 percent for barristers) came from this successful mercantile background. There was no inevitable movement from commerce to law when a merchant's family attained prosperity.[15]

Legal families considered the barrister's status sufficiently distinguished to break with the ideal of occupational stability from generation to generation. Even when a father had an office or practice to pass on to his children, he frequently placed his eldest son (and heir) at the bar. The attorney Jean Monserrat Lagarrigue, for example, made his eldest son, Jean, his heir but reserved the attorney's office for another child.[16] Jean Lagarrigue became a barrister, and his younger brother assumed the family office. Bernard Etienne Arbanere, Pierre Belin, and

[13]See Henri Hauser, "Le 'Parfait Négociant' de Jacques Savary," *Revue d'histoire économique et sociale* 13 (1925): 7.

[14]G. Marinière, "Les marchands d'étoffes de Toulouse à la fin du XVIIIe siècle," *Annales du midi* 70 (1958): 251.

[15]Dawson found that men from commercial backgrounds were not prominent among non-noble judges. See *Provincial Magistrates*, pp. 108-9. Career patterns of merchants' children merit more attention. Apparently, law and commerce offered rather separate and distinct career "tracks."

[16]*A.D.*, 3E-10872, no. 164, testament of Lagarrigue.

Jean Valette were other eldest sons of attorneys who became barristers.[17] Notaries, too, placed their eldest sons and heirs at the bar.[18] In legal families, then, barristers were not cadets who had been pushed out on their own while an older brother assumed the greater part of the family's wealth and status. On the contrary, the eldest son raised the honor of the family by entering the bar, leaving the inferior legal office to a younger child.

In the case of commercial families, however, the intergenerational pattern was much less consistent and clear. Both eldest sons and cadets entered the bar, with the latter predominating. It appears that smaller merchants (perhaps some were only prosperous shopkeepers) were more willing to place eldest sons at the bar than were established traders. Such career patterns, however, did not indicate that larger merchants scorned the legal world; rather, these patterns reflect different values and family aspirations.[19]

Outside the legal world the families of *bourgeois* (that is, *rentiers*) were another important source of barristers. They, of course, lacked the commercial alternative available to sons of merchants. Many "advocates without cases" differed from rentiers only in their possession of legal degrees and professional title. In terms of life style the bourgeois and barrister were close, and this may explain the migration to the bar of families "living nobly."

If the bar attracted most of its practitioners from the legal professions, it was particularly open in a geographic sense. New men from all over the jurisdiction of the Parlement and beyond established practices in Toulouse. The marriage contracts reveal that 46 percent of the barristers were sons of nonresidents. However, this source is biased in favor of Toulousans; the true proportion of non-natives at the bar was surely over half.[20] Some came from distant places, but most were natives of villages and towns within fifty miles of Toulouse (see figure II–1).[21] About a third of the non-native barristers were from rural communities around Toulouse, where their fathers had frequently been bourgeois or notaries.[22] Jean Philippe Boun, for example, was the

---

[17]*A.D.*, 3E–21571, fol. 228; 3E–13919, fol. 3; 3E–11867, fol. 10348.

[18]See, for example, the case of Corail, *A.D.*, 3E–11095, fol. 220; and Lafage, whose father was a notary, but not in Toulouse, 3E–11087, fol. 174.

[19]When merchants were ennobled, their sons usually became barristers. This indicates their respect for the legal profession.

[20]Natives of the city were more likely to wed women from Toulouse, thereby leaving a marriage contract with a Toulousan notary. Marriage contracts are only one possible source for the study of internal migration. For the problems and prospects of research on migration, see the special issue of *Annales de démographie historique* (1970).

[21]For Toulousan migration in general, see M. L. Larnaudie, "L'immigration à Toulouse de 1750 à 1775" (D.E.S., University of Toulouse, 1969). More studies of the migratory patterns of different social groups are needed.

[22]There are no studies of the "bourgeoisie rurale" for the region of Toulouse. For Burgundy, see Pierre de St. Jacob, *Les paysans de la Bourgogne du Nord au dernier siècle*

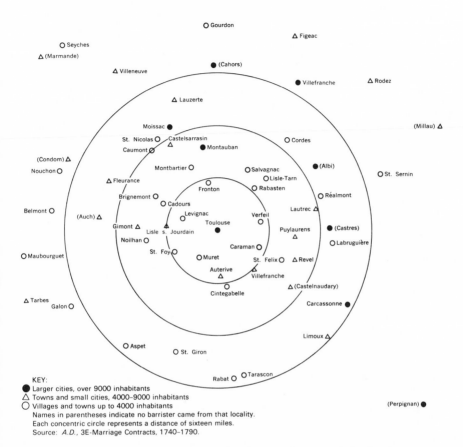

FIGURE II-1.   Geographic Origins of Forty-Nine Non-Native Barristers

son of a bourgeois of Maurens, a village of nearly 300 inhabitants 32 kilometers southeast of Toulouse.[23] The important barrister Jean Baptiste Lafage was the son of a notary of Cintegabelle, a larger village in the diocese of Toulouse.[24] Nearly half of the non-native advocates came from towns and urban areas of 3,000 to 5,000 inhabitants. Their fathers had been legal men (especially barristers, judges, and notaries) or rentiers. Children of leading families in these towns were not uncommon at the Toulousan bar. Jean Bernard Bellomaire, for example, was the son of a mayor of Verfeil, a town of about 2,500, east

de l'ancien régime (Paris, 1960), pp. 525-28. St. Jacob emphasizes their exploitation of the cultivators and their domination over rural justice.

[23] A.D., 3E-10760, fol. 128. For the populations of towns and villages, I have used Georges Frêche, "Dénombrement de feux et d'habitants de 2973 communautés de la région toulousaine," Annales de démographie historique, 1968, pp. 389-421; and 1969, pp. 397-471.

[24] A.D., 3E-2652, fol. 8.

of Toulouse.[25] The grandfather of Antoine Flottes had been a municipal officer of Cordes,[26] while Antoine Cahusac was the son of the
"royal magistrate" of Gimont, a town near Auch.[27] Barristers from
villages and towns outnumbered those from the large cities (other than
Toulouse). Natives of Montauban, Castres, Albi, and Carcassonne were
not numerous at the bar, even if these cities had concentrations of well-
to-do legal professionals.[28] Perhaps residents of these cities were
satisfied with the cultural and social opportunities available there. But
well-off families outside these large urban areas sought wider horizons
by placing sons at the Toulousan bar.

Thus far, we have been examining the background of Toulousan
barristers without distinguishing between tribunals. However, the
varying degrees of prestige attached to each court created different
patterns of recruitment. The Parlement readily attracted non-natives
and eldest sons, even those of merchants. The lesser courts of the city
were staffed largely by Toulousans whose families were in commerce or
law. Of six barristers at the Seneschal Court, one was the son of a
barrister at this court, three were younger sons of Toulousan merchants, and two were sons of magistrates at the Seneschal Courts of
Toulouse and Cordes respectively.[29] A similar pattern may be detected
for barristers at the minor courts of exceptional jurisdiction, though
documentation is, admittedly, poorer. Only the Parlement attracted
sons of legal men, rentiers, even *seigneurs*, from afar.

A study of the social origins of attorneys completes and confirms
what has been said about the professional milieux of recruitment of
barristers (see table II-1). Like the barristers, attorneys were usually
sons of legal men, along with an important element of rentiers.
Artisans' sons were excluded by the price of the office and, perhaps, by
other restrictions imposed by the Community of Attorneys.[30] It is
noteworthy that barristers' sons did not become attorneys; apparently,
the profession was insufficiently honorable in their eyes. The Parisian
barrister Barbier, in fact, exhibited great disdain for attorneys, claiming
that their sons "had no birth at all."[31] This was not simply a prejudice

---

[25]Jules Villain, *La France moderne. Grand dictionnaire généalogique, historique, et
biographique (Haute-Garonne et Ariège)*, 4 vols. (Montpellier, 1911), 1: 311–12.

[26]*Ibid.*, 2: 978–81; marriage contract of Flottes, *A.D.*, 3E–11093, fol. 58.

[27]*A.D.*, 3E–13995, fol. 211, marriage contract of Cahusac.

[28]One might add the cities of Auch, Condon, Cahors, and Béziers, too. Three
barristers (de Vier, Fraissiner, and Villefranche), however, came from Villefranche-de-
Rouergue, which had a population of about 9,300.

[29]See the marriage contracts of Loubers, *A.D.*, 3E–13933, fol. 218; Augé, 3E–5973, fol.
54; Guion, 3E–10981, fol. 109; for Bordes, 3E–10893, fol. 291, list of witnesses. See
genealogies of Purpan and Flottes in Villain, *Grand dictionnaire*, 2: 978 and 4: 1604–8.

[30]In the 1760s, this group paid 6,000 livres to liquidate an office. See Florentin
Astre, *Les procureurs près le Parlement de Toulouse* (Toulouse, 1858), p. 32.

[31]E. J. F. Barbier, *Journal historique et anecdotique*, 8 vols. (Paris, 1884), 1: 103.

peculiar to barristers; it was a generally accepted evaluation. No nobles or *seigneurs* made their sons attorneys but they did place offspring at the bar. Attorneys and barristers, so akin by function, were socially quite distant.

The legal status and wealth of the barristers' families further defined their milieu of recruitment. By no means were all barristers sons of commoners. In fact, the Toulousan bar may well have had a higher portion of noble pleaders than any other in France; about one in ten belonged to the Second Estate. The source of this anomalous situation in Toulouse was the ennobling municipal office of *capitoul*, which barristers frequently held. Postponing a detailed discussion of these capitouls for later, it need only be said here that, in the last fifty years of the Old Regime, thirty-nine practicing barristers served as capitouls.[32] These barristers and their sons made up most of the noble pleaders at the bar, but their presence encouraged other nobles, *écuyers*, and *seigneurs* to enter it.[33] The nobles enhanced the status of the profession and, as we shall see, set standards and aspirations for their colleagues.

How wealthy were the families who placed sons at the Toulousan bar? This important question is not easily answered, for direct indications of the fathers' economic status are hard to gather. Their far-flung geographic origins and their disappearance at death from tax rolls, even when they had resided in Toulouse, necessitate the use of indirect measures of wealth. One convenient, though rough, index of family fortune was the dowries given to barristers by their brides. The dowry itself was a direct reflection of the wealth in the bride's family. Its size was ultimately determined by the portion of her parents' estate she would inherit ("la légitime tel que de droit"). The dowry varied, to be sure, with the number of siblings, the desirability of the match, and the parents' generosity. But the most important determinant was her parents' fortunes. What made the dowry a rough index of the *husband's* wealth was the very strong tendency for families of equal fortune to intermarry. That this was true in eighteenth-century Toulouse has recently been confirmed by Jean Sentou.[34] Certainly, the

---

[32]There are many lists of capitouls, some unreliable. I have used the list in Alexandre DuMège, *Histoire des institutions . . . de Toulouse*, 4 vols. (Toulouse, 1844), 2: 459–72. I am grateful for the advice of M. Charles Pistre, who is working on a study of the capitouls.

[33]A barrister with a particularly distinguished background was Joseph Durban, baron of Sananezan, member of a parlementaire family. See *A.D.*, 3E-11090, fol. 164. His case should be distinguished from those of the many parlementaires' sons who became barristers only as a momentary step on their way to a magistracy.

[34]*Fortunes et groupes sociaux à Toulouse sous la Révolution* (Toulouse, 1969), p. 55 (chart), and p. 58. The marriage contracts I studied did not usually state the amount the husband received from his parents, the *apport masculin*. Professor Sentou believes that, on the average, it was very close to the dowry.

dowry can indicate no more than the general magnitude of the wealth in the barristers' family, and nothing further will be claimed. Whenever firmer data are available, however, they support the accuracy of this index.

The average dowry received by barristers was quite large, amounting to 14,300 livres.[35] Their ability to attract such sizeable dowries indicates that the barristers themselves came from well-to-do families. Only 6 percent of the marriages in Toulouse during the revolutionary period entailed such large transfers of wealth. Indeed, four-fifths of the dowries in Toulouse were less than a tenth of this.[36] Our rough index, then, shows that barristers came from very favorable economic backgrounds. To be sure, they were considerably below the parlementaires and *noblesse de race*, whose average dowries were over 44,000 livres in 1785.[37] The barristers were, however, well within the economic group immediately below the aristocracy.

Our sample of 152 dowries received by barristers indicates a considerable diversity of family fortune, with a concentration at the more elevated financial levels (see table II-2). The range of dowries was immense: from the 300 livres received by Meric Ricard from his illiterate wife, to the 60,000 livres received by Jacob Londois, the son of a Montaubanais merchant.[38] Nearly 70 percent of the dowries received by barristers surpassed 10,000 livres. At most, 5 percent of the entire Toulousan population might have attracted dowries of this magnitude.[39] Thus it seems that barristers came predominantly from a narrow range of wealthy families.

If dowries of 14,000 livres were exceptional in Toulouse, with its concentration of aristocrats and wealthy *roturiers*, they must have been much more outstanding in the villages and small towns of the region. Yet, the non-native barristers did attract dowries of this magnitude.[40]

[35]*A.D.*, 3E-marriage contracts of 152 barristers, 1740–1790. My findings differ somewhat from the average dowry found by Sentou (*Fortunes et groupes sociaux*, p. 215). The disruptions of the Revolution may have caused the disparity. There was also an important change in legal personnel after 1789, and this surely had an impact on the size of dowries.

[36]Sentou, *Fortunes et groupes sociaux*, p. 66 (chart). Sentou's figures are the average of the male and female *apports*; mine represent the dowry of female *apport* only. Since the two were generally the same, this should make no difference for the comparison I am drawing.

[37]Jacques Godechot and Suzanne Moncassin, "Structure et relations sociales à Toulouse en 1749 et 1785," *Annales historiques de la Révolution française* 37 (1965): 134, 138.

[38]*A.D.*, 3E-7362, fol. 199 and 3E-11094, fol. 171.

[39]Sentou, *Fortunes et groupes sociaux*, p. 66. Sentou shows that less than 6 percent of the *apports* were above 10,000 livres. The very poor, of course, did not make marriage contracts.

[40]Their average dowry was 13,750 livres. Studies of the socioeconomic structure of towns and villages in the region are needed. An examination of sixty-eight marriage contracts in the Lauraguis countryside (nineteenth century) revealed that fourteen were

TABLE II-2.   Size of Dowries Received by Barristers, 1750-1790

Dowry (livres)	Number	Percent
0-999	1	0.6
1,000-4,999	15	9.6
5,000-9,999	34	22.4
10,000-14,999	34	22.4
15,000-19,999	26	17.0
20,000-24,999	28	18.1
25,000-29,999	2	1.5
30,000 and over	12	8.4
Total	152	100.0

Source: A.D., 3E. This table is based on 152 marriage contracts of barristers.

Their fathers must have been rural or town residents of quite uncommon wealth.

These large dowries were not characteristic of the barristers at all Toulousan courts, which, in fact, recruited their pleaders from different economic levels. The sizeable dowries discussed so far were characteristic primarily of the barristers at the Parlement, who were clearly from the wealthiest families. Barristers at the Seneschal Court received an average dowry of only 7,200 livres, indicating a less favored economic background. The pleaders at the Merchants' Court received an average of only 4,100 livres, which was not much more than a prosperous retail merchant could expect from his bride. Thus, the varying economic levels of the barristers' families corresponded to the hierarchy of the courts and helps to explain recruitment into each. The barristers at the Parlement, where success was most difficult, came from the wealthiest families and could most afford the risks. Those of the Seneschal Court needed the greater opportunities for earning fees that their relatively uncrowded tribunal afforded. Finally, the modest family wealth of barristers at the minor courts explained their need for the small fees earned by handling procedure and by serving in several legal capacities at once. These variations in social background reinforced the differences in professional status among the barristers of the Toulousan courts.

---

less than 100 livres, forty-four were 100 to 1,000 livres, ten were above 1,000 livres. See Germain Sicard, "Société et comportement juridique: une enquête sur les contracts de mariage au XIX siècle," *Annales de la Faculté de Droit . . . de Toulouse* 18 (1970): 249. A socioprofessional analysis of some large and small villages in Quercy indicates that the "rural bourgeoisie" rarely formed more than 2 to 4 percent of the population—and only a small minority of these could have attracted such large dowries. See Denise Leymond, "La communauté de Duravel au XVIIIe siècle," *Annales du midi* 79 (1967): 370; Pierre Valmary, *Familles paysannes au XVIIIe siècle en Bas-Quercy* (Paris, 1965), p. 71. For a market town of about 4,000, see Pierre Gérard, "Citoyens actifs de Grenade-sur-Garonne," *Annales du midi* 70 (1958): 309-16.

In the end, the recruitment pattern at the Toulousan bar was shaped by the absence of formal restrictions on entry but also by the delayed-earning period, the limited opportunities for success, and the cultural barriers that discouraged even those with the financial prerequisites. This made the bar—especially that of the Parlement—a stronghold for the wealthiest 5 to 8 percent of Toulousan families and a much narrower elite in the towns and villages of the region. Unusual sacrifice, risk, or ambition was required for families outside this elite to place sons at the bar, so they were, accordingly, less numerous. Such a recruitment pattern provided a bar that was diversified in origin, to be sure. But behind this diversity was a very qualified openness.

MARRIAGE AND THE QUEST FOR NOBILITY

The son of the unfortunate barrister Etienne Joseph Martel was known for his "lightness" of character, his indolence, and his propensity for trouble. Barrister Martel died with concern for this son on his mind. He entrusted the youth to a relative, instructing the guardian to find his son a wife distinguished by the "respectability [*honnêteté*] of her birth, her good morals, and by her real and effective fortune."[41] Despite the special problems presented by his son, Martel's marriage policy was a typical one for barristers. Good birth and substantial fortune were the desired qualities for an advocate's wife.

Marriage was a serious, long-pondered act for barristers, one which they postponed long beyond their entry into professional life. The average barrister wed (for the first time) 9.4 years after beginning his practice.[42] Since twenty-four was the average age for entering the bar, most advocates were surely over thirty when they took a wife. The Toulousan barrister, thus, married two to three years later than the sober French peasant and perhaps a dozen years after the average duke and peer in Paris.[43] Indeed, their bachelorhoods were no shorter than those of such notorious celibates as the gentlemen of Victorian England and the patriciate of Geneva.[44]

---

[41]*A.D.*, 3E-14178, fol. 194, testament of Martel.

[42]I have arrived at this average by comparing the date of the marriage contracts with the year the barrister took his professional oath, listed in the *Almanach historique de la province de Languedoc* (Toulouse, 1789).

[43]Louis Henry, "The Population of France in the Eighteenth Century," in *Population in History*, ed. D. V. Glass and D. E. C. Eversley (London, 1965), p. 455.

[44]The average age at first marriage for the Genevan was 31.5 years, according to Louis Henry, *Anciennes familles genèvoises* (Paris, 1956), p. 55. The Victorian gentleman or liberal professional is thought to have married in his very late twenties or early thirties. See Joseph A. and Olive Banks, *Feminism and Family Planning in Victorian England* (New York, 1964), pp. 29-30.

The lengthy delay served an important economic purpose: the barrister did not have to wait long after establishing a family to inherit his parents' property. This was highly desirable because, as we shall see, the family fortune was usually a barrister's most important source of income. However, the delayed marriage was not simply the product of economic necessity; it had become an integral part of the barristers' expectations and life style. Barristers from some of the wealthiest families—Londois, Cahusac, Dessolles, Durban, and Vidal—waited until their mid-30s before marrying. The long period of celibacy suggests a large measure of self-discipline, no doubt made less conscious by habit and custom.[45]

The maturity of the barrister at marriage assured him a definite voice in the selection of his wife. Fathers or elder relatives still arranged matches, which the barrister usually accepted,[46] but his consent was the result of shared values and opinions, not of compulsion. A practicing pleader for several years, he could hardly have been forced into matrimony through economic pressure. Frequently, too, the father had died before the son's marriage, so the barrister was the effective family head. In any case, we can be confident that the values and attitudes displayed in selecting a wife were the barrister's own, not attitudes forced upon him by his family.

The substantial dowries that the barristers received demonstrated their success in meeting Martel's requirement for "real and effective fortune." As for "respectability of birth," they attained this by marrying within the professional milieux from which they had been recruited (see table II-3). Though artisans' daughters were unacceptable matches, barristers readily wed into families of large merchants, legal professionals, and rentiers.[47] It was quite common for a barrister to take a wife from his father's occupational group. If marriage within one's own profession (to the daughter of a colleague) survived at all as an ideal, it had a weak hold on the barristers. Intermarriage among barristers' families was quite frequent, but it seems to have been more a matter of circumstance than of conscious design. Family occupations

[45]I have found only two instances in which barristers fathered illegitimate children. Both Louis Jean Gaudens Raynal and Jean (?) Vincens left sizeable legacies to "natural children" born to their servants—presumably their own children. See their testaments, *A.D.*, 3E-10875 and 3E-11857, no. 8985.

[46]An uncle arranged Bertrand Barère's marriage, and the barrister accepted it. Leo Gershoy, *Bertrand Barère, A Reluctant Terrorist* (Princeton, 1962), p. 32.

[47]The barristers who married artisans' daughters were sons of artisans in each case. The famed Parisian *avocat* Pierre Berryer wed the daughter of an attorney in order to receive some of his father-in-laws' rich clients. See Pierre Berryer's *Souvenirs de M. Berryer*, 2 vols. (Paris, 1839), 1: 99–103. Toulousan barristers might have made more matches with attorneys' daughters if this had been a significant factor in their marriage policies.

TABLE II-3.   Marriage Alliances of Barristers, 1750–1790

Occupation of Wife's Father	Barristers	
	No.	%
Merchant[a]	34	22.8
Barrister	32	21.4
Seigneur, écuyer	25	16.7
Bourgeois	16	10.7
Attorney	13	8.7
Civil officer	10	6.7
Notary	6	4.1
Master artisan	5	3.4
Medical profession	3	2.1
Huissier, greffier	3	2.1
Military noble	2	1.3
Total	149	100.0

Source: A.D., 3E, marriage contracts.

[a]This category includes both négociants and marchands. There were only eight cases of marchands.

over a fairly wide range seemed less important than the size of the dowry, the personal traits of the bride, and the local reputation of her family.[48] There was, however, one milieu above all others into which barristers sought to marry: the nobility.

Barristers were strongly attracted to alliances with noble families, and it was a sign of their high social standing that such matches were frequent. Over a fifth (22 percent) of the Toulousan avocats married into noble families (or, in two or three cases, into families whose noble pretensions may have been stronger than their legal claim).[49] Three-quarters of these alliances involved barristers who were commoners themselves. It was significant, too, that twenty-two of our thirty-two noble marriages concerned second-generation barristers. This suggests that after a generation at the bar families were particularly ready to form a noble alliance. Altogether, these matches were the most striking aspect of the barristers' marriage pattern.

The barristers married into two types of noble families: those recently ennobled—often via the capitoul's office—and those of the hoberaux, or poor country gentlemen. The marriage of advocate

[48]Dawson (in Provincial magistrates, pp. 109–12) suggests that intermarriage among non-noble judges was significantly less frequent than it had been a century earlier. My impression is the same for the Toulousan barristers.

[49]Table III-3 includes these alliances under the rubrics seigneur, military noble, écuyer, barrister, and, in one case, civil officer. In order to determine how many of the families had a legitimate claim to noble status, I consulted Louis de la Roque, Catalogue des gentilhommes de Languedoc qui ont pris part . . . aux assemblées de la noblesse pour l'élection des députés aux Etats Généraux . . . (Paris, 1862). With the exceptions of two or three doubtful cases, the families appeared to have been genuinely noble.

Dominique Arrivat to a daughter of Noble de Glaçon exemplifies the latter. Arrivat's father-in-law was an *écuyer* and a former captain in the infantry.[50] The Glaçon family had obviously seen better days; so had the ancient family of Bigorre into which the Toulousan barrister and future revolutionary Bertrand Barère married.[51] Such nobles were not completely impoverished, but the 5,000 to 10,000 livres in dowry they could afford was hardly on a par with the aristocratic families of Toulouse. Considerably more often, the barrister married into a family whose noble pedigree was only one or two generations old. These noble matches flattered the barrister's self-image, drew his family closer to privileged status in a psychological sense, and gave his children what they took to be a foothold in the Second Estate.[52]

The marriage alliances of the noble advocates deserve special attention because they had an important impact on their colleagues' social outlook and aspirations. The numerous marriages among *anoblis* (from law and commerce alike) created a social stratum just below the aristocracy: the second most exclusive milieu in Toulouse. These alliances illustrate the increasing compartmentalization of Old Regime society despite channels of social advancement, a phenomenon which Alexis de Tocqueville noted long ago.[53] Yet at the same time this stratum of new nobles had the important psychological effect of making nobility seem near, familiar, and feasible as an aspiration for many barristers.

The noble barristers endeavored to marry their children to other *anoblis* as frequently as possible. Their alliances formed a reticulum too complicated to follow in detail here, but a striking demonstration of this network occurred at the wedding of barrister (and future capitoul) Jean Raynal to the daughter of barrister-capitoul François Amblard in 1761. Present at the ceremony were five related capitoul families, Rolland St. Rome, Cucsac, Tilhol, Morrot, and Saremejane.[54] These, in turn, were allied to other noble families. The Rolland St. Rome family, originally rich merchants, were tied by marriage to the barrister-capitoul Jean Marie Delort and to Jean Pierre de Bouttes.[55]

---

[50]*A.D.*, 3E-2110, register 2, fol. 142.

[51]Gershoy, *Barère*, pp. 32-33.

[52]Barrister Lamarque proudly noted his mother's noble blood in his marriage contract, *A.D.*, 3E-5077. And Barère claimed noble status on the basis of his mother's nobility (Gershoy, *Barère*, pp. 5-6).

[53]Alexis de Tocqueville, *The Old Regime and the French Revolution*, trans. Stuart Gilbert (New York, 1955), pp. 81-96.

[54]*A.D.*, 3E-13965, fol. 266, marriage contract of Raynal.

[55]*A.D.*, 3E-1175, fol. 97; 3E-14009, fol. 44. De Bouttes had married the daughter of Delort, and the son of this marriage wed a Rolland St. Rome. Saremejane married a daughter of capitoul Daunaussan (3E-3900, fol. 606). A Borrel was married to the capitoul-merchant Desazars (3E-2777, register 2, fol. 16).

The Rollands were also cousins of another merchant-capitoul family, the Roussillous. A Roussillou married the daughter of the barrister-capitoul Jerome Taverne, and a child of this match married the son of the ennobled advocate Jean Baptiste Jouve.[56] Another of Jouve's sons married Rose d'Arexi, the daughter of Pierre Arexi; and he, in turn, had wed the daughter of the minor nobleman Jean Catala de Catellan.[57] We could easily extend our enumeration of these intermarriages, but it ought to be clear how these capitouls formed an exclusive circle and a "family"—much like the extended family of parlementaires—on the edge of the aristocracy.

To enter this restricted milieu was the hope of non-noble barristers, and a substantial number did so. Capitouls were not always wealthy enough to endow each of their daughters with the 20,000 to 25,000 livres required for a husband from their own circle. This was especially a problem in large families with several daughters. So, the *anoblis* sought promising barristers as sons-in-law; such pleaders were likely to become capitouls themselves. Thus, Marie Amblard married Jean Raynal while he was still a commoner, but Raynal was ennobled several years later. The merchant-capitoul Borrel gave his daughter's hand to Jean Baptiste Viguier, the most outstanding barrister during the last decade of the Old Regime.[58] Distinguished advocates who did not attain this noble stratum might hope that their descendants would. The highly respected barrister Guillaume Dirat had never become a capitoul himself, so he was probably very pleased when his daughter married the son of capitoul Berdoulat, ensuring a noble descent.[59] Altogether about one in four marriages involving *anoblis* drew non-noble barristers into this exclusive "family." In this way, many successful pleaders were placed in intimate contact with the nobility.

The intertwining of this noble circle with the most distinguished portion of the bar had very important social consequences. The noble barristers not only provided social and professional leadership for their colleagues, but they facilitated an identification with the Second Estate on the part of non-noble barristers. Hence their attachment to the extended trappings of nobility, the *seigneurie*, and the noble particle, as well as their eagerness to marry noble families. The distinction between noble and commoners was not always a clearcut one among the Toulousan barristers.[60]

[56]*A.D.*, 3E-26524, fol. 102, and Villain, *Grand dictionnaire*, 3: 1730–31. The capitoul Pyron married his daughter to a Roussillou (3E-13989, fol. 167).

[57]Villain, *Grand dictionnaire*, 1: 11–14, 3: 1730–31.

[58]*A.D.*, 3E-2111, register 1, fol. 264, list of witnesses. Viguier never became capitoul, despite his prominence at the bar.

[59]*A.D.*, 3E-26537, fol. 146, marriage contract of Berdoulat. Dirat's pleasure at his daughter's match was demonstrated by the large dowry he provided, 30,000 livres.

[60]De Tocqueville underscored the importance of clear-cut, legal divisions in Old Regime society. Without denying the significance of these divisions in 1789, it may

LEVEL OF FORTUNE

The barristers' very respectable social origins and their favorable marriage alliances placed them in a social position immediately below the aristocracy. Did they possess wealth commensurate with this position? Born to well-off families, for the most part, it would have been surprising if many barristers did not have substantial fortunes. How large these were and how they compared to others in Toulousan society must now be considered.

Several sources are available for a study of the barristers' wealth, but none is complete or fully satisfactory in itself. In all cases, these sources deal exclusively with the barrister's personal, invested wealth (land, houses, annuities) and neglect his professional income entirely. The head tax (*capitation*) was, very roughly, 1 percent of annual return on capital.[61] Its utility lies more in its comprehensiveness than in its reliability in individual cases. The average head tax paid by barristers was 25.1 livres, suggesting a yearly revenue of 2,500 livres and, assuming a 5 percent return on invested wealth, a total fortune of 50,000 livres. In contrast, the rolls of the first revolutionary imposition, the *Quart*, provide a much lower estimate of the barristers' fortunes—no doubt because each declared as small a revenue as he dared.[62] Nearly a hundred barristers paid the *Quart*, declaring an average income of 1,310 livres. Much more reliable were the acts of succession, depositions of the barristers' estates made by their heirs. Professor Jean Sentou has found that the average succession of fifty-nine barristers who died during the revolutionary period was 34,000 livres.[63] Finally, there were the declarations for the Forced Loan of 1793.[64] The statements of forty-seven barristers included in this "loan" averaged slightly above 50,000 livres. However, this imposition was levied on "the rich," so the sample was not fully representative of the Toulousan bar.

If the different sources are weighed on the basis of reliability and comprehensiveness, they suggest an average fortune at the end of the Old Regime of 35,000 to 40,000 livres. This was substantial wealth, 25 to 30 percent more than the mean for Toulousan property-owner. It

---

well have been that until the Revolution many commoners were more conscious of their connections to the nobility than of their exclusion from it. See Colin Lucas, "Nobles, Bourgeois, and the Origins of the French Revolution," *Past and Present*, no. 60 (1973), pp. 88, 93, *passim*. Also, Maurice Agulhon, *La vie sociale en Provence intérieure au lendemain de la Révolution* (Paris, 1970), pp. 103–23.

[61]*A.M.*, CC-rolls of *capitation* and 1K–6 for St. Etienne in 1790. For the value of the head tax, see Sentou, *Fortunes et groupes sociaux*, pp. 22–23.

[62]*A.M.*, 2 G–2.

[63]*Fortunes et groupes sociaux*, p. 215. During the Revolution, barristers were entitled "hommes de loi" or "avocat." Sentou provides different average fortunes for the two groups. My figure is a weighted average of these two.

[64]*A.M.*, 2 G9–16.

was twice the wealth of most retail tradesmen and four times that of a master artisan. Certainly, no more than one in ten or fifteen Toulousan families could have hoped to attain this economic level, and such wealth was certainly much more exceptional outside the city.[65]

A discussion of "averages," however useful, obscures the diversity of fortunes among the barristers; and this diversity was considerable. The Merchants' Court pleader Pierre Bonnet paid no head tax, while Jean Boubée, at the Parlement, paid the very high *capitation* of 123 livres.[66] Declarations for the forced loan ranged from 12,000 livres to 133,000 livres. The wealthiest barrister was probably Guillaume Louis Daram, who declared a yearly revenue of 11,698 livres in 1793 and had a fortune of about 230,000 livres.[67] Pierre Alexandre Gary and Jean Prévost also had fortunes of over 200,000 livres.[68] These barristers were perhaps twelve times wealthier than the most humble barristers.

The hierarchy of courts compounded the complexity of the barristers as an economic group. The richest barristers were exclusively in the Parlement, while, with one exception, the pleaders in the Seneschal Court had only middling or modest fortunes.[69] Their average head tax of 12.2 livres was less than half the average for the bar of the Parlement (29.1 livres). The barristers at the courts of exceptional jurisdiction were still more modest, with an average head tax of only 7.2 livres. The differences of wealth among the bars of each court undoubtedly resulted from their different milieux of recruitment.

Even the exclusive circle of noble barristers was not an economically unified group. With an average head tax of 49.5 livres, many of these barristers were quite wealthy, and the majority certainly had fortunes over 60,000 livres. Nonetheless, this group defined itself by legal status rather than wealth, and some noble barristers were not distinctively well-off. Etienne Dominique Taverne, son of the very distinguished barrister-capitoul Jerome Taverne, died in 1790 with a fortune of only 34,000 livres.[70] Jean Marie Saremejane, also the son of a capitoul, possessed a fortune of only 30,000 livres.[71] So, this social elite at the bar was not always an economic elite, and this explains their intermarriages with non-nobles.

A careful analysis of the different fiscal sources permit us to estimate the personal fortunes of 229 barristers. As displayed in table II-4, these

[65]Sentou, *Fortunes et groupes sociaux*, pp. 61, 66, 293, 350.
[66]*A.M.*, 1 K-6 for Boubée; CC-1056 for Bonnet.
[67]*A.M.*, 2 G-16.
[68]*A.M.*, 2 G-2, for Gary; Sentou, *Fortunes et groupes sociaux*, p. 264 for Prévost.
[69]The rich barrister in the Seneschal Court was Jean Antoine Romiguières, with a fortune of about 70,000 livres. He declared a revenue of 3,600 livres for the Quart (*A.M.*, 2 G-2) and paid a head tax of 36 livres.
[70]Sentou, *Fortunes et groupes sociaux*, p. 268.
[71]Henri Martin, ed., *Documents relatifs à la vente des biens nationaux, District de Toulouse* (Toulouse, 1916), p. 243, and *A.M.*, 1 S-70.

TABLE II-4.   Fortunes of the Toulousan Barristers (1789)

Fortune (livres)	Number	Percent
Below 10,000	26	11.4
10,000–19,999	52	22.9
20,000–29,999	35	15.4
30,000–39,999	30	13.2
40,000–49,999	22	9.6
50,000–59,999	18	7.9
60,000–69,999	13	5.4
70,000–79,999	13	5.4
80,000–100,000	8	3.5
Over 100,000	12	5.3
Total	229	100.0

Sources: A.M., CC, rolls of capitation; 2 G-9-16; 2 G-2; Acts of succession from Jean Sentou, Fortunes et groupes sociaux à Toulouse sous la Révolution (Toulouse, 1969).

figures represent the economic structure of the bar in 1789. They do, however, understate the financial situation of barristers in two significant ways. First, our approximations are likely to be minimal ones, based as they are on the advocates' own declarations of wealth. More important, these data include the fortunes of many young men whose wealth could have grown with their maturity. Nonetheless, the barristers were still well-off compared to other Toulousans. At least half the city residents were essentially propertyless and cannot be included in any comparison.[72] Two-thirds of those who did have property possessed fortunes between 1,585 livres and 63,000 livres according to the invaluable study by Professor Sentou.[73] Most barristers were in this range, but at the top of it. Figure II-2 illustrates how barristers were relatively and absolutely most numerous at the top of the Toulousan economic hierarchy. If only one Toulousan property-owner in ten possessed wealth above 63,000 livres, a quarter (24 percent) of the barristers did so, and the barristers were certainly much more of an elite in the context of the regional economic structure. Thus, their financial position reflected their origins: though modest men were not excluded, a narrow stratum of wealthy families were disproportionately represented.

The barristers as an economic group compared favorably with the socioprofessional groups from which they were recruited and with which they allied in marriage. They were far richer than the average

[72]The "laboring poor" of Toulouse have not been studied. In Orléans, Bayeux, and Montauban, however, half the population depended on their daily wages for subsistence. See Georges Lefebvre, Etudes orléanaises, 2 vols. (Paris, 1962), 2: 212; Olwen Hufton, Bayeux in the Late Eighteenth Century (Oxford, 1967), p. 58; Daniel Ligou, "Etude fonctionnelle de la population de Montauban à la fin de l'ancien régime," Actes du 86ᵉ congrès nationale des sociétés savantes (Paris, 1962), pp. 579–89.

[73]Fortunes et groupes sociaux, p. 66 (graph).

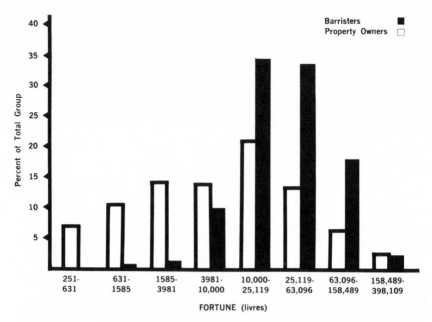

Sources: *A.M.*, 2 G- 9-16; 2 G-2; Sentou, *Fortunes et groupes sociaux*, p. 66

FIGURE II-2.   Fortunes of Barristers and of All Toulousan Property-Owners.

court clerk and *feudiste*, whose average head tax was about ten livres. The attorneys, so scorned by the barrister in a professional sense, were not so far behind the barristers economically. The attorneys' average succession was about 4,000 livres less than the barristers', while the average head tax was 20 percent below the barristers' (20 livres compared to 25.1 livres).[74] Two professional groups in the legal world, notaries and Seneschal Court judges, were, on the average, wealthier than the barristers.[75] However, the number of very wealthy men at the bar was greater than in either of these professions, and barristers dominated the economic elite of the legal world. For example, the twenty wealthiest legal professionals (of 108) to leave acts of succession during the revolutionary period included two attorneys, three notaries, two judges, and thirteen barristers.[76]

In this eminently legal city, barristers were not economically inferior to the dominant commercial groups. There was a striking similarity in size and range of fortunes between the barristers and the

[74]*A.M.*, CC–rolls of capitation; Sentou, *Fortunes et groupes sociaux*, p. 215.

[75]Sentou, *Fortunes and groupes sociaux*, pp. 215, 259. Seneschal Court officers paid an average head tax of twenty-eight livres; notaries paid one of thirty-four livres.

[76]I am very grateful to Professor Sentou for allowing me to examine the individual acts of succession recorded on perforated cards. A print-out of these acts is now on deposit in the Departmental Archives.

négociants, as illustrated in figure II-3. This may explain the many intermarriages between the two groups. Only the commercial elite, the textile traders, were clearly a good deal wealthier than the barristers.[77] If merchants were found less often in local positions of power and prestige than barristers, it was because their wealth did not surpass the barristers' by enough to compensate for their lack of cultural achievements and institutional connections.

Though well-to-do in absolute terms and in relation to most other socioprofessional groups, barristers were far below the parlementaires in wealth. The magistrates' average succession was 339,000 livres,[78] nine times the average barrister's fortune. Indeed, a larger gap existed between the average barrister and parlementaire than between the barrister and the average master artisan. The wealthiest 5 percent of the avocats barely attained the economic level of the least prosperous magistrates, who were only cadets of more important families. The parlementaires were the richest Toulousan aristocrats, but only four in a hundred barristers attained the economic level of even the most modest sector of the aristocracy, the nobles without professions.[79] In total, there could not have been more than a dozen barristers in Toulouse who were affluent by aristocratic standards.

The barristers were not an economically homogeneous group, and some humble men pleaded, especially at the lesser tribunals. But there were enough moneyed barristers to place the group in a dominant position among legal men, to make barristers the equals of most merchants, and ultimately to give them a place just below the aristocracy in the economic structure of the city and of the region. Moreover, the barristers' social power rested as much, if not more, on their professional and cultural attainments as on their wealth.

COMPOSITION OF FORTUNES

The type of property owned by the barristers reflected their interest in procuring status, security, and steady revenue from their wealth.[80] This was particularly important to the many barristers who derived only a marginal revenue from their professional activities. Nearly two-

[77]Marinière, "Marchands d'étoffes."

[78]Sentou, *Fortunes et groupes sociaux*, p. 84. Another student of the parlementaires calculates their average fortune at 400,000 livres. See Philippe de Peguilhan de Larboust, "Les magistrats du Parlement de Toulouse à la fin de l'ancien régime" (D.E.S., University of Toulouse, 1965), p. 87.

[79]Sentou, *Fortunes et groupes sociaux*, p. 121. They had average successions of 128,000 livres.

[80]The sources which yield most information on the composition of the barristers' estates are the Forced Loan (*A.M.*, 2 G-9-16); Martin, *Documents relatifs à la vente*; and Sentou, *Fortunes et groupes sociaux*. The analysis presented in this section is based on a study of sixty-nine barristers' estates.

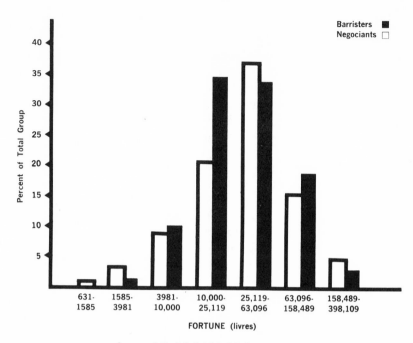

Sources: *A.M.*, 2 G- 9-16; 2 G-2; Sentou, *Fortunes et groupes sociaux*, p. 159.

FIGURE II-3.   Distribution of Fortunes of Barristers and *Négociants*

thirds (63.7 percent) of their fortunes were invested in real estate, urban
and rural, which returned a reliable 3 to 5 percent on capital a year.
Constituted rentes, paying 4 to 5 percent annually, composed an
average of 30 percent of their fortunes. The remainder was invested
primarily in personal furnishings. The overall composition of the
barristers' fortunes differed little from that of most Toulousan property
owners, who also had two-thirds of their wealth in real estate.[81]

Rural land was the single most important component of the
barristers' fortune. It was a very attractive investment, not only for its
steady return but also for reasons of prestige. Landowning was the
mark of a *gentilhomme*, and the barrister never felt more like an
aristocrat than when he spoke of "his sharecropper," or when he was
addressed as "maître" at harvest time.[82] Perhaps this was why six out of
ten barristers owned some rural property, a large proportion. Not even
one in three Toulousan property owners in general possessed land in
the countryside.[83]

[81]Sentou, *Fortunes et groupes sociaux*, p. 61.
[82]See Robert Forster, *The Nobility of Toulouse in the Eighteenth Century* (Baltimore,
1960), p. 44.
[83]Sentou, *Fortunes et groupes sociaux*, p. 148.

The basic unit of rural property was the "domain," usually consist-ing of a farm (*métairie*) of moderate size, plus a few fields and some buildings. The *métairie*, complete with its own name, was the source of considerable pride. At midcentury, the average size of the barristers' domains was 63.9 acres (46.2 *arpents*).[84] A typical domain was the one owned by Jean François Catala in the community of Pechbusque. It consisted of a country house in which Catala spent his yearly vacations, 47.4 acres (34 *arpents*) of wheat field, 8.4 acres of vineyard, 1.4 acres of meadow, and 5.4 acres of wood. Such a domain produced for Catala a net annual revenue of about 510 livres. In addition, Catala owned scattered fields in other villages: 2.8 acres in Merville and another field of the same size at Auzeville.[85] Catala's domain was typical not only in size but in composition. The barrister's domain was primarily arable (75 percent) with a small amount of meadow and forest. Most landown-ing barristers had one such principal domain plus a few scattered fields. The less prosperous had smaller domains (farms of 15 to 20 acres) or perhaps only a few scattered fields or acres of vineyard.

Despite their interest in owning rural property, not even modest barristers desired the small vineyards and country residences in the suburbs of Toulouse. Barristers associated this type of property too closely with the "populace," the shopkeepers and artisans who did own the vineyards in the communities surrounding the city.[86] Attor-neys, it should be noted, did not disdain to hold such property, but barristers did.[87] Only the domain, which gave him the opportunity to be "maître" to his sharecropper, suited the barrister's self-image. Land was partly an investment in symbolic status, and the barristers ex-pressed their separation from inferior social groups through it.

Though the barristers certainly owned more land than the average property owner of Toulouse, their holdings, like their fortunes, hardly compared with the aristocracy. Sixty percent of the nobles possessed over 100 *arpents* of land;[88] it is doubtful that more than 15 percent of the barristers owned such large domains. In most of the villages in the diocese, nobles were the principal landlords; barristers could claim this distinction in only 7 of the 200 or more communities in the diocese of Toulouse.[89]

---

[84]*A.D.*, C-1331-1346, declarations for the *vingtième* tax, 1750. I have found fifty-eight declarations by barristers in these rolls. Most rolls did not specify occupations, so identification was difficult.

[85]*A.D.*, C-1325, -1322, -1331. For the revenue, I have used the estimates provided in Forster, *Nobility of Toulouse*, appendix A.

[86]See the *vingtième* rolls for Cugnaux, Coloniers, Gratentour, Lespinasse, Portet: *A.D.*, C-1331-1346.

[87]Five attorneys owned such property in Gratentour alone. *A.D.*, C-1336.

[88]Forster, *Nobility of Toulouse*, p. 36.

[89]*A.D.*, C-1331-1346.

Aside from rural land, barristers invested substantially in constituted rentes. This form of wealth accounted for 30 percent of their fortunes, on the average, and varied less in importance than did urban and rural real estate. Investment in rentes may have been an extension of their legal practices, for clients needed long-term loans when they consulted barristers about dowries, portions, pensions, or jointures. This would explain the barristers' preference for rentes "on individuals" rather than "on the state" or on bodies such as the Estates of Languedoc. Over a tenth of the barristers had fortunes composed primarily of rentes. Claude Castor Bragouse, for example, possessed a large fortune of 120,000 livres, 90 percent of it in rentes.[90]

Urban real estate was the third important element in the barristers' personal fortunes though its importance varied from case to case. Modest barristers had the largest portion of their wealth in houses. As fortunes grew, more went into land and rentes. Nearly a tenth of the advocates owned only urban property, and overall, this type of wealth constituted 27 percent of the barristers' wealth.

Barristers were not very active in the urban housing market. Unlike the parlementaires of Paris, the Toulousan barristers did not speculate in housing despite the lucre to be made as a result of a growing urban population.[91] If they purchased a house, it was for their own use, and a surprisingly large number did not own even this. Apparently, barristers felt no social stigma about renting apartments, so even advocates with large fortunes sometimes did not own residences in Toulouse.[92] They probably placed their wealth in rural property, which gave them more status.

Above all, the barristers were cautious spenders and "prudent" investors. Their debts were small in relation to their fortunes, rarely more than one or two years' revenue. What obligations they did incur had usually been contracted for normal family charges: the settlement of an estate or the provision of dowries and pensions. Moreover, the barristers were decidedly a creditor group, their rentes amounting to a good deal more than their debts.[93] Barristers frequently made loans to one another and occasionally had the honor of advancing funds to aristocrats.

[90]The declarations for the Forced Loans, *A.M.*, 2 G-9-16, provide the most detailed information on the rentes held by barristers.

[91]For the speculative activities of the Parisian parlementaires, see François Bluche, *Les magistrats du Parlement de Paris au XVIIIe siècle (1715-1771)* (Paris, 1960), pp. 178-80. The barristers' lack of interest in the urban housing market can be seen through the registers of the *centième dernier*, *A.D.*, 2 C-3023 ff.

[92]Barristers Lafage and Senovert, with fortunes of 53,000 livres and 70,000 livres respectively, did not possess houses in Toulouse. See *A.M.*, 2 G-12, -16.

[93]The Forced Loan declarations include enumerations of the barristers' debts. See *A.M.*, 2 G-9-16.

Conscious of the need to preserve their fortunes, the barristers avoided risky forms of investment. The only stocks that they owned were shares in the local mills, and a barrister rarely invested more than 3,000 livres in these. Only one advocate of the forty-nine subject to the forced loan had placed capital (other than rentes) with a merchant. This barrister, Jean Marie Lautier, invested only 6,000 livres in commerce and received 5 percent on his money.[94] The barristers preferred very traditional, secure, status-laden forms of wealth to commercial ventures in Toulouse or elsewhere in the kingdom.

STYLE OF LIVING

Difficult as it is to define, "style of living" must be a subject of central concern to the social historian.[95] It was an expression of the material standards that individuals could afford, and also (and more intriguingly) an exhibition of their self-image, cultural level, and sense of values. The Toulousan barristers displayed greater homogeneity in their life styles than in their economic status. And surely their daily decisions on expenditures and investments, the arrangement of their household and family life, were at least as indicative of their place in society as their wealth and social origins.

The economic conditions and social values of eighteenth-century Toulouse were not conducive to a high level of consumption. The most elevated social strata did not often earn large and regular revenues from outside sources; their income came from invested wealth, so heavy expenditures threatened future revenues in an immediate manner. Moreover, a very important source of status in this society was land, and no expenditure on luxury items could quite equal the prestige of investment in rural property. Thus, even the very wealthy did not live opulently. The parlementaires, the richest group in Toulouse, rarely spent more than 3 percent of their fortunes on personal effects, including furniture, apparel, and mode of transport.[96] This sum was somewhat less than a year's revenue. Even the august magistrate had chairs, wall hangings, and clothing that were noticeably threadbare.[97]

---

[94]*A.M.*, 2 G-9.

[95]Not much archival research on style of living has been done for nonaristocratic groups. The older study by Albert Babeau, *Les bourgeois d'autrefois* (Paris, 1886), is still very useful. More recent is André Bouton, *Le Maine. Histoire économique et sociale, XVIIe et XVIIIe siècles* (Le Mans, 1973), pp. 328-46.

[96]This estimate of 3 percent is based on the successions published in Sentou, *Fortunes et groupes sociaux*, pp. 86-112. See, also, Forster, *Nobility of Toulouse*, chap. 7.

[97]The near "millionaire" counselor Blanquet de Rouville possessed effects worth only 7,255 livres, less than 1 percent of his wealth. See Sentou, *Fortunes et groupes sociaux*, p. 90.

Certainly these aristocrats also possessed luxuries, but even at its highest, their mode of existence was not opulent.

The barristers, with much smaller fortunes than the magistrates, had to spend a greater portion of their wealth on personal furnishings. On the average, about 7 percent of their wealth was devoted to this, but as fortunes grew larger the portion spent on personal effects usually declined.[98] Even the more affluent barristers were quite circumspect and restrained in their expenditures.

The parlementaire's mode of living was well above that enjoyed by the barristers. Every magistrate possessed a few elements of real luxury. One counselor owned tapestries worth over 2,000 livres; another possessed gold bracelets and a locket surrounded by precious stones.[99] Nearly all the rooms in their homes were decorated with tapestries and large mirrors, the symbols of a respectable household. Though not extravagant, the magistrates did spend part of their wealth on objects of art, beauty, and cultural interest.

The parlementaires would have been struck by the lack of ornamentation and variety in the homes of the barristers, even the very wealthy ones. For the most part, barristers lived comfortably and possessed a superabundance of the common objects of daily use—kitchenware, linen, table service, and so on. What they lacked were the luxuries, the articles intended as much for display as for use, objects of individual taste or aesthetic appeal.[100] The walls of all but the principal rooms were bare; tapestries, usually confined to the drawing room and perhaps a chamber or two, were inexpensive and often very old.[101] Chandeliers of any sort were rare. Only a minority of barristers had silver, usually no more than a half-dozen spoons or forks.[102] Their table service, though abundant, was made only of earthware, never of porcelain.

It is worth comparing the drawing room of a wealthy and ennobled barrister like Pierre Arexi with the parlor of a magistrate. Arexi

[98]The major sources for studying the values of the barristers' personal possessions are the twenty-one acts of succession published in Sentou, *Fortunes et groupes sociaux*, and the thirty-two inventories of barristers' possessions in the Departmental Archives (*A.D.*, 3E-11871–11966) and Municipal Archives (*A.M.*, 1 S–"Biens des Emigrés.") The stated values, however, are often deceptive because they included "moveables" like farm equipment and animals, which did not contribute to a "style of living." Care must be taken to eliminate these elements.

[99]Martin, *Documents relatifs à la vente*, pp. 193, 205, 156.

[100]See the inventories of barristers accused of being *émigrés*, *A.M.*, 1 S. Altogether, I have examined thirty-two inventories of barristers' personal effects and furnishings.

[101]A wealthy law professor, Julien, had wall-hangings worth only 190 livres. Those of counselor Bonnemain were worth ten times as much. *A.D.*, 3E-11919; 3E-11874.

[102]Only fourteen of the thirty-two inventories inspected indicated that the barristers possessed silver. Only one (*A.D.*, 3E-11917, inventory of Ginisty) mentioned valuable jewelry.

decorated this, the principal room of his home, with eighteen arm-chairs, a sofa, and two small wooden tables covered with green cloth. The walls were decorated with two moderate-sized mirrors over the fireplace. There was also a small chandelier, which was a rarity in a barrister's home.[103] By comparison, the drawing room of counselor Jean Paul David was elaborately furnished. A "fine" tapestry repre-senting battle scenes hung on the wall along with a larger mirror. For the guests, there were two sofas and twelve armchairs, a large marble table, and three smaller wooden tables. The room was decorated with four ornamental folding screens, a carpet, some inlaid furniture, and a birdcage with two birds.[104] Although David's house was not luxurious, it was much more ornate and even aristocratic than the sober home of Arexi.

The barristers' furnishings demonstrated a spirit of cautious spend-ing. Their life style could not be described as "severe" for, along with civil officers and rich merchants, they lived better than all but impor-tant nobles and parlementaires; but there certainly was an element of restraint and an avoidance of needless expenditures. Even highly cultivated barristers—and, as we shall see, there were several at the bar—possessed none of the musical or scientific instruments which magistrates owned.[105] Rich or modest, the barristers aimed for solid comfort and not much more.

A distinction should be drawn between status-laden investments, of which the barristers approved, and the purchase of luxuries, which was not acceptable to them. Barristers were apparently eager to acquire seigneurial rights, and about a tenth of them had done so.[106] Hôtels were also an attractive investment for those barristers who could afford them.[107] However, barristers manifested little desire to compete for prestige among their peers through high levels of consumption. In this sense, their "consumer mentality" was entirely different from such elite groups as the court nobility or the financiers of Paris.[108] The Tou-lousan barristers sought other ways of expressing their respectable social standing, and they channelled their wealth into real estate or, perhaps, into good dowries for their daughters.

[103]A.M., 1S-72.

[104]A.D., 3E-11896.

[105]See, for example, the inventory of the academician-barrister Jamme, A.M., 1 S-59.

[106]Actually, barristers were usually co-seigneurs, owning a minor portion (one sixth or one eighth) of the rights. Few purchased full seigneurial rights. See A.D., C-3010-3034, dénombrements.

[107]The former capitouls Arexi, Taverne, Gary, Laviguerie, and the non-noble barristers Sudre and Gratian owned hôtels. See J. Chalande, Histoire des rues de Toulouse, 3 vols. (Toulouse, 1913), 1: 48, 63, 183-97, 212-15, 340, 360.

[108]Jean-Pierre Labatut, Les ducs et pairs de France au XVIIe siècle (Paris, 1972), pp. 300-310; Julien Dent, Crisis in Finance: Crown, Financiers, and Society in Seventeenth-Century France (London, 1973), pp. 182-83.

In this society of extreme inequality of wealth, solid comfort was itself the mark of a fairly elevated social standing. But what identified the barristers as a high-status group was not so much their material possessions as the manner in which they organized their households. The barristers, along with aristocrats and other wealthy commoners, sought family privacy, a regulated social life, and the relegation of occupational concerns to their proper sphere. In these goals the higher social strata differed markedly from artisans and most merchants, whose daily existence was organized around the trade.[109] Artisans and shopkeepers lived in cramped quarters above the shop; their one or two rooms contained only essential furnishings and served for eating, sleeping, and socializing. Life was centered about the shop below. Those who lived in this manner may well have been able to afford something better, but they did not aspire to anything more.[110]

Barristers (along with the magistrates, rentiers, and large merchants, with whom they shared this life style) organized their households and family lives very differently. They attempted to provide a forum for socializing as well as a stronghold for family and personal privacy. The very existence of a *salon de compagnie*, a room for the specialized purpose of socializing, was a mark of social superiority. This was the principal room in the barrister's home, and he decorated it as well as his sober habits of spending would allow. Into this room he put a very large number of chairs (often fifteen or twenty)—a provincial symbol of affluence to this day. The best furniture went into this room, while the more worn chairs and practical effects (armoires and coffers) were placed elsewhere. Social life was made as comfortable as possible in this room, with its fireplace, tapestries, and mirrors. Any paintings or ornamental objects were in the *salon*, too.[111] The barrister's family and social lives went on in this room, and the rest of the house was subordinated to it.

Barristers did not feel obligated to own homes, but they did seek a certain respectability in the style of their residences. The house with carriage gates (*portes cochères*) was thought desirable as a symbol of wealth and standing.[112] If they leased apartments, barristers made certain that their principal rooms were on the first living floor; and

[109]The following is an impressionistic description, based on the examination of inventories-after-death of ten artisans and ten *marchands*.

[110]See, for example, the inventory of the shoemaker Dupuy (*A.D.*, 3E–11904). He owned a house in Toulouse, a vineyard outside the city, and left 1,800 livres in cash, but he lived as described above.

[111]A minority of barristers possessed ornamental (apart from religious) objects. The few pictures inventoried were religious in subject and not very valuable (2–3 livres). Only one barrister possessed a family portrait.

[112]For documents on home ownership, value, size, and style see *A.M.*, 1 G, "Contribution foncière," in addition to the inventories-after-death.

above all, they desired large residences. Jean Marie Saremejane, for example, lived in a three-story house with ten rooms. Jean Bernard Chipoulet and his wife lived alone in apartments of seven rooms.[113] Only newlyweds, who often boarded in their parents' home, and widowers resided in confining quarters on the second floor or above.[114]

These large residences permitted individual and family privacy. Many homes had a bedroom for each child. The domestics were kept at arm's length. They slept in the kitchen or a separate bedroom and ate in the kitchen; the family had a dining room for its use. Barristers also segregated their professional and family lives. Their offices (*cabinets*) were located near the principal entrance to the house, so clients could come and go without disturbing the family.[115] The barrister's secretary was never part of the household. By contrast, the clerks of the attorneys and notaries resided with their masters.[116] The barrister's household was thus a more exclusive circle, composed of family, relatives, and invited friends, while all others were defined as "outsiders." It was through this organization of home and family life that barristers expressed their *honnêteté*.

Barristers were imitating the aristocracy of the city in adopting this life style, and many of the differences between the parlementaire's household and that of the advocate resulted from the disparities in their wealth. One has the sense that with more money barristers would have lived even more like their social superiors. However, some differences in life style were based not on financial inequalities but rather on divergent norms, values, and self-images. The most interesting of these was the barristers' attitudes toward public displays of opulence, which they eschewed for themselves but expected of the aristocracy. Barristers dressed in somber colors: black, grey, and maroon. Their suits were made of plain wool, though a rich barrister might have one of silk or velvet. This dress might be compared to the wardrobe of counselor David: two suits of green taffeta, a coat and breeches in scarlet with gold braiding, a satin coat, several pairs of velvet breeches, a plum-colored suit with gold buttons and braiding, and two coats of white satin with gold braiding.[117] Even if a barrister could have purchased such apparel, he would have felt self-conscious wearing it.

---

[113]*A.M.*, 1 S–41, for Saremejane; *A.D.*, 3E–11887, inventory of Chipoulet.

[114]See, for example, the inventories of two widowers, Louis Antoine Clausolles and Guillaume de Pérès, *A.D.*, 3E–10756, fol. 164 and 3E–2117, register 2, fol. 356.

[115]Before the eighteenth century, barristers received clients in the same "general purpose" rooms in which they ate, slept, and conducted family life. See Philippe Ariès, *Centuries of Childhood: A Social History of Family Life*, trans. Robert Baldick (New York, 1962), p. 310. I have not been able to determine exactly when this changed.

[116]*A.M.*, CC–rolls of *capitation*. These rolls listed the servants and other adults residing in the household with the family.

[117]*A.D.*, 3E–11896, inventory of David.

The barristers' attitude toward domestic servants was another sign of their disinclination for public displays of wealth. Servants were a necessary part of a respectable household, and at least two-thirds of the barristers employed one.[118] Most advocates could not afford more than a single servant, for wages and board cost at least 500 livres a year.[119] Only 20 percent of the barristers had two domestics, and very few employed more than two, no matter how well-off they were. This limit was psychological and cultural, not financial. For example, Jean Prévost (de Fenouillet), one of the richest pleaders, with a fortune of 214,000 livres, employed only two servants. The parlementaire Joseph de Rigaud had a fortune of 211,000 livres, but he had eight servants.[120] The marquis de Palarin, who paid the same head tax as Prévost, employed five domestics.[121]

The type of servant was as important as the number, and there had been some recent shifts of habit in this area. Before 1750, all capitouls and rich barristers had employed valets; a few even had lackeys.[122] By the last decades of the Old Regime, noble barristers had dismissed such servants from their households. Valets and lackeys invoked too much the tone of extravagance, so they employed only servants and chamber maids. The parlementaires and nobles of older extraction were the only ones to retain lackeys and valets. This change may have been induced by the rising cost of keeping servants,[123] but it is interesting that noble barristers chose to economize in this manner. Was it simply that symbols of status were shifting, or could it have been that barristers were sensing more deeply their separation from the aristocracy of the city?

AN INTERMEDIATE SOCIAL GROUP

The social structure of Toulouse was, to be sure, a continuum, but a continuum with fissures at different points. These fissures were of varying depths, and they found varying forms of expression. No single criterion alone—wealth, social origin, life style—could reveal each cleavage, but a study of all these factors identifies at least some of them. There was, of course, an important break which isolated the artisan

[118]*A.M.*, CC-rolls of *capitation*.
[119]John McManners, *French Ecclesiastical Society in the Old Regime: A Study of Angers in the Eighteenth Century* (Manchester, 1960), p. 141. This was the annual cost of servants in the 1760s. It undoubtedly rose with the price of food thereafter.
[120]*A.M.*, CC-1056; CC-1041; Sentou, *Fortunes et groupes sociaux*, pp. 98, 264. Aristocrats employed an average of seven servants.
[121]*A.M.*, CC-1008.
[122]See, for example, *A.M.*, CC-1071 (for 1735) and CC-1077 (for 1740).
[123]This is the argument of Bernard Marcoul, "Les domestiques à Toulouse au XVIIIe siècle" (D.E.S., University of Toulouse, 1960).

from most liberal professionals and larger merchants. All that has been said so far indicates a more subtle fissure separating the middling professions (notaries, attorneys, doctors, law clerks) from barristers, most judges, and the wealthiest of merchants and *rentiers*. This fissure was based only partly on professional prestige, so particularly wealthy individuals in the middling occupational groups might belong to the higher stratum. Moreover, this was not an impermeable division. Mobility through it was frequent; the crossing from one level to another involved subtle but telling changes in life style, status symbols, cultural activities, and attitudes. The fact that an attorney might have a vineyard in the suburb and keep a clerk in his household while his son, a barrister, did away with both, was significant. So was the one-way social movement, as the notary strove to place a son at the bar while the barrister never wanted to see his son a notary, attorney, or *greffier*. These changes mark the fissure between the middling occupational groups and the barristers.

Above the barristers' level was another important cleft; one that was, perhaps, as large as the break separating the *peuple* from the middling groups. This second cleft divided the barristers, civil officers, and rich merchants from the aristocracy of parlementaires and *noblesse de race*. Thus, the barristers were part of an intermediary group between the middling professions and the aristocracy. This intermediary stratum cut across the legal Orders. At its lower limits were the barristers of no special distinction, and at the top were the ennobled barristers and their children, who formed an exclusive circle of minor nobles.

Such was the social structure of Toulouse and the barristers' position in it as measured by their wealth, marriage alliances, and life styles. These, however, were not the only important determinants of social relations. Until we adopt a dynamic analysis and assess the prospects of crossing each fissure, and until we examine cultural and political alignments, our comprehension of the barristers' social world will remain incomplete.

III

SOCIAL AND ECONOMIC ADVANCEMENT

Toulousans implicitly recognized the barrister's respectable social standing when they addressed his wife as "Madame," the same title they used for the wife of a parlementaire. Spouses of notaries and attorneys, it seems, were only "Mademoiselle."[1] A barrister undoubtedly derived much satisfaction from his social station just below the aristocracy. But was he in a favorable position to maintain or enhance his status? This depended, to a very large degree, on the possibilities for professional and economic advancement at the bar, and also on his personal ambitions and aspirations. In his getting, spending, and securing the status of his progeny, the Toulousan barrister revealed much about himself and about his society.

The Family Settlement

Judging from the large number of printed legal briefs that have survived in the libraries of Toulouse, a very substantial portion of the barristers' cases involved family disputes over inheritance. In his role as *paterfamilias*, the barrister had to settle his *own* estate, and the manner in which he did so was an expression of his family concerns and of his aspirations on his children's behalf.

The barrister's family settlement was intended to maintain each member at a "respectable" level and give the first-born somewhat greater material comfort or opportunity. In keeping with this purpose, the usual settlement made the eldest child the heir and granted full portions to the younger children. These portions were equal and were calculated on the basis of one half or one third of the estate, depending upon the number of offspring, in accordance with Roman law.[2] A settlement such as this was determined at the marriage of the eldest son

---

[1]Georges Lefebvre, *The Coming of the French Revolution*, trans. R. R. Palmer (Princeton, 1947), p. 47.

[2]Portions were taken on half the estate if there were more than four children, and on a third of the estate if there were four children or fewer. Paul Viollet, *Histoire du droit civil français* (Paris, 1893), p. 837.

and instituted in his marriage contract. The parents usually donated to him all their possessions, reserving the usufruct or part of it for themselves. Provisions would be made to give the heir some immediate income or support from the estate. The heir, in turn, bore the responsibility of paying portions to his siblings, and the marriage contracts of the younger children complemented the settlement. Each younger child received a dowry or a donation (the *apport*) that was more or less equivalent to his legal share.[3] The father's testament completed this settlement, and through limited legacies to charities and to collaterals the estate was kept within the immediate family. Only those barristers who died childless gave freely to brothers, cousins, nephews, or to charitable institutions. All other barristers wanted to pass on their estates intact to their children, and within certain limits, to *all* their children.

This type of settlement was not unique to the barristers; most families at their social level instituted the same policies, reflecting their common concerns and values.[4] However, these provisions did contrast in some significant ways with the family settlements of parlementaires and *noblesse de race*, and the differences defined some very important social and psychological cleavages between the aristocracy and members, even noble ones, of the intermediate stratum. Though barristers did not usually treat their children with complete equality, neither were they so firm as aristocrats in subordinating interests of their progeny to a transcendent notion of family or "line."[5] A key intention of the aristocratic settlement was to reduce the part of the estate devolving upon the younger children. This was accomplished through entailing and through the "voluntary" renunciation of portions by children. With an entailing clause in the marriage contract of the eldest son, the family head in each generation received possession of half the family estate, the rest being donated to the unborn child of the newlyweds. Consequently, younger children of the marriage received portions on a quarter (or a sixth) instead of half (or a third) of the full fortune. Moreover, a combination of parental pressure and a voluntary sense of moral obligation to the family directed many younger children to renounce their portions in return for gifts and pensions below the value of the legal share. The same pressure encouraged sons to remain celibate and daughters to take religious vows, an act which abrogated

[3]Discrepancies between the anticipated portion and the actual share to which a child was legally entitled could be rectified after the father's death.

[4]It would be very interesting to know if groups below this position employed the same type of settlement, and at what social level testaments ceased to be used. The legal comportment of social groups is just beginning to receive serious attention.

[5]See Robert Forster, *The Nobility of Toulouse in the Eighteenth Century* (Baltimore, 1960), chapter 6, for the details that follow.

their claims to the estate. The ideal aristocratic settlement included celibate cadets and the marriage of at most one daughter.

That transcendent notion of family which inspired and compelled sacrifice among the children of aristocrats did not have the same force in the barristers' household. Their children hardly ever renounced a succession, except one encumbered by debt.[6] Among the twenty-four families we have been able to reconstruct, nearly two-thirds of the daughters (twenty-five of thirty-eight) married, and only two entered convents. In contrast, about a third of the daughters in aristocratic households wed, and up to 1760 at least, about a fourth of them took vows.[7] While it is true that barristers' sons frequently entered the Church, this was more a response to vocational opportunities than an act of sacrifice for the family interest; otherwise, they married.[8] Moreover, not even wealthy, ennobled barristers with sizeable landed holdings (100 acres or so) entailed their estates. Nor did any barrister attempt to reduce the portions to which younger children were legally entitled by making large donations to the heir, above and beyond his share. Minimizing the dispersal of the family fortune was apparently not the barrister's overwhelming concern.

In a fairly sizeable minority of cases, the benefits of the eldest child disappeared entirely in favor of equal treatment for all children. The desire to ensure an *"honnête"* status for each child was undoubtedly the motivation behind such a settlement, which was employed, significantly enough, by barristers at both the top and bottom of the economic scale. Bernard Rey and Jean Degeilh, two advocates at the Merchants' Court, evidently preferred to divide their small estates equally among their sons rather than give one son a portion that was extremely small.[9] But why would rich, noble barristers like Jean Baptiste Jouve and Pierre Albaret divide their estates equally among their children? Aristocrats would have condemned such a settlement as a sacrifice of future family distinction to imprudent sentiments; they would have preferred a more "businesslike" settlement that bore down heavily upon the younger children. Given the different aim of the barristers—to maintain each child at an honorable status—the egalitarian settlement made social sense. Pierre Albaret was one of the wealthiest barristers, with an estate of 103,000 livres, but he also had fourteen children.[10] Had each daughter been endowed with only her

[6]Renunciations were registered in the *insinuations* and *centième dernier, A.D.,* 2C. These registers hardly ever contained the renunciation of a barrister's child.

[7]For the aristocratic family, see Forster, *Nobility of Toulouse,* pp. 129–30. The twenty-four barristers' families were reconstructed through notarial documents, mostly testaments, in *A.D.,* series 3E.

[8]More will be said about the careers of barristers' children later in this chapter.

[9]*A.D.,* 3E–14162, fol. 118; 3E–2122, register 1, fol. 399.

[10]Jules Villain, *La France moderne. Grand dictionnaire généalogique, historique, et biographique (Haute-Garonne et Ariège),* 4 vols. (Montpellier, 1911), 1: 2–4. For his

legal share, she would have received less than 5,000 livres. It would have been impossible to make suitable matches. Even with each daughter an heiress, the dowries came to only 12,000 livres, and the girls found very respectable, though non-noble, husbands.[11] Jean Baptiste Jouve employed the same family policy, apparently for the same reasons. Calculating his wealth at 105,000 livres, Jouve gave each of his seven children 15,000 livres.[12] Had he "given an advantage" to one child, the rest of his progeny would have received only 7,500 livres. As an heiress, Jeanne Françoise Jouve was able to marry the very talented barrister Jean Douyau. Jouve and Albaret were not necessarily aberrant cases, but when capitouls had smaller families they might conform more closely to the model aristocratic settlement (except for entailing).[13] On the whole, then, the families of the municipal nobles were a transitional group in which the immediate status of each family member weighed more or less heavily as a concern.

The barristers' interest in each child's standing and their relative freedom from concern about dispersing the family fortune was also demonstrated by their generosity in endowing daughters. The majority of daughters married, and the barrister sought an honorable match for each. He was usually willing to give each one her full portion in dowry, sometimes supplemented by a small donation, on terms favorable to the groom.[14] Table III-1, presenting all cases for which the dowry and the barrister's fortune are known, shows that marriage charges consumed a very sizeable part of the father's estate. On the average, a barrister agreed to disperse about 20 percent of his wealth with each daughter's marriage.[15] This undoubtedly meant selling some property or transferring rentes to the groom. If the dowry was not paid at once, the father covered the interest on it or provided the newlyweds with room and board. At any rate, a daughter's marriage was a burden on the barrister's estate, and he did not take important measures to reduce its weight.

Despite their habitual frugality, some barristers seemed willing to incur debts for the sake of a good match for one of their daughters. Joseph Marie Duroux borrowed heavily in order to give his elder daughter a dowry of 18,000 livres, and this, apparently, permanently

---

wealth, see the computer print-out of successions studied by Professor Sentou, on deposit at the Departmental Archives.

[11] See the marriage contracts for two of his daughters: 3E-5077 and 3E-5068, fol. 145.

[12] See marriage contracts of his son and daughter: 3E-26523 and 3E-26538.

[13] See Villain, *Grand dictionnaire*, for the genealogies of several capitoul families.

[14] The dowry could be paid in full at once or given to the groom in installments. If the barrister did not provide the full dowry at marriage, he usually gave the groom interest on the unpaid portion.

[15] The average dowry given to our sample of twenty barristers' daughters was 14,000 livres. Part of this came from the maternal estate and from relatives.

TABLE III-1. Dowry Size of Barristers' Daughters

Name	Total Dowry	Portion of Dowry from Paternal Estate[a]	Father's Wealth	Percentage of Father's Wealth Contributed
Prévost	50,000	28,000	214,000	12
Albaret	12,000	10,000	101,000	10
Sudre	20,000	8,000	28,000	28
Bernard	20,000	14,000	54,000	26
Dirat	30,000	30,000	110,000	26
Villefranche	6,000	1,600	16,500	10
Duroux	18,000	18,000	36,800	50
Bourdeil	12,000	6,000	20,000	30
Clausolles	12,000	8,000	35,000	26
Jouve	15,000	15,000	113,000	13
Bernadou	10,000	—	5,000	—
Dutour	8,000	—	20,000	—
Chabanettes	30,000	30,000	120,000	25
Averages	17,100	15,400		20

Sources: A.D., 3E, marriage contracts; A.M., 2G-2; 2G-9-16; Jean Sentou, Fortunes et groupes sociaux sous la Révolution (Toulouse, 1969).

[a] In Toulouse, the régime dotal was in force; the property of the husband and wife was separate.

weakened his financial situation.[16] The leading pleader Guillaume Dirat endowed his daughter with 30,000 livres so that she might marry into the capitouls' circle; this was such a burden that he could not leave legacies to his grandchildren six years later.[17] Marriage charges were clearly an exception to the barristers' sober spending habits. A good match for a daughter was an important family event, a source of pride that could not easily be resisted.

The barrister's family settlement was a sort of intermediate step between equal division of the patrimony and the energetic efforts made by aristocrats to keep the family fortune in the hands of the heir. This was a society in which celibacy was frequent, however, especially among elite groups,[18] and prominent features of the noble settlement—institution of an heir, sons in Church vocations—were shared by the barristers. But they did seem to demonstrate more concern with the status of each child. The family was not necessarily a less central

[16]A.M., 2G-16; see the declaration by Duroux.
[17]A.D., 3E-11869, no. 13299, testament of Dirat.
[18]We lack studies of celibacy rates at different social levels. Louis Henry believes that these rates were quite high at the upper strata. Among Genevan patricians from 1750 through 1799, 18 to 20 percent of the males and 32 percent of the females over fifty were unmarried. (Louis Henry, "The Population of France in the Eighteenth Century," in D. V. Glass and D. E. C. Eversley, Population in History [London, 1965], pp. 452-53.) The Toulousan barristers may have had an equally high proportion of male celibates; my evidence suggests a smaller proportion of unmarried daughters, though.

institution for the barrister and his progeny than it was for aristocrats, but it did involve a different set of relationships and obligations.

PROFESSIONAL REVENUE AND ENRICHMENT

Contemporary professional manuals spoke about the barristers' financial rewards in an apologetic or defensive tone. They piously reiterated that the bar brought honor, not wealth, to its practitioners.[19] And barristers, more than other "liberal professionals," were careful not to discuss their fees in public.[20] Indeed, they were not even in the habit of keeping account books of their earnings.[21] Reimbursing a barrister was, apparently, a very private and discreet transaction between pleader and client.

Unfortunately, the absence of disclosure about professional revenues prevailed in official fiscal documents, too. The barristers were subject only to impositions on returns from capital; their professional revenues escaped taxation and recording entirely. Hence, it is hardly possible to examine their legal earnings directly on a year-to-year basis. Still, we can derive from other data a general picture of both the barristers' capacity to expand their total fortunes through their practices and the opportunities that the bar afforded for enrichment over a lifetime. These estimates will hardly be precise, but it would be most difficult to comprehend the barrister's ambitions, aspirations, and professional motivations without some notion of his potential for enrichment.

Assessing the barristers' lifetime professional earnings first requires an indication of their wealth at the outset of their careers. This would be the amount (the male *apport*) that an advocate received from his parents' estate to establish a household. As Professor Sentou has demonstrated, this was usually of the same magnitude as the dowry (or female *apport*).[22] Thus, 14,000 livres was roughly the average (nonprofessional) wealth of a young barrister. The acts of succession indicate the size of the barrister's estate at the end of his career. They show an average size of about 34,000 livres, indicating a mean lifetime enrichment of about 20,000 livres.

Of course, the barrister did not derive all of this increment from legal fees. Donations from relatives, dowries of deceased wives, and

---

[19]Armand-Gaston Camus, *Lettres sur la profession d'avocat* (Paris, 1777), p. 5.

[20]Toulousan physicians sometimes published their fees in the local newspaper. See Denyse Muller, "Médecins et chirurgiens à Toulouse de 1740 à 1830" (D.E.S., University of Toulouse, 1961), p. 141.

[21]Inventories-after-death listed the private papers kept by the deceased. These inventories never mentioned account books.

[22]Jean Sentou, *Fortunes et groupes sociaux sous la Révolution* (Toulouse, 1969), p. 55 (graph). I have found seven marriage contracts in which both the male and female *apports* were given. The average dowry for these was 12,000 livres, and the average male *apport* was 14,000 livres.

accruements from invested wealth may have been the source of some or most of these gains. To assess the contribution of legal revenues alone, we must compare the lifetime enrichment of barristers to the increases experienced by groups having no professional revenue at all. Fortunately, there were several such categories: women from well-to-do families, rentiers, and "nobles without profession" were a few. In each case, the fortunes of these nonremunerative groups tended to double over a lifetime. Professor Sentou has found that the wealth of rentiers ("bourgeois" and "proprietaires") increased 2.2 times over their lifetimes. The enrichment of nobles without professions was very close to this. Wives of *négociants*, of liberal professionals, and of nobles made even larger gains, perhaps because family expenditures fell disproportionately on the husband.[23] Thus, only part of the 20,000 livre average increment for barristers can be attributed to his legal fees.

If the barristers' private wealth of 14,000 livres doubled without income from their practices, their average gain from legal fees was about 6,000 livres. This was a *net* increment, after expenditures of all kinds. Certainly, the barristers enjoyed a considerably higher overall revenue than rentiers with equal private wealth, yet their professional earnings were not impressive when compared with the incomes of other occupations. The attorney, the advocate's inferior, earned over 14,000 livres during his career, more than twice as much as a barrister.[24] Notaries acquired still more through their *cabinets*, and the average *négociant* may have added nearly 25,000 livres to his fortune over a lifetime of commercial activity.[25] The superiority of the barrister's profession to most others was based on the honorability of its function, not on its potential for enrichment.

In a twenty-five-year career, the average barrister would have received a net gain from professional fees of only 240 livres annually. One can only guess how much this might represent in gross income but, certainly, a barrister who received fees of 1,000 livres was doing well, and one deriving 2,000 livres from his practice was far more successful than most pleaders.[26] In most cases, professional earnings must have been a supplement, of varying importance, to a more substantial private income of 1,200 to 2,000 or more livres a year.

[23]*Fortunes et groupes sociaux*, pp. 121, 155–56, 186, 214. In contrast, the wealth of merchants increased five-fold, and artisans' fortunes expanded more than thirteen times in their lifetimes.

[24]*Ibid.*, p. 215.

[25]*Ibid.*, pp. 151, 215. Most Toulousan textile merchants had a gross professional revenue of 2,000 livres a year. Nearly a third had incomes of between 4,000 and 8,000 livres. See G. Marinière, "Les marchands d'étoffes de Toulouse à la fin du XVIIIe siècle," *Annales du midi* 70 (1958): 281.

[26]Baron Francis Delbèke, in his *L'action politique et sociale des avocats au XVIIIe siècle* (Paris and Louvain, 1927), pp. 122–36, suggests that 2,000 livres was the average income for barristers. If he meant professional revenue, his estimate is clearly too high.

Given the very unequal distribution of cases and clients among the barristers, it is not surprising that the amount of professional enrichment varied enormously from barrister to barrister. It seems that a small number of leading advocates could increase their fortunes substantially over their careers. Table III–2 lists the wealth of the most distinguished barristers along with the dowries they received, as a rough index of their initial fortunes. Their average wealth after thirty-four years of practice was quite substantial and the dowries do not suggest they began their careers with such fortunes. One of the most important barristers, Jean Desirat, once claimed a professional income of 6,000 livres, and this, if accurate, was probably the most a Toulousan barrister could earn.[27] The few barristers with both large private incomes and lucrative practices might have had annual revenues of 4,000 to 7,000 livres a year, which approached the level of Toulousan aristocrats. Thus, substantial enrichment was a *possibility* at the Toulousan bar.

Enrichment was certainly not a probability, though, for most barristers. Even among the masters of the bar were some who failed to earn a sizeable fortune. Certainly, Joseph Marie Duroux and Jean Mascart were among the most distinguished and frequently-employed pleaders of the century. Yet after twenty-four years of practice, Duroux had a fortune of only 36,000 livres; and Mascart died, after forty years at the bar, with an estate of only 40,000 livres.[28] Another very distinguished pleader and legal scholar was Théodore Sudre, whose estate at death was less than 28,000 livres.[29] Even when leading barristers were well-off, their wealth did not necessarily come from pleading. Jean Bastoulh, for example, possessed the large fortune of 73,000 livres after fifteen years of practice, but 65,000 livres came from his wife's dowry.[30] That barristers of such professional prominence did not earn much suggests that there must have been many more *petites affaires* than lucrative ones. But, then, Toulouse was hardly a great commercial or financial center like Paris, where great ventures engendered large fees.[31] We must draw the distinction between a large practice and a lucrative one. Though large practices were not the rule, financially rewarding ones were still less so.[32]

---

[27]*A.D.*, C–276, letter of Desirat to intendant, 24 October 1757. The circumstances under which Desirat claimed such an income may have led him to exaggerate its size.

[28]*A.M.*, 2G–16, for Duroux; Sentou, *Fortunes et groupes sociaux*, p. 231, for Mascart.

[29]See computer print-out of successions studied by Sentou, in the Departmental Archives.

[30]*A.M.*, 2G–12.

[31]Pierre Berryer, the Parisian advocate, discusses some enormously profitable cases in his autobiography, *Souvenirs de M. Berryer*, 2 vols. (Paris, 1839), 1: 88–89.

[32]Jean Egret has found literary evidence for the same income structure at the bar of Grenoble. See *Le Parlement de Dauphiné et les affaires publiques dans la deuxième moitié du XVIIIe siècle*, 2 vols. (Grenoble, 1942), 2: 82.

TABLE III-2.   Fortunes of Some Leading Barristers (in livres)

Name	Wealth	Dowry Received[a]	Years of Practice[b]
Bastoulh	73,000	65,000	15
Bragouse	133,000	30,000	15
Duroux	36,800	—	24
Douyau	20,000	15,000	24
Dirat	110,000	—	55
Gary	200,000	—	34
Gez	30,000	6,000	26
Jouve	113,000	11,000	50
Jamme	60,000	6,000	30
Laviguerie	100,000	—	32
Mascart	40,000	—	42
Mayniel	16,000	—	20
Merle	75,000	20,000	42
Monyer	70,000	—	28
Roucoule	40,000	—	13
Sudre	28,000	—	53
Albaret	103,000	—	48
Arexi	65,000	—	46
Savy-Brassalières	190,000	9,000	49
Averages	75,000	20,250	33.8

Sources: Sentou, Fortunes et groupes sociaux; A.M., 2G-2; 2G-9-16; A.D., 3E, marriage contracts.
[a] In some cases this amount is unknown.
[b] The "Years of Practice" column does not go beyond 1790.

Below this group of very distinguished barristers, opportunities for substantial enrichment were even more restricted. Table III-3 lists the wealth of barristers who were not masters of the bar but still had respectable careers. Their mean fortunes of 35,600 livres was hardly more than the average for all barristers, including many obscure pleaders. It would seem that their professional revenues were too small to create important net gains in wealth. Indeed, when we are able to examine in detail the sources of a barrister's fortune, it is difficult to discern the amount derived from professional revenues. Jean Marie Saremejane, for example, was a barrister of importance, appearing regularly at the bar through the 1770s and turning to consultation and instruction afterward. He received 15,000 livres from his father when he married in 1770,[33] and he must have gained his first wife's dowry of 15,000 livres sometime before 1785, for he remarried in that year.[34] When his possessions were confiscated in 1793, he had 26,000 livres in real property and 3,470 in rentes.[35] Of course, part of his wealth was

[33] A.D., 3E-3900, fol. 606, marriage contract of Saremejane (stating male apport).
[34] A.D., 3E-13894, fol. 33.
[35] A.M., 1S-70; Henri Martin, ed., Documents relatifs à la vente des biens nationaux (Toulouse, 1916), pp. 243-44.

TABLE III-3.   Wealth of Barristers with Important Practices (in livres)

Name	Fortune	Years of Practice [a]
Arbanere	40,000	14
Ozun	28,600	42
Pouderoux	22,000	22
Raynal	30,000	30
Saremejane	30,000	30
Taverne	34,000	30
Ardenne	25,000	15
Barère	25,000	15
Bellomaire	55,000	29
Dabatia	45,000	23
Detté	6,000	23
Faure	25,000	18
Gratian	35,000	22
Lafage	50,000	22
Latapie	12,000	24
Londois	51,000	20
Verieu	25,000	13
Guizet	26,000	24
Legendre	5,000	17
Lheritier	62,000	29
Bonnet	80,000	40
Roques	25,000	15
Soulé	24,000	22
Malpel	166,000	30
Nuly	70,000	20
Planet	73,800	38
Averages	35,600	23.3

Sources: A.M., CC-Capitation rolls; A.M., 2G-2, 2G-9-16; Sentou, Fortunes et groupes sociaux.

[a] The "Years of Practice" column does not go beyond 1790.

dissipated through expenditures, but he did not appear to have lived beyond the usual standards of comfort[36] or to have had children to whom he might have given large dowries and donations. It seems reasonable to conclude that his professional revenues had not been very substantial. A close examination of the financial history of Gérard Lheritier yields a similar conclusion. This respectable barrister declared revenues of 3,100 livres in 1793, indicating an estate of 62,000 livres.[37] Most of this wealth, however, did not come from his practice, for in 1782 he had inherited 54,000 livres from a relative, and 6,000 livres more came from his wife's dowry.[38] Apparently this barrister, too, was unable to accumulate much capital from the fees he earned in court.

[36]He possessed personal effects worth only 1,750 livres in 1793. See his inventory in A.M., 1S-70.
[37]A.M., 2G-12.
[38]A.D., 2C-3027, register of centième dernier, entry of 25 February 1782; A.M., 2G-12.

Below this second professional echelon were the many barristers at the Parlement with small practices or with no clients at all. A large portion of these were titular barristers who sought no cases and who intended to live on their private fortunes. Other barristers earned a slender professional income—it could hardly have been more than a few hundred livres—but had large enough private fortunes to live comfortably. There were still twenty to thirty pleaders at the Parlement with neither large estates nor sizeable practices. Among these were young men below the average marriage age, and they may have lived at their father's expense at home.[39] But a few men undoubtedly had to struggle to live respectably, and they especially bore the brunt of the rapid expansion of the Sovereign Court bar.

It may have been easier for each pleader to earn a moderate livelihood at the nonsovereign tribunals, but opportunities for substantial enrichment seem to have been almost entirely absent there. Two leading barristers of the Seneschal Court, Michel Martin and Guillaume Bordes, had both been professionally active for over forty years and had both served as arbitrators and as seigneurial officers.[40] In addition, Bordes had been counsel to the Dames of Refuge for over twenty years.[41] Despite their very full careers, neither was well-off. In 1789, Martin paid a head tax of only 9 livres, and Bordes declared a revenue of only 800 livres in 1790. Indeed, Martin was able to give his daughter a portion of only 4,000 livres in 1785.[42] Thus, success in the Seneschal Court was very unlikely to bring substantial wealth.

In all but a few cases, then, a legal practice provided only the supplement to a more important private income or, at best, a moderate livelihood. The number of pleaders who dramatically raised their financial status through their profession does not seem to have been more than ten or so each generation. For many or most of its practitioners, the barrister's profession was—like the magistracies at all levels—a very honorable civic and social function from which one could not expect sizeable pecuniary rewards.[43] The bar did attract some ambitious men from modest backgrounds, because talent could bring success and a comfortable living. But as the recruitment patterns show, most barristers were aware that a respectable private fortune was a well-advised accompaniment to a career at the bar. For the most part, the professional manuals were correct in stressing the supremacy of honor over lucre as the motivating force in the profession.

---

[39]There were eighteen barristers at the bar in 1789 who had been practicing less than seven years and who did not seem to have developed even minimal practices.

[40]*A.D.*, B-registers of sessions of Seneschal Court; B-seigneurial justice.

[41]*A.D.*, L-4249, fol. 113.

[42]*A.M.*, 2G-2; CC-1056; *A.D.*, 3E-10911, fol. 243.

[43]For *bailliage* magistracies, see Philip Dawson, *Provincial Magistrates and Revolutionary Politics in France, 1789-1795* (Cambridge, Mass., 1972), pp. 82-83.

In this sense, the bar played a conservative or stabilizing economic role in Toulousan society. Men from well-to-do families became barristers, settled their children well, and preserved their status. The bar rarely generated a great deal of new wealth or raised families much beyond the financial position achieved before entering the bar. The barrister's profession, at least as it was practiced in Toulouse, could not easily accommodate the acquisitive.

MANAGEMENT OF INVESTED WEALTH

The secure, status-laden property in which the barristers invested could not be made to yield more than 4 to 5 percent, but there were ways of maximizing, or at least increasing, the returns. The parlementaires and nobles of older extraction did so through careful, even aggressive, estate administration.[44] Since the barristers depended so heavily on their private sources of revenue, they had an incentive to manage their wealth shrewdly; however, they seem to have been passive recipients of rents and interest, neither expending much attention on their property nor attempting innovations. As with their professional revenues, the barristers placed considerations of prestige above personal gain.

It must be admitted at once that the documents dealing with the barristers' estate management are very scarce. No family papers or financial records have survived; inventories-after-death indicate that barristers never even kept account books, a fact which is significant in itself. But tax rolls and notarial acts do shed some light on their methods of handling rural property and attest to their lack of shrewdness and their unbusinesslike methods.[45] The barristers leased their land to sharecroppers at half fruits. Even if they possessed a few scattered fields that were not organized into a farm, they found sharecroppers to work them for half the yield. This method of management was most appropriate for a country gentleman, who spent six to nine months on his estate and could exercise sufficient supervision and control over the sharecropper.[46] The barrister, however, busy as he was at court from 12 November (St. Martin's) to the beginning of September, could not give his domain much supervision, and he might not receive his full share of the harvest. The money lease (*fermage*) was a more suitable managerial method for nonresident proprietors.[47] Parle-

[44]Forster, *Nobility of Toulouse*, chapters 2–4.
[45]The most useful sources for studying the barristers' rural property are the declarations for the *vingtième* of 1750, *A.D.*, C-1312-1346. These provide information on the size of the holdings, the lease, the crops grown, and the yields.
[46]Forster, *Nobility of Toulouse*, p. 155 and *passim*.
[47]For the extensive supervision needed in sharecropping, see Marc Venard, *Bourgeois et paysan au XVIIe siècle* (Paris, 1957), p. 69. For this reason, Parisians rarely used *métayage*.

mentaires, who were also confined to the city for most of the year, sometimes employed money leases,[48] but we know of only one instance of a barrister doing so. The barristers preferred sharecropping because it was customary and, perhaps, because it was more compatible with their image of the country squire's lifestyle.

Shrewd, efficient land management frequently meant being a rigorous landlord, a role which Toulousan aristocrats readily assumed.[49] There are several indications, however, that barristers were not demanding landlords and did not seek to extract all they could from the cultivators. The contract between the barrister-proprietor and his tenant-sharecropper was frequently an oral, informal agreement renewed each year.[50] Accustomed as the barrister was by profession to the scrutiny of documents, his use of an oral agreement denotes a certain casualness about the conditions by which his land was worked. Moreover, this oral agreement was an imprecise accord in which tradition and personal trust governed the relations between tenant and proprietor. It could hardly have been used as the instrument by which sharecroppers were reduced to the position of wage laborers, a practice of many aristocratic landlords in the region.[51]

Instances of generosity toward the cultivators were much more evident than cases of severity and increasing exactions. Barristers quite frequently bequeathed a hundred livres or so to the poor of the parishes in which they held land. The Toulousan aristocrats, several times wealthier than the advocates, rarely gave more than this.[52] In a few cases, barristers even canceled the small debts owed to them by the cultivators of their villages. Jean Poisson, barrister and former capitoul, posed as the beneficent *seigneur* by leaving 100 livres to the poor of Fenouillet and Gagnac and by granting to the cultivators "what they have borrowed from me up to twenty livres."[53] Barrister Jean Dumec abrogated without qualification all arrears owed to him by the residents of his village.[54] The parlementaires and important nobles left no such provisions for debt cancellation in their wills. In fact, they often used arrears to force small cultivators to sell their land.[55] Certain barrister-proprietors may have taken the paternalistic ideals of a

---

[48]Forster, *Nobility of Toulouse*, pp. 58–59.

[49]*Ibid.*, pp. 47–65.

[50]*A.D.*, C-1312–1330. See, for example, the declarations of Quinquiry (C-1328), Labordie (C-1321), and Dejeans (C-1314).

[51]Forster, *Nobility of Toulouse*, pp. 56–58.

[52]*Ibid.*, chap. 6.

[53]*A.D.*, 3E-11855, no. 8097, testament of Poisson.

[54]*A.D.*, 3E-11831, no. 3375, testament of Dumec. Perhaps more barristers would have made such gestures of *largesse* if they had not wanted to pass on all they could to their families.

[55]Forster, *Nobility of Toulouse*, pp. 50–53. Professor Forster tells me that he found no cases of debt cancellation provisions in the wills of the Toulousan nobility. They rarely did more than leave a gift of 100 or so livres to the parish poor.

country gentleman all the more seriously because they were only aspiring to be true *gentilhommes.*

However much the barrister wished to emulate the country gentleman, he was primarily an urban dweller. Perhaps it was for this reason that the problems of land management rarely impinged on his consciousness. Indeed, raising the productivity of the land seems never to have occurred to the barristers, although Toulousan aristocrats were sometimes "improvers." Most nobles had initiated the cultivation of maize, which was an intermediate stage between biennial and triennial rotation.[56] By mid-century, no barrister had planted maize. Their property grew only the traditional grains—wheat, oats, barley—and retained the biennial rotation in its pure form, half grain, half fallow.[57] The barristers were also far behind the nobility in clearing new land. The intendant's list of land-clearers rarely contained a barrister, though their domains had uncultivated areas.[58] The only improvement taking place on the barrister's domain was the replacement of old vines with new ones—a change of questionable import, since the intendant thought too many vines had been planted anyway.[59]

Not only did Toulousan aristocrats take a more active role as landlords, but their position as proprietors of substantial holdings enabled them to adjust more profitably to the expanding food market. The middling size of the barristers' landed holdings prevented them from benefiting fully from the buoyant market even if they were inclined to do so. Barristers may well have been sympathetic to speculation in grain, but it was rarely possible for a middle-sized proprietor. His margin of surplus over taxes, wages, seed, and personal consumption was small.[60] The steep price increase in wood was a boon to the aristocrats, for they owned most of the forest. The barrister owned an average of only 1.3 acres of woodland, so he could have hardly sold commercially.[61] Furthermore, in the case of the noble estate of 200 to 300 acres, it was worthwhile to transport the grains directly to market, eliminating the middleman and selling at the seasonal high price. The barrister could not undertake the cost and reponsibility of grain transportation, so he had to sell to the small grain merchants (*blatiers*) who scoured the countryside. The aristocrats even made financial use of their seigneurial rights through careful account-keeping and foreclosures on those who could not pay arrears.[62] Most barristers did not possess seigneurial rights, but even for the 10 to 15

---

[56]*Ibid.,* p. 62.
[57]*A.D.,* C-1312-1346.
[58]*A.D.,* C-108-109.
[59]Forster, *Nobility of Toulouse,* p. 99.
[60]*Ibid.,* p. 76.
[61]*Ibid.,* pp. 91–94; *A.D.,* C-1312-1346, *vingtième* declarations of 1750.
[62]Forster, *Nobility of Toulouse,* chaps. 2-3.

percent who did, the rights were ornamental, not lucrative. Though they gloried in the title "seigneur de . . . ," barristers were almost always minor co-seigneurs with a sixth or an eighth of the rights.[63] Any "seigneurial reaction" on their part would have had little effect on the cultivators. Thus, many opportunities for agricultural profits were closed to barristers as middling proprietors.[64]

It seems that raising returns from rural property required social prominence in several ways. The time, incentives, interest, and extensive holdings needed to profit most fully from the growing agricultural markets were possessed mainly by country gentlemen. Furthermore, squeezing the cultivators may have required a self-confidence—or at least an absence of self-consciousness—about one's status. Barristers, as would-be *gentilhommes*, seemed to have lacked both the psychological and physical prerequisites for businesslike land management.

The manner in which barristers directed their nonlanded wealth is still more obscure, for lack of documents. The little we can observe denotes, once again, a passive posture rather than a vigilance in maintaining or enhancing their financial position. Holding rentes offered several conveniences,[65] but it was imprudent for barristers to invest such a large portion of their estates in annuities during an inflationary period. The decline in real value of invested capital depended on the age of the rente, and since the barristers' annuities were often older ones, inherited from relatives, the loss may have been considerable. For example, the noble barrister François de Senovert possessed the sizeable fortune of 73,000 livres, all in rentes.[66] If most of these were constituted prior to 1770, Senovert may have found the real value of his estate reduced one-sixth by 1789.[67] Investment in rural property would have been preferable, but annuities continued to make up a large portion of the barrister's wealth. There is also some evidence that barristers kept significant amounts of liquidity, suggesting a failure to make every *sou* productive. The Merchants' Court barrister Jean Degeilh died in 1765, leaving 26,400 livres in a strongbox;[68] this

[63]See, for example, *A.D.*, C-1313, declaration of Carrière; C-1318, declaration of Albaret; C-1318, declaration of Prévost.

[64]A few of the largest proprietors, usually ennobled barristers, may have behaved more like the aristocracy. See the example of the advocate Faget in Forster, *Nobility of Toulouse*, p. 76.

[65]See François Bluche, *Les magistrats du Parlement de Paris au XVIIIe siècle (1715-1771)* (Paris, 1960), p. 214 for a discussion of the conveniences of investment in rentes.

[66]*A.M.*, 2 G-12.

[67]The general price level rose about 20 percent between 1750-1770 and 1771-1789. See Camille-Ernest Labrousse, *Esquisse du mouvement des prix et des revenues en France au XVIIIe siècle*, 2 vols. (Paris, 1933), 1: 147; 2: 598-99.

[68]*A.D.*, 3E-11905, inventory-after-death of Degeilh.

was probably most of his fortune. The law professor Julien possessed 3,000 livres in gold coin at his death.[69] One wonders, too, whether the 10,500 livres in idle funds that Jacob Londois had in 1793 or the 18,000 livres in gold belonging to Jean Lafage marks their hoarding of coin during the Terror or their lack of diligence in making their cash yield returns.[70]

Maximizing revenues, whether professional or personal, was apparently not an important concern of most barristers. They depended on a good marriage or an inheritance to enhance their economic position; barring these fortunate occurrences, they accepted their economic state and faced daily monetary concerns by holding expenditures to a respectable minimum. The barristers were hardly alone in seeking status through a conspicuous conformity to traditional (and financially unrewarding) standards. But such an economic psychology was not appropriate to the long-term realities of their socioeconomic position, for social advancement required, above all else, expanding wealth.

INTRAGENERATIONAL MOBILITY

The absence of formal restrictions on entry to the bar, the recognition which the profession accorded to personal merit, and the potential for ennoblement through the capitoul's office all offered the barristers considerable opportunity for social advancement. The most prevalent pattern of social promotion was limited and undramatic, to be sure, but still meaningful to those who experienced it. This was the movement from the inferior, middling, and commercial occupations to the bar. At least 40 percent of the barristers exercised a more esteemed profession than their fathers.[71] Their ascension to the bar had taken them across that fissure separating middling occupations from the barristers' intermediary stratum and had involved changes in life style and attitudes that marked them off as "better" people. Their new profession, unlike their fathers', was assuredly an honorable one. Even the attorney, whose functions seem to us so close to those of the barrister, had to defend himself against charges of exercising a "vile and mechanical" occupation.[72] The barrister was never so disparaged, and the many young men who came to the bar from below surely appreciated this.

[69] *A.D.*, 3E-11919, inventory-after-death of Julien.

[70] *A.M.*, 2G-9; 2G-16. The Revolution introduced incentives for hoarding coin, so this evidence is not as solid as the pre-1789 examples.

[71] They were the sons of attorneys, *bourgeois*, notaries, *greffiers*, artisans, and most civil officers and merchants.

[72] *A.D.*, E-1190, deliberations of Community of Attorneys (letter of syndics to Parlement of Pau, 26 June 1770; also, *mémoire* of attorneys of Pau).

The receptivity of the bar to merit ensured substantial professional mobility to a smaller number of talented barristers. These men usually came from well-off but otherwise undistinguished backgrounds, and they rose to become highly respected men in the legal world. Such success did not necessarily bring notable increases in fortune, but it was accompanied by contacts with important people and by enhanced prestige. The career of Jean Joseph Gez demonstrates the rewards which talent and application might normally bring a barrister. The son of a prosperous retail merchant, Gez became a highly respected barrister and even entered the prestigious Academy of Sciences. His prominence at the bar probably helped him win the hand of a minor nobleman's daughter.[73] These honorific rewards, however, were never matched by pecuniary ones, for his fortune surely remained below 40,000 livres.[74] The accomplishments of Gez were certainly more typical than those of his brother-in-law, the celebrated advocate Alexandre Augustin Jamme, who gained not only respectability but wealth. Jamme was the son of a modest rural notary and received a dowry of only 6,000 livres in 1764.[75] After a most distinguished literary and legal career, he was one of the 600 most heavily taxed men in the Département under Napoleon.[76]

The bar witnessed a few more dramatic successes, in which "self-made" men ascended from the *peuple* to wealth, prominence, and even ennoblement. Guillaume Chabanettes presents the most striking example of this. The son of a master baker,[77] he rapidly rose to the top of the profession, receiving all the honors a consummately successful legal career could bring. After thirty-two years of practice, his talent and legal successes were rewarded with ennoblement through municipal office. Chabanettes established a family of minor nobles, his son becoming an *écuyer* and his daughter marrying in the capitouls' circle with a dowry of 30,000 livres.[78] Another self-made man was Jacques Marie Rouzet, the son of a tailor.[79] He was never capitoul, but he did build a successful practice in Toulouse, become the advisor to an important nobleman, and develop very lucrative connections in Ver-

[73]*A.D.*, 3E–7644, fol. 138, marriage contract of Gez.

[74]*A.M.*, 2G–7, declaration of wealth by public notoriety. This roll greatly exaggerated the wealth of those on it, so Gez almost certainly had a fortune smaller than the 40,000 livres attributed to him.

[75]*A.D.*, 3E–7634, fol. 134.

[76]Pierre Bouyoux, "Les 'six cents plus imposés' du département de la Haute-Garonne en l'an X," *Annales du midi* 70 (1958): 325.

[77]*A.D.*, 3E–26487, fol. 184, marriage contract of Chabanettes.

[78]*A.D.*, 3E–1986, fol. 30, marriage contract of J. F. Facieu to Catherine de Chabanettes.

[79]See Pierre Arches, "Les origines du conventionnel toulousain Jacques-Marie Rouzet," *Annales du midi* 83 (1971): 431–39.

sailles.[80] Only two or three other barristers even approached the successes of Chabanettes and Rouzet. Most pleaders began from positions considerably above the *peuple* and attained neither ennoblement nor outstanding wealth.

What social opportunities confronted the twenty or so distinguished barristers who reached the top of their profession? Was a respected judgeship the normal course of promotion? After 1788, men envisioned the magistracy as a reward for successful pleaders, but this was not the pattern of advancement before the Revolution. Leading barristers did not view their function as at all inferior to the magistrate's, and they manifested no desire to sit on the bench of a nonsovereign court.[81] In fact, the barristers of the Parlement considered the judges of the Seneschal Court, the second tribunal of the city, their professional inferiors. On at least one occasion the Seneschal Court magistrates were publicly ridiculed as former advocates who had failed at the bar.[82] While untrue, this claim was probably appreciated by the barristers, since they never sought an office in the Seneschal Court.[83] Only a magistracy in the Parlement would have been a clear social advance for them.

A seat on the *fleur-de-lys* bench, however, was not a realistic aspiration for even the most successful pleaders,[84] and there is no evidence that barristers expected such a position. Admission to the Parlement was a matter of birth, wealth, and connection, not of legal expertise. While the bar was the place for a great legal mind, the parlementaire had to be more than a legal expert; he had to assume the position of "father of the people" and defender of provincial liberties and constitutional forms. To fulfill this role required independence, steadfastness, and attachment to the *patrie*; and these qualities came—so it was thought—only from impressive wealth, long-standing social prominence, and generations of service to the province.[85] Such

[80]Rouzet, *Lettre de M. Rouzet à un de ses amis* (n.p., 1790), pp. 4-6.

[81]See John Henry Merryman, *The Civil Law Tradition* (Stanford, 1969), pp. 109-19, for a discussion of the prestige of the bar in civil law countries.

[82]André Bordeur, "Les magistrats toulousains non-parlementaires à la fin de l'ancien régime" (D.E.S., University of Toulouse, 1967), p. 75.

[83]I have found only one successful pleader who abandoned the bar for an office in the Seneschal Court. This was Jean-François-Rose Duroux, who married the daughter of the king's advocate and received the office as part of the dowry. See the marriage contract, *A.D.*, 3E-10790, fol. 215. Bertrand Barère received an office at the Seneschal Court of Tarbes, but he continued to practice at the bar of Toulouse. See Leo Gershoy, *Bertrand Barère, A Reluctant Terrorist* (Princeton, 1962), pp. 15-16.

[84]There were certain subaltern offices within the Parlement, like substitute to the attorney-general or judge in the *département des eaux et forêts*, which were accessible to barristers but did not appeal to them. They were expensive and apparently not so prestigious as a leading place at the bar.

[85]This may not have been equally true of all sovereign courts. Those in Metz or Douai, for example, were more like other *savonnettes à vilain*. But the Parlements in

was the rationale behind the very exclusive recruitment policy of the Parlement, and the barristers seemed to accept it.[86]

The Parlement of Toulouse was one of the most exclusive sovereign courts in France and had hardly ever deigned to admit barristers.[87] Only two practicing advocates became parlementaires in the eighteenth century—and that took place under special conditions. The two, Jean Baptiste Lapomarède-Laviguerie and Pierre Théodore Delort, were admitted by the Maupeou parlement in 1774 for essentially political reasons.[88] With the reestablishment of the pre-Maupeou court in 1775, the parlementaires did not hesitate to expel the new judges, noble though they were.[89] Even when the Sovereign Court did admit an occasional commoner (or man of dubious nobility), he was never a barrister. Between 1735 and 1750, at least four non-nobles entered the Parlement, but each gained entry as a result of his wealth and connections, not because of his success at the bar. Pierre François Astruc was the son of the consulting doctor to the Parlement.[90] Pierre de Lassus was the grandson of a subdelegate and the son of a civil officer.[91] Another new magistrate was a titular barrister from Paris, and the fourth was the son of a financier and himself the president of the *élection* of Commenges.[92] In 1775–1790, only one non-noble, Pierre de Guiringaud, was accepted into the Parlement,[93] and he was not a practicing barrister in Toulouse. Although we cannot ascertain why these men in particular were received by the court, their wealth and connections were surely much superior to those of the barristers.

Strictly speaking, one ought not to infer attitudes about social mobility from the patterns of advancement themselves; but it is

---

Toulouse and elsewhere were clearly not mere sources of noble status, similar to other ennobling offices. This is a point which is not clearly made in some discussions of social mobility. See, for example, Elinor Barber, *The Bourgeoisie of Eighteenth Century France* (Princeton, 1955), chap. 6.

[86]See below, chap. 5, for a further discussion of the relation between barristers and parlementaires.

[87]Philippe de Peguilhan de Larboust, "Les magistrats du Parlement de Toulouse à la fin de l'ancien régime" (D.E.S., University of Toulouse, 1965), p. 51. See Jean Egret, "L'aristocratie parlementaire française à la fin de l'ancien régime," *Revue historique* 208 (1952): 9–10. Egret is mistaken in recognizing five non-noble parlementaires. Actually, four of these entered the Department of Waters and Forests. There was only one non-noble who entered the Parlement after 1775.

[88]*A.D.*, B-1961, fol. 420–22. See below, chap. 5, for a discussion of the Maupeou Parlement and the bar.

[89]Despite his expulsion, Laviguerie was so proud of his former position in the Parlement that he took the title "ancien conseiller au Parlement." See the marriage contract of his daughter, *A.D.*, 3E-10792, fol. 197.

[90]*A.D.*, B-1946, fol. 17–18.

[91]Villain, *Grand dictionnaire*, 4: 1894.

[92]These were Etienne Desprez and Pierre Belloc. For the latter see *ibid.*, 2: 678–79.

[93]Larboust, "Les magistrats," pp. 35–36. By this point, the Parlement may have decided upon a secret resolution not to admit commoners.

difficult to comprehend how barristers could have aspired to enter the Parlement. Their exclusion was complete and justified by widely-held notions connecting family prominence with magisterial "independence." That they were not "destined" to be parlementaires was simply a fact of life which probably never troubled them during the Old Regime. At most, entering the Sovereign Court might have been a vague aspiration for their descendants Successful barristers sought a less exalted social reward for themselves: ennoblement.

With a seat on the *fleur-de-lys* bench beyond his horizons, the barrister could realistically hope for ennoblement through the capitoul's office. Capping off a successful legal career as an *anobli* was possible, even likely, for a very distinguished barrister. But this was *not* because the capitouls were always recruited among the most outstanding Toulousan commoners; in fact, the procedure for choosing capitouls was very corrupt and subject to outside interference. Distinguished pleaders gained the office almost incidentally, as a matter of circumstance.

In theory, the king selected eight capitouls annually from a list of honorable Toulousan residents drawn up by incumbent capitouls and scrutinized by local notables and officials. These nominees were supposedly drawn from the ranks of barristers, merchants, and *bourgeois* of the city.[94] The actual selection process, however, was quite different. In November of each year (until the reform of 1778) the incumbent capitouls received a list of six to eight names, called the *norme* of the court, which emanated from Versailles.[95] The capitouls obediently placed these names in nomination even though many candidates were not even Toulousan residents. Almost inevitably, these nominees became the new capitouls. To have one's name placed on the *norme* required the favor of leading regional or administrative figures. The First President of the Parlement, the intendant of Languedoc, and the governor of the province (the comte d'Eu) each had the right to name one person to the *norme*.[96] Three or four other capitouls were selected by the minister of state, St. Florentin, and these were men "whom he names at the solicitation of seigneurs, ladies or of his first secretary."[97]

---

[94]For details, see Roger Sicard, *L'Administration capitulaire sous l'ancien régime* (Toulouse, 1952), and L. Dutil, "La réforme du capitoul toulousain," *Annales du midi* 19 (1907): 305–63.

[95]My description of the actual selection of the capitouls is based on administrative correspondence, *A.D.*, C-269-289.

[96]*A.D.*, C-287, Raynal, "Mémoire sur la nécessité de la réformation de l'administration municipale . . . ." At some time the archbishop may also have had a nomination.

[97]Cited in Gérard Lavergne, "Un perigourdin capitoul de Toulouse," *Annales du midi* 49 (1937): 265.

The favor of the great usually came at a price. One Jean Léonard Gaillard, for example, became capitoul in 1758, though he was an inhabitant of Perigord and had no intention of living in Toulouse even for a year. However, he did pay the duc de Nivernais a hundred *louis d'or* (2,400 livres) to intercede on his behalf with St. Florentin.[98] Influence alone, unsupplemented by coin, was apparently a less effective means of acquiring the office. Voltaire attempted to have Theodore Sudre, the respected Toulousan barrister and defender of Jean Calas, named capitoul. The celebrated writer used his own influence and wrote to the marquise de Boufflers-Remiencourt and the comte d'Argentel on Sudre's behalf, but in vain. This barrister, whom Voltaire so admired, was never named to the *norme* of the court.[99]

As a result of these practices, three or four "barristers" became capitouls each year—but they were not usually practicing advocates or residents of Toulouse. All royal officers received the title *avocat*, and once even the the wood-merchant Berdoulat was qualified as a barrister.[100] So, official lists of capitouls were no guide to the number of barristers who became capitoul each year.

Under this selection process, it was almost possible to dismiss the interests of the city and concerns about the qualifications of nominees. However, the royal administrators could not allow this to happen entirely. The intendant was obligated to see that Toulouse had a few competent, resident capitouls for practical reasons, and barristers in particular were needed. The capitouls' judicial functions required some legal experience, and each year a barrister who had already served as capitoul was needed to direct the other alderman as *chef de consistoire*. The intendant had to ensure that such barristers would be available each year, so he could not allow only titular advocates and "foreigners" to hold the ennobling office.[101] If no other nominator did so, the intendant probably saw to it that a distinguished barrister became capitoul fairly often.

This would explain how thirty-nine practicing barristers—most of them masters of their profession—became capitouls in the last fifty years of the Old Regime, despite the corruption of the selection process (see table III-4). Between 1740 and 1778, when the municipal govern-

[98]*Ibid.*, p. 266. This price was said to be a bargain. The usual price was 2,000 *écus* (6,000 livres).

[99]Voltaire (François-Marie Arouet), *Correspondence*, ed. Theodore Besterman, 107 vols. (Geneva, 1962), 63: 162–64 (letters 12832–33).

[100]*A.D.*, C-277, "Notes sur les 18 sujets qui ont été retenus"; C-276, letter of subdelegate Amblard to intendant, 11 November 1757. Nonresidents could make their candidacy "legitimate" by having their names added to the tax rolls in retrospect. See C-276, letter of Amblard to intendant, 6 August 1757.

[101]*A.D.*, C-277, letter of Seneschal Chalvet to intendant, 27 November 1761; letter of Chalvet to intendant, 30 November 1762; C-278, Letter of Chalvet to intendant, 19 October 1767.

TABLE III-4. Practicing Barristers Who Became Capitouls, 1740–1789 [a]

Capitouls, 1740–1778	Year(s) of Tenure
de Cominhan	1740
Sicard	1740
Laviguerie	1741, 1752
Quinquary	1741
Laporte	1745, 1746
Tournier	1745, 1758
Prévost	1746, 1751
Courdurier	1747
Pujos	1748
Tilhol	1750, 1755, 1756
Fabry	1751
Amblard	1752, 1759
Desirat	1753, 1757
Furgole	1754
Daurier	1755, 1760
Pons	1756, 1766, 1767
Carrière	1756, 1762
Faget	1757, 1761
Taverne	1760
Gouazé	1762, 1768–70
Gary	1764
Ricard	1765
Savy de Brassalières	1766, 1774
Chabanettes	1767
Raynal	1767
Jouve	1768
Dupuy	1768
Albaret	1770
Cahusac	1772
Carbonel	1774, 1775–78
Mascart	1775–78
Manen	1775–78

Capitouls, 1778–1789	Year(s) of Tenure
(Savy)	—
(Gouazé)	—
Senovert	1778–80
Monier	1778–80
Arexi	1778–80, 1782
(Gary)	—
Ginisty	1781
Merle	1786
Manent	1786
Duroux	1786

Source: Alexandre Du Mège, *Histoire des institutions religieuses, politiques, judiciares, et littéraires de la ville de Toulouse*, 4 vols. (Toulouse, 1849), 2: 459–72.

[a] By "practicing" I mean those who were inscribed on the table of the Order of Barristers.

ment was reformed, thirty-two barristers entered the Hôtel de Ville; this was nearly one each year. A few of these, like Jean Prévost de Fenouillet or Antoine de Cahusac, were not leading pleaders and probably purchased the influence necessary to acquire an office.[102] Two others, François Amblard and his son-in-law Jean Raynal, became capitouls by first serving as subdelegates. The rest, however, were all highly respected barristers whose professional success brought them public prominence.[103]

The municipal reform of 1778, about which more will be said later, returned the selection of capitouls to local bodies and decreased the number of available ennobling positions to four and then to two. These changes reduced the rate of ennoblement somewhat but certainly did not eliminate this avenue of advancement. Those who suffered most from the reform were the "foreigners" and unqualified nominees, not the Toulousan barristers. In the ten years following the reform, six more barristers entered the Hôtel de Ville, and possibilities for a higher number of ennoblements existed.[104]

Thus, the many eighteenth-century moral critics who decried the "mixing of ranks" would not have been comforted by the social situation at the bar. In contrast to its conservative economic function, the bar was a source of considerable social relocation. To be sure, conservation of status and small advances were the rule, and highly visible exceptions like Chabanettes or Rouzet should not obscure this fact. But the bar enabled numerous men to exercise a more distinguished progression than their fathers, allowed the talented and ambitious to achieve success and respect, and permitted a select few to enter the nobility. Even if an office in the Parlement was beyond the barrister's social horizons, he still found very important avenues to higher status open to personal merit.

Intergenerational Mobility

Most of the social promotion at the Toulousan bar, as we have seen, was dependent on individual merit. Only the few who had substantially increased their wealth or acquired noble status could ensure their progeny a permanently higher social position, and even this fortunate

---

[102]Actually, there were very few cases of rich, but totally undistinguished barristers who "bought" the office. There was probably some strong feeling against such a practice at the Toulousan bar.

[103]One advocate, Pons, was not a well-regarded pleader, but the subdelegate thought him qualified because of his friendship with the distinguished barristers Ricard and Faget. See *A.D.*, C–278, table of candidates, 1765–66.

[104]The reform also introduced a new pattern of advancement into the Hôtel de Ville, the result of which was the inclusion of more non-noble barristers in the municipal government. For details, see Edmond Lamouzèle, *Essai sur l'administration de la ville de Toulouse à la fin de l'ancien régime* (Paris, 1910).

elite had not established their families so solidly that they could be unconcerned about their childrens' social standing. This, of course, explains the barristers' family settlement, which aimed at providing each child with the means of acquiring a respectable position. Now, we shall want to examine their success in doing so and their descendants' opportunities for further social advancement.

There were two different career patterns and perspectives among barristers' children. The progeny of the wealthy and ennobled advocates had vocational possibilities that differed from the families of less successful colleagues. First, we shall consider the occupational choices facing children of undistinguished pleaders; this establishes a "lower limit" to the social attainments at the bar. We shall see that opportunities were rather restricted by choice and circumstance, but these children usually found positions that were *honnête*.

The difficulties in tracing the career patterns of obscure legal families are considerable. Genealogies are rare, and homonyms impeded research in the notarial archives. We have, however, been able to reconstruct twenty-four families.[105] Of the forty sons in this group, eighteen became barristers; sixteen were priests; two became merchants; two, financial officers; one, an engineer; and one, a "bachelor of law." Data from incompletely reconstructed families confirms the overwhelming importance of the bar and the priesthood as vocations for barristers' sons, and it is not difficult to understand why this was so. The barristers were reluctant to place their children in "inferior" middling professions; civil offices were costly and may not have represented an improvement in status, in any case. So, family circumstances and social structure restricted the career choices of the barristers' children to the Church and the bar; but there were many attractive aspects of these professions that made them most appropriate for barristers' children. Both involved the study of Latin and classical culture, so much a part of the advocates' sense of respectability. Both priests and barristers were in positions of authority and honorability, and once the necessary education was acquired, entry into either profession was unrestricted and inexpensive.

The barristers seem to have regarded the priesthood and the bar as equally acceptable alternatives. Their eldest sons and heirs became either clerics or pleaders with nearly equal frequency. Advocates sent their sons to the university for degrees in either theology or law, and the sons who became priests sometimes acquired both. It may well have been that barristers were more conscious of the similarities between the two professions as honorable social positions than of their differences,

---

[105]My major sources are the barristers' testaments, *A.D.*, 3E–11809–11858. Marriage contracts have also been helpful. I have not undertaken the arduous task of family reconstitution through parish registers, however.

an attitude which would have been characteristic of their thinking about occupations.[106] The only restriction which a barrister may have imposed on his sons in choosing between the two vocations derived from the overcrowded conditions at the bar. Advocates rarely placed more than one son at the bar as practicing pleaders, and in large families the father may have expected or encouraged one or more of his children to enter the priesthood.

The role of the Church in providing places for children of aristocratic families is well-known; but ecclesiastical positions were just as much a part of the barristers' family settlement. Very often a *cure* passed from uncle to nephew, so one son had a family position in the Church reserved for him.[107] For example, the brother of barrister Bernard Molinier was the *curé* of Saint Nicolas in Toulouse, and Molinier's son "inherited" this position.[108] A religious vocation incidentally contributed to a successful family settlement, for it reduced the division of the patrimony. The son in the Church received his legal share of the family estate, but he then left it to his brother's heir, thereby reconstituting the family wealth. The Church was, thus, very much a part of the social framework around which the barrister constructed his family plans and vocational aspirations.

The barristers' children entered other types of professions only if they had special interests and aptitudes (in science, for example, which might lead to a medical or an engineering occupation). It is worth noting the still limited, but growing, attraction of careers in overseas trade. The children of barristers never became merchants in Toulouse, but several did migrate to the port cities and engage in the colonial trade. The barrister Jean Lavaysse granted his eldest son freedom to select a career, and this son chose overseas commerce.[109] The fact that Lavaysse was Protestant did not make his case a unique one. The eldest son of the respected barrister Noel de St. Pierre became a merchant in Lorient and died during a voyage to the Indies.[110] A child of the distinguished pleader Jean Mayniel and a grandson of the noble law professor Jean Delort went into colonial commerce, too.[111] The opportunities for wealth and adventure offered by this career created an interest in it, but entry into overseas trade was not yet widespread.

Ultimately, the limited professional perspectives of these barristers' sons were self-imposed as much as they were dictated by circumstances.

[106]See the remarks on "function and profession" in chapter 1, above.
[107]See Dominique Julia, "Le clergé paroissial dans le diocèse de Reims à la fin du XVIIIe siècle," *Revue d'histoire moderne et contemporaine* 13 (1966): 208.
[108]*A.D.*, 3E-14153, fol. 105 (see list of groom's attendants).
[109]D. Lavaysse, *Mémoire de Me David Lavaysse, avocat en la cour . . . pour le sieur Lavaysse, son troisième fils* (Toulouse, n.d.), p. 5.
[110]*A.D.*, 3E-1170, no. 173, testament of St. Pierre.
[111]*A.D.*, L-302, L-326, dossiers of Mayniel and Delort.

True, positions demanding family prominence or great wealth were closed to them. But they chose the bar and the church because these were familiar, secure professions that embodied the barristers' notions of respectability.

What social positions might the families of wealthy, successful, and ennobled barristers attain? These children had all the advantages that a distinguished career at the bar could provide and so, in effect, defined the upper limit of social mobility for this socioprofessional group. Not even with these advantages, though, could barristers' children expect to enter the Parlement. In the few, and increasingly rare, instances in which a capitoul's son became a magistrate, he was almost never the son of a successful, practicing barrister. As table III–5 demonstrates, the majority of parlementaires throughout the century were sons or relatives of parlementaires. In the years 1735–50, about one out of ten new parlementaires was the son of a capitoul, but this trickle from the city hall to the Parlement did not include a single son of a practicing advocate. The father of counselor Joseph Marie Cucsac, for example, was a rich judge at the Court of Coinage and a capitoul.[112] Cucsac's colleague Joseph Luc de Vaisse descended from a wealthy taille-receiver.[113] Capitouls Delherm, Carrère, Cantalouze, and Miramont, all of whom placed sons in the Parlement, had been either écuyers or only titular barristers.[114] It is clear that these families had gained their wealth and influence outside the bar.

The entry of a few recently ennobled men continued until the Maupeou coup (1771), but, as before, there was almost no access from the bar to the bench of the Parlement. Counselor François Joseph Foulquier, for example, was a son and grandson of capitouls and had entered the Parlement only after enriching himself as Intendant of Guadeloupe.[115] The newly admitted magistrates Pierre Bonhomme Dupin and André de David d'Escalonne were sons of wealthy écuyers who became capitouls.[116] Only one new parlementaire, Antoine de Miegeville, was the son of a barrister. His father, however, had not been "an advocate of the first order," according to the subdelegate,[117] and

---

[112]*A.D.*, B-1947, fol. 218-220.

[113]Alphonse Brémond, *Nobiliaire toulousaine*, 2 vols. (Toulouse, 1863), 2: 483.

[114]*A.D.*, B-1947, fol. 243-245 for Delherm; Brémond, *Nobiliaire*, 1: 175 for Carrère; Villain, *Grand dictionnaire*, 1: 49 and P. V. Poitevin-Peitari, *Mémoire pour servir à l'histoire des Jeux Floraux*, 2 vols. (Toulouse, 1815), 2: 231 for Miramont.

[115]Villain, *Grand dictionnaire*, 3: 1277.

[116]*Ibid.*, pp. 1443-46; Robert de Roton, *Les arrêts du Grand Conseil portant dispense du marc d'or de noblesse* (Paris, 1951), p. 314.

[117]*A.D.*, C-269; see table of candidates for capitoul, 1733. The subdelegate wrote, "Le sieur Miegeville n'est point un avocat du premier ordre mais il passe pour un honnête homme."

had probably become capitoul through purchased influence rather than professional distinction. The new counselor possessed a fortune of nearly 100,000 livres and his wife owned rural property valued at nearly 300,000 livres.[118] If these were the prerequisites for a seat on the *fleur-de-lys* bench, it is clear why barristers' sons so rarely became parlementaires.

In the last fifteen years of the Old Regime, admission into the Parlement became even more exclusive. As table III-5 illustrates, a new pattern of recruitment was developing in which titled nobles became magistrates with increasing frequency (both relative and absolute) and the sons of the recently ennobled were excluded. No capitoul's son entered the Parlement from 1775 to 1790; the only *anobli* was Bernard de Cerat, president of the *Bureau des finances*, a man whose urban property alone surpassed the entire fortunes of many advocate-capitouls.[119] As with the municipal reform of 1778, the people most hurt by this new pattern were not the barristers, but the commoners of exceptional wealth, those who had possessed fortunes equal to the aristocracy. Moreover, this increasing exclusiveness was not solely the result of a heightened sense of "caste" among the parlementaires.[120] There had also been a sharp decline in the number of openings on the bench. In the years 1735–50 sixty-one lay counselors had entered the Parlement for the first time, whereas during 1775–90 the number of new magistrates was only twenty-nine.[121] Part of this decrease was attributable to the suppression of the Third Chamber of Inquests, an act which was one of the few permanent accomplishments of Chancellor Maupeou. Had there been more offices, more capitouls' sons might have entered the Parlement. But, judging from past experience, these would not have been barristers' sons, anyway.

Distinguished, ennobled barristers could not pass on enough wealth to their children to make them eligible for the Sovereign Court. Their mean fortune of about 75,000 livres, though very sizeable by most standards, was only a fourth of an average parlementaire's estate. Moreover, the barristers had to distribute their wealth among their children, so the sons of some of the richest barristers had not the

---

[118]Sentou, *Fortunes et groupes sociaux*, p. 96.

[119]See Roton, *Arrêts du Grand Conseil* for ancestry of entrants into Parlement after 1774. For the urban property of Cerat, see Martin, *Documents relatifs à la vente*, p. 159. He had property valued at 77,000 livres.

[120]See William Doyle, "Was there an 'Aristocratic Reaction' in Pre-Revolutionary France?" *Past and Present*, no. 57 (1972), 97–122 for a discussion of a sense of exclusiveness among parlementaires.

[121]B. Faucher and T. Gérard, *Inventaire sommaire des Archives . . . Série B, Tome V: Enregistrement des actes du pouvoir royal* (Toulouse, 1965). The number of new counselors for 1755–1770 was comparable to 1735–1750.

TABLE III-5.   Recruitment into the Parlement of Toulouse[a]

Social Background	1735-1750		1775-1790	
	No.	%	No.	%
Parlementaire family	35	57.4	20	68.9
(son)	(26)	(42.6)	(14)	(48.2)
(relative)	(9)	(14.8)	(6)	(20.7)
Anoblis	7	11.5	1	3.4
(son of capitoul)	(6)	(9.8)	0	0
(other)	(1)	(1.6)	(1)	(3.4)
Simple noble	5	8.2	2	6.9
Titled noble	1	1.6	4	14.0
Noble civil officer	2	3.2	1	3.4
Non-noble	4	6.6	1	3.4
Unknown	7	11.5	0	0
Total	61	100.0	29	100.0

Sources: A.D., B, letters of registration; works by Villain, Bremond, Larboust, and Roton, as cited in bibliography.

[a]Excluded from consideration are the counselor-clerks and the subaltern offices, such as the substitutes to the attorney-general.

slightest chance of becoming magistrates.[122] But even if they had settled their estates differently or had only one child, they could not have competed with sons of financiers and other exceptionally wealthy men for the few places open to the recently ennobled.

Thus, the high magistracy was nearly closed to the children of barristers, and it remained so. Had there been other sovereign courts in Toulouse (such as the *Chambres des comptes et aides* of Rennes, Bordeaux, Aix, or Dijon) there might have been places on the bench for sons of ennobled barristers.[123] As it was, only two sons of capitouls acquired high judicial offices after 1775, both in Paris. A son of one of the richest advocates, Prévost, became a counselor at the *Chatêlet de Paris*. Pierre Derrey (de Roqueville), the son of a very wealthy Toulousan merchant and capitoul, became the advocate-general at the *Requêtes de l'Hôtel*.[124] The bench of the Parlement in Toulouse was occupied by an aristocracy, not just a nobility. Only after several

[122]Two sons of the rich Pierre Albaret had a combined landed fortune of less than 12,000 livres. (Martin, *Documents relatifs à la vente*, p. 148). A son of the wealthy barrister Jouve had a fortune of only 45,000 livres. See *A.D.*, 3E-26538, fol. 145, marriage contract of Jouve *fils*.

[123]See Charles Carrière, "Le recrutement de la cour des comptes, aides, et finances d'Aix-en-Provence à la fin de l'ancien régime," *Actes du 81ᵉ congrès nationale des sociétés savantes. Rouen-Caen* (1956), pp. 141-59.

[124]Roton, *Arrêts du Grand Conseil*, pp. 14, 281.

generations of prosperity and good fortune could an ennobled family hope to enter the Sovereign Court.[125]

With distinguished magisterial positions in Toulouse all but closed to them, the sons of noble barristers entered the army and the Church, though they remained at the bar quite often as well (see table III-6). Almost every barrister-capitoul placed one and sometimes two sons in the army.[126] Despite the supposed prestige of a military career, though, it was not usually the eldest son and future family head who became the army officer. There was no firm pattern, but the eldest son usually entered the bar, while the cadets took the military vocation. These younger sons received the 3,000 to 6,000 livres needed for a military charge as part of their portions, while the barrister became the heir. In Toulouse, that legal city, the sword was second to the robe as the profession for the family head.[127]

Sons of ennobled barristers sometimes became merely titular advocates and made no attempt to duplicate their fathers' professional success. Yet it is indicative of the proud and dedicated spirit of the Toulousan bar, permeated with its own sense of importance and with the reflected glory of the Parlement, that sons of capitouls were just as often hard-working, respected legal men. And this was the case not just for noble barristers of moderate wealth, like Saremejane, Taverne, or Furgole, who surely welcomed the added revenues from their practices. The children of very wealthy capitouls, Jean Bernard Lapomarède de Laviguerie, Alexandre Gaspard Gary, and Guillaume Jean Desazars de Montgaillard, all had very considerable private wealth but were also conscientious pleaders and consultants. A tradition of dedication to the bar ran in their families, and the barristers' profession was acceptable to them as noblemen.

The Church was another possible place for the progeny of ennobled advocates. However, their ecclesiastical careers were often surprisingly humble. A few managed to acquire canonries or abbacies; the best-placed one was probably Etienne Taverne, abbot and vicar of the parish of Dalbade in Toulouse.[128] But several capitouls' sons were vicars and even curates of rural parishes: Albaret's son at Castelginest,

---

[125]The Lespinasse family, which first had a capitoul in 1606, waited nearly a century and a half to place a member in the Parlement. See *ibid.*, pp. 316–17.

[126]The Ségur Law of 1781 was effective in excluding the recently ennobled from the army. See David D. Bien, "La réaction aristocratique avant 1789: L'example de l'armée," *Annales: économie, société, civilisation* 29 (1974): 23–48, 505–34. There may have been changes in the vocational patterns of capitouls' sons after this, but I lack information for the brief period 1781–1789.

[127]This career pattern was similar in parlementaire families. See Forster, *Nobility of Toulouse*, p. 127. Movement between the three major career "tracks"—law, commerce, and the army—may not have been so frequent, overall, as is often assumed.

[128]See *A.M.*, 1S-57, inventory of Abbé Taverne.

TABLE III-6.   Professions of Sons of Some Barrister-Capitouls

Name	Barrister	Army	Church	Esquire
Jouve	1	1	1	—
Albaret	—	2	1	—
Delort	1	1	—	—
Bouttes	—	2	—	—
Malefitte	1	—	1	—
Gary	1	—	—	—
Lafue	—	1	—	—
Senovert	—	1	—	—
Carrière	1	1	1	1 (?)
Duroux	1	1	—	—
Saremejane	1	1	—	—
Taverne	1	1	2	—
Delessert	—	1	—	1
Pyon	—	—	2	—
Clausolles	2	—	—	—
Furgole	2	—	2 (?)	—
Merle	1	—	1	—
Chabanettes	—	—	—	1
Total	13	13	11	3

Source: J. Villain, La France Moderne, 4 vols. (Montellier, 1911).

for example, or Carrière's son at Fronton.[129] These, clearly, were not enviable positions for men from wealthy, ennobled families, and the situation reflected some of the social problems created by a prolific source of noble titles, like the *capitoulat*. But it should be remembered that the cadets of the parlementaires seldom became more than canons of cathedral chapters, often obscure ones.[130] Finding suitable careers for cadets was a problem even for aristocratic families.

As for the daughters of the ennobled barristers, they had no more success in marrying parlementaires than their brothers experienced in entering the Sovereign Court. We have found no cases in which barristers' progeny allied with those of the magistrates.[131] In the few instances in which the magistrates went below their social level for a match, it was with daughters of the wealthiest merchants.[132] As long as these few parlementaires intended to soil their lineage with a misalliance, they wanted to receive the largest possible dowry (and fortune, if the daughter was an heiress) in compensation. The wealthiest of

[129]Villain, Grand dictionnaire, 1: 2-4, 3: 306-7. Jouve's son was curate at St. Germer de Muret.

[130]Forster, Nobility of Toulouse, p. 127.

[131]In one case, the son of the famed barrister Carrière married the sister of a parlementaire; her family was new to the Parlement. See A.D., 3E-11094, fol. 196.

[132]Marinière, "Marchands d'étoffes," p. 297. For the huge fortunes of two merchants who married daughters to parlementaires, Gounon and Julia, see A.M., 2G-13 and Sentou, Fortunes et groupes sociaux, p. 165.

barristers made alliances only within their own circles of *anoblis*. The rich Prévost married his daughter to the former capitoul Antoine de Cahusac, and Pierre Gary, one of the wealthiest advocates, gave his daughter to the son of capitoul Nicol.[133]

The upper limits of social mobility for a barrister's family, then, were honorable but hardly glorious. Many continued at the bar, others became military nobles or esquires without profession, but very few advanced beyond their circle of minor nobles. And only the more fortunate families, those that attracted new wealth and good marriages, would eventually become a part of the local aristocracy. In the final analysis, the bar might have provided rapid social advancement into the second most exclusive social milieu in Toulouse; but this rise was followed by a generation or two of stability, which would determine whether a family might enter the aristocracy.

To a duke-and-peer or to an ancient military family of the provincial Estates, the parlementaires were men of no overwhelming distinction. These *Grands* probably regarded a magistracy as another *savonnette à vilain*, somewhat better than, but of the same order as, the capitoul's office. This majestic view of society was not shared by the Toulousan barristers. They had no chance of entering the Parlement but, surprisingly, there is no evidence of resentment, not even in 1789. The barristers were probably proud of their positions just below this stable aristocracy of magistrates, many of whose families had been in the Parlement since the early seventeenth century.[134] No doubt the advocates were preoccupied with the immediate goals of living at and maintaining a respectable position; beyond this, they hoped for ennoblement, which some achieved. So even if the barristers' most ambitious dreams were unattainable, their society allowed them to achieve their immediate aims and some of their aspirations.

[133]*A.D.*, 3E-13995, fol. 211, marriage contract of Cahusac; *A.D.*, 2C-2988 (entry of 26 March 1772), articles of marriage for Nicol and Gary.

[134]Franklin Ford, *Robe and Sword, The Regrouping of the French Aristocracy After Louis XIV* (New York, 1953), pp. 128–29.

IV

IDEAS AND REFORMS
IN THE AGE
OF ENLIGHTENMENT

The highly esteemed Toulousan bar attracted men of intelligence and talent from all over the southwest. The mere acquisition of a law degree required little ability, but barristers with even a moderately successful practice must have had superior intelligence, memory, and verbal acuity. Occasionally, men of exceptional and multi-faceted talents came to the Toulousan bar. One of these was Alexandre Augustin Jamme, who won official recognition as a brilliant law student and still found time to study science and write prize-winning poetry. He became not only a leading barrister but also a member of the prestigious Academy of Floral Games and of the local Academy of Science.[1] No less exceptional was Jamme's colleague, Pierre Fermin de Lacroix. Before seriously practicing law, Lacroix tried a literary career in Paris and won the encouragement of Fontenelle. Even after he renounced literature as an occupation and returned to Toulouse, he wrote a letter imitating Rousseau's style that circulated at Versailles. His legal career also flourished, as he pleaded the winning side of several *causes célèbres*.[2]

How did these intelligent, sometimes exceptional, men perceive their government and society in this age of intellectual ferment? Fortunately, the barristers were engaged in the debates of their day and left a sizeable body of published writings. These sources, of course, represent disproportionately the opinions of prominent, highly articulate advocates or those with literary ability; care must be taken to determine when a position was shared by most colleagues and when it was peculiar to a few of them. Furthermore, our sources are largely public in nature and may well omit opinions which barristers held privately. Still, the barristers were capable of bold and critical thought

[1]Tragans, "Eloge de M. Jamme," *Recueil de l'Académie des Jeux Floraux*, 1819.
[2]M. de Lacroix, "Pierre Fermin de Lacroix, avocat au Parlement de Toulouse," *Revue des pyrénées* 20 (1908): 528–48; 21 (1909): 97–123.

even on a public level, so these writings do provide some valuable insights into the thought of the barristers in the Age of Enlightenment.

EXPANDING CULTURAL HORIZONS

During most of the Old Regime, Toulousan barristers had not been encouraged by their families or colleagues to take an interest in belles-lettres, science, or philosophy. Jurists condemned nonlegal pursuits as frivolous and incompatible with a serious legal career. By the mid-eighteenth century, however, men at the Toulousan bar were taking a more profound interest in literature, philosophy, and science than ever before. This important cultural transformation was closely related to a similar and prior evolution among the parlementaires, a development which should be examined before considering the barristers.

In the late seventeenth century, those who frequented aristocratic salons did not expect to discover charm, gaiety, politeness, or worldliness among the magistrates of the sovereign courts. Gravity, sobriety, diligence in attending to law—these were the virtues of the magistrates, and those who found the magistrates refined or *galant* were surprised.[3] The intellectual endeavors of the high robe were usually heavy, learned histories or immense and incredibly dull collections of court decisions. Their life style was supposed to lack elegance; the chancellor d'Aguesseau once said that the magistrates' residences should have "the severity of edicts."[4] By the mid-eighteenth century, however, the cultural world of the high robe had become much more receptive to current fashion. The magistrates continued to produce legal works and classical commentaries, but they also found time for the intellectual passions of their age—science, economics, belles-lettres, and travel accounts. Some critics occasionally deplored the magistrates' interest in the new artistic and intellectual currents, but the expansion of cultural interests among the magistrates was irreversible.[5] Ovid had taken a place beside Cato on their library shelves.

The magistrates of the Parlement of Toulouse took part in this cultural reorientation. While they did not lose their reputation for severity and diligence, their failure to produce any new collections of legal decisions, in emulation of their seventeenth-century ancestors,

[3]Franklin Ford, *Robe and Sword: The Regrouping of the French Aristocracy after Louis XIV* (New York, 1953), pp. 75, 204; Marcel Bouchard, *De l'humanisme à l'Encyclopédie* (Paris, 1929), p. 501; Lionel Gossman, *Medievalism and the Ideologies of the Enlightenment* (Baltimore, 1968), p. 12.

[4]Cited in François Bluche, *Les magistrats du Parlement de Paris au XVIIIe siècle (1715-1771)* (Paris, 1960), p. 326.

[5]Ford, *Robe and Sword*, pp. 214, 217; Bluche, *Magistrats*, p. 334. Montesquieu exclaimed that "To please in a vain and frivolous conversation is the only merit today. For this, the magistrates abandon the study of law."

was indicative of an important change. In 1768, a friend of Voltaire, the abbé Audra, wrote to the great *philosophe* that "the youth of the Parlement, many in the center, and a few heads of the Court are devoted to you."[6] The parlementaires were at least showing fashionable interest in the great ideas and literary figures of their time. The president du Bourg, an ardent admirer of Rousseau, named a son Emile.[7] The wife of the counselor de Maniban (comte d'Orbessan) offered her chateau to Rousseau as a refuge in 1766.[8] It was at the hôtel of Mme. du Bourg that Mesmer was to be received in Toulouse,[9] and by far the fullest collections of the philosophes' works available in Toulouse were to be found in the homes of President de Cambon and Advocate-General Resseguier.[10] The magistrates of the Parlement enjoyed a richer cultural life than any other group in their provincial capital.

The Toulousan barristers were only beginning to participate in a fuller cultural life when that wider outlook had already become a well-established fact among their social superiors. The opprobrium surrounding literature and nonlegal pursuits began to dissipate by mid-century, and in the 1740s and 1750s law students engaged in a varied cultural life. University students like Jean François Marmontel entered literary contests and formed poetry circles.[11] By the 1760s, the barrister Philippe Poitevin could discern a much more positive attitude toward literary studies among his colleagues.[12] Not only did advocates now admit the compatibility of a serious legal career and the study of letters, but they came to value literature and philosophy as inherently worthwhile pursuits. Poitevin attributed this "happy revolution" to the example set by his colleagues Pierre de Lacroix and Thomas Verny, who "reconciled letters and jurisprudence by excelling in both."[13] To this explanation, we might add the very puissant force of fashion, as the barristers sought once again to emulate the magistrates. And, beneath these explanations, it would be fair to posit a growing sense of dignity and confidence, as barristers defined for themselves a more

---

[6]Voltaire (François-Marie Arouet) *Correspondence*, ed. Theodore Besterman, 107 vols. (Geneva, 1962), vol. 70, letter 14327.

[7]Pierre-Joseph Monbrun, "Les Jeux Floraux et Jean-Jacques Rousseau," *Bulletin de littérature ecclésiastique* 4 (1912): 311.

[8]Roger Vives de Regie, *Les femmes dans la société de nos derniers parlementaires toulousains* (Toulouse, 1901), p. 113.

[9]Clément Tournier, ed., *Le Mesmérisme à Toulouse suivi de lettres inédits sur le XVIIIᵉ siècle d'après les archives de l'hôtel du Bourg* (Toulouse, 1911), p. 21.

[10]Claude Delpla, "Etude du niveau intellectuel des émigrés toulousains (d'après les inventaires bibliothèques)" (D.E.S., University of Toulouse, 1959).

[11]Jean-François Marmontel, *Oeuvres complètes: Mémoires*, 2 vols. (Paris, 1819), 1: 88-106.

[12]Philippe Poitevin-Peitari, *Mémoire pour servir à l'histoire des Jeux Floraux*, 2 vols. (Toulouse, 1815), 2: 187-90, 376-83 and *passim*.

[13]*Ibid.* Verny was a very respected barrister who had always desired a literary career. In 1782, after inheriting the wealth of a rich uncle, he retired to Montpellier.

ambitious cultural role. They were no longer content to be learned jurists; they wanted to be well-informed, cultivated men. The self-imposed restrictions and limited self-awareness of a corporate-based society were slowly breaking down at the Toulousan bar.

Those barristers who wanted reassurance that letters and law were compatible had only to look to their colleagues, among whom were several distinguished pleaders with serious literary accomplishments. Aside from Jamme, Lacroix, and Verny, there was Joseph Nicolas Gez, Jamme's brother-in-law. Gez delivered a well-received discourse on literary taste at the Academy of Rouen and won the praise of Voltaire for it. Then he returned to his legal career and pleaded frequently in the Parlement.[14] Like Jamme, he was a member of both the Academy of Floral Games and Academy of Sciences. The young Jean Baptiste Mailhe won several literary contests in Toulouse and became a member of the Academy; at the time of the Revolution he was among the most promising young barristers.[15] Finally, Jerome Taverne, probably the most important advocate at mid-century, somehow found time in his busy legal career to write poetry. He won three Academy contests, thereby becoming a "master" of the Floral Games.[16]

Ever since Daniel Mornet's pioneering study of private libraries in 1910, historians have investigated the intellectual interests of a social group by examining the books which individuals in that group owned.[17] On this basis, can we assess the extent of exposure to literature and nonlegal culture at the Toulousan bar? Inventories of fifteen libraries have survived to inform us of the works they possessed.[18] Their collections were sizeable, averaging 181 titles or 250 volumes. But the evidence from these libraries is disappointing and even misleading. These were professional collections, composed almost totally of legal reference works. They attest more to the sober spending habits of the barristers, who apparently bought only necessary and vocationally useful books, than to their intellectual interests. An average of 86.6 percent of their books were professional: collections of decisions, treatises on special questions, commentaries on ordinances.[19] The most

---

[14]Axel Duboul, *Les deux siècles de l'Académie des Jeux Floraux*, 2 vols. (Toulouse, 1901), 2: 117–18.

[15]Geneviève Thoumas, "La jeunesse de Mailhe," *Annales historiques de la Révolution française* 43 (1971): 221–47.

[16]Duboul, *Académie*, 2: 517–22.

[17]Daniel Mornet, "Les enseignements des bibliothèques privées (1750–1780)," *Revue d'histoire littéraire de la France* 17 (1910): 449–97. For a critique of this method, see Robert Darnton, "Reading, Writing, and Publishing in Eighteenth Century France," *Daedalus*, Winter 1971, pp. 214–56.

[18]These may be found in the collections of inventories-after-death, A.D., 3E–11871–11966 and inventories of *émigrés*, A.M., 1S. They all fall within the years 1770 to 1793.

[19]Their libraries almost entirely lacked works on legal theory and natural law like Burlamaqui, *Principes du droit naturel*, Grotius (de Groot), *Le droit de la guerre et de la*

frequently possessed works were the *Corpus Juris Civilis* and the *Arrêts* of Maynard and Combolas. The twenty most common books were all juridical, and only one library was less than 80 percent professional in composition.[20] Even among the nonlegal works, divided fairly evenly among history, religion, and letters, there were many books which had definite professional uses.[21]

The narrow composition of these libraries may indicate that some ambivalence about the cultural pursuits befitting a barrister still persisted, but it should not mislead us into underestimating the changes that had occurred. Even the academician Jean Baptiste Mailhe, who surely had a rich intellectual life, possessed a library that was 83 percent professional.[22] Other types of evidence clearly demonstrate that literary activity was common at the bar. After 1750, at least sixteen practicing Toulousan barristers won poetry or essay contests sponsored by the Floral Games.[23] This included even a barrister at the Seneschal Court. The advocate Jean François Corail de St. Foi was a member of the Academy of Béziers,[24] and Jacques Marie Rouzet, an important pleader, wrote a play (though not a very successful one).[25] There are indications, too, that verse writing was a fashionable, if not very serious, pastime among young advocates.[26] It does seem, then, that an active interest in literature was a common and quite acceptable pursuit after the 1760s.

One significant and highly visible manifestation of this cultural expansion was the increased participation of barristers in the intellectual elite of the city, the academies. The most coveted literary honor was inclusion among the august forty of the Academy of Floral Games, reputedly the oldest such society in the world. Every Friday afternoon from January to August, this prestigious cultural circle met for critical reading and serious examination of ancient or contemporary works.[27] Superior literary talent was the ostensible basis for membership; but ability had to be accompanied by high social standing, as was clearly

---

paix and Pufendorf, *Le droit de la nature et des gens.* Only eight of the fifteen collections had Jean Domat's *Les loix civiles dans leur ordre naturel.*

[20]This was the collection of Jean Bernard Blanc, *A.D.*, 3E-11882. It contained only twelve titles, 75 percent of them legal.

[21]Institutional histories and dictionaries were often cited in legal briefs.

[22]*A.M.* 1S-52. The library of Taverne (1S-57) was also composed almost solely of jurisprudence.

[23]Duboul, *Académie,* vol. 1, contains a list of all prize-winners.

[24]*A.D.*, 3E-11095, fol. 220, marriage contract of Corail.

[25]*Lettre de M. Rouzet, avocat, à un de ses amis* (n.p., 1790), pp. 2-3.

[26]See *Affiches, annonces, et avis divers, ou Feuille hebdomadaire de Toulouse,* 22 avril 1789, p. 69.

[27]Poitevin, *Mémoire,* 1: 126.

indicated by the letters patent of the Academy, stating that members "should be chosen among the considerable citizens, not only by their enlightenment and their talents, but also by their rank, birth, profession, and employment."[28] Such criteria led to a quota system of sorts and, given the structure of Toulousan society, the parlementaires inevitably dominated the Academy. Throughout the second half of the century, fifteen to twenty of the forty academicians were magistrates of the Sovereign Court.[29] Some may well have "inherited" their seats regardless of their literary discernment or interest.[30] In addition to the parlementaires, the Academy welcomed prelates, like Dillon, archbishop of Toulouse, and titled nobles. Six to ten seats went to socially undistinguished men, who had to compensate for their lack of status by having talent. Increasingly, the barristers were dominating the commoners' seats in the Academy.

There had been barristers in the Academy of Floral Games since at least 1713 and probably much earlier.[31] However, their participation had been quite limited during the first half of the century. In 1750 there were only two advocates, Jean de Souberian and Jean François Duclos.[32] By 1755 these two had died, and only one new barrister, Jean Castillon, had been admitted.[33] After this, the position of the barristers began to expand, first slowly and then much more rapidly. New barristers took seats in 1756 and 1761. By 1770, the Academy had apparently adopted a much more generous quota for advocates; two new ones were admitted that year. By 1779, there were five members of the bar in the Academy: Castillon, Verny, Lacroix, Martel, and Jamme. The admission of five more in the 1780s (and the death of Lacroix in 1786) brought the total number of barrister-academicians to nine on the eve of the Revolution. They had become a major social element in the Floral Games.

The Academy of Sciences underwent a similar evolution in social composition. Only titular barristers were among its founding members in 1749; the first practicing advocate, Jean Raynal, was admitted in

---

[28]*Ibid.*, p. 107.

[29]Membership lists of the Academy appeared in various almanacs. I have used the *Calendrier de Toulouse* (Toulouse, 1750-1790). For comparisons with other academies, see D. Roche, "Milieux académiques et sociétés des lumières," in François Furet et al., *Livre et société dans la France du XVIIIe siècle*, 2 vols. (Paris, 1965), 1: 93-185.

[30]The son of M. d'Orbessan was admitted as soon as he reached the minimum age, twenty-two.

[31]The barrister de Cormouls was on the list for that year.

[32]*Calendrier de Toulouse*, 1750. It is possible that neither was a practicing barrister. Duclos was said to be "more an academician than an advocate." See Duboul, *Académie*, 2: 222-25, 334-35.

[33]Castillon is often cited as a contributor to the *Encyclopédie*. Actually, his brother Jean-Louis wrote for the "Supplément." See Frank Kafker, "A List of Contributors to Diderot's *Encyclopédie*," *French Historical Studies* 3 (1963): 120.

1751.[34] He remained the only one until 1770, after which the number of barristers grew rapidly. By 1779, there were four barristers in the Academy of Sciences, and by 1789, there were seven (including a law professor).[35] Aside from the scientific professions (surgeons, physicians, and engineers) the barristers were the major vocational group from the Third Estate.

This increasing participation of the barristers in the leading academic circles accurately reflected their position as the most intellectually active element among Toulousan commoners. No judges of the Seneschal Court, no *bourgeois*, attorneys, or notaries, and few civil officers of any sort entered the Floral Games. It is not even clear that these groups experienced an expansion of cultural horizons; and if they did, it was certainly not so profound as the barristers' intellectual evolution. This development reinforced the barristers' claim to the position just beneath the parlementaires in Toulousan society.

To what extent did this cultural reorientation bring the barristers in contact with the ideas and great names commonly associated with the Enlightenment? Here again, their libraries may be misleading. There were few books written by the philosophes in the barristers' small collections of nonlegal works. The classical authors typically read in *collège*—Horace, Cicero, Ovid, and Seneca—dominated this portion of their libraries. Of the moderns, Boileau was the most popular, followed by Molière.[36] Half the libraries contained no works whatsoever by a philosophe, not even *The Spirit of the Laws*. One in three had a work by Voltaire, usually a history, and only two (of fifteen) had writings by Rousseau. Completely absent from the collections we have examined were Descartes, Locke, Bayle, Diderot, Helvétius, and Fontenelle.[37] Yet, there is compelling evidence that barristers did read and absorb the

[34]See Eugène Lapierre, *Histoire de l'Académie* (Toulouse, 1905), p. 71, for a list of the founding members, and the *Biographie toulousaine, ou Dictionnaire historique*, 2 vols. (Paris, 1823), 2: 271.

[35]*Calendrier de Toulouse*, 1779 and 1789. In 1789, there were thirty-eight regular members.

[36]The only interesting philosophical works were those by Gassendi and St. Evremont in Chabanette's library (*A.D.*, 3E-1987). Taverne owned a work opposing the philosophes, *L'Anti-Lucrèce* (*A.M.*, 1S-57).

[37]These libraries differed so much from the collections examined by Mornet (which included forty-three Parisian barristers) that we may have to recognize regional variations in book-buying habits. Robert Darnton has noted in a recent article ("The *Encyclopédie* Wars of Prerevolutionary France," *American Historical Review*, no. 78 [Dec., 1973], pp. 1149–1151) that numerous copies of the *Encyclopédie* were sold in Toulouse; in Besançon, "lawyers" frequently purchased the work. Whether this is another example of regional buying habits or whether the inventories I have found were not completely representative, I am unable to determine. At any rate, the Toulousan barristers were familiar with the *Encyclopédie* whether they purchased it themselves or borrowed copies, which were evidently numerous in the city.

thought of the philosophes. Guillaume Martel, for example, wrote enthusiastic poetry about Fontenelle, Malherbe, and the physiocrats Quesnay, Mirabeau, and Mercier de la Rivière.[38] Gélibert and Barère both quoted the outspoken Parisian Simon Henri Linguet.[39] Barère, apparently interested in English culture, read Richardson's *Clarissa* and compared it with Rousseau's *La Nouvelle Héloise*.[40] Mailhe's writing demonstrated a familiarity with Raynal's *History of the Two Indies*.[41] More than just being familiar to the Toulousan advocates, the philosophes were taking their place beside traditional literary giants. As early as the 1760s, some barristers had come to regard Fontenelle, Voltaire, and Montesquieu as "geniuses" in the same category as Virgil, Cicero, and Racine.[42] Occasionally, an instructing advocate— even one of no particular literary distinction—quoted a philosophe in a brief; it was no longer extraordinary to find references to Voltaire and especially to Montesquieu along with others to Cujas.[43] Indeed, by the end of the Old Regime, the advocates could cite the *Encyclopédie* even in their most serious and urgent public pronouncements. Jamme wrote a letter to the Keeper of the Seals in protest over the edict of 8 May 1788, and this letter, signed by twenty-five barristers, quoted the *Encyclopédie* twice and Abbé Mably once.[44]

Rousseau, by virtue of his ideas, his personality, and his *sensibilité*, made an important impression on some Toulousan barristers.[45] Espic and Mailhe, especially the latter, formed an intimate appreciation of Rousseau and a personal identification with him. Mailhe imagined that in his own dream world Jean Jacques could find happiness.[46] The desire to be "men of feeling" and of humanity prompted Gez, Barère, and thirty other advocates to establish a Conference of Charity, in-

[38]Guillaume Martel, "La mort de Fontenelle" and "Les muses philosophiques," *Recueil de l'Académie des Jeux Floraux*, 1769, pp. 4, 17, and "L'économie politique," *ibid.*, 1770, p. 1.

[39]Gélibert, "Epitre à mon robe de Palais," *Recueil de l'Académie des Jeux Floraux*, 1783, p. 4.

[40]Bertrand Barère, "Eloge de Jean Jacques Rousseau, citoyen de Genève," *Recueil de l'Académie des Jeux Floraux*, 1786, p. 199.

[41]Thoumas, "Jeunesse de Mailhe," pp. 233–40.

[42]Espic, "Discours," *Recueil de l'Académie des Jeux Floraux*, 1765, p. 15; Alexandre A. Jamme, "Eloge de Clémence Isaure," *ibid.*, 1770, p. 37.

[43]See the reference to "the celebrated Voltaire" in Fréydier, *Plaidoyer curieux pour la Demoiselle Marie Lajon* (Toulouse, n.d.), p. 14.

[44]*Lettre des avocats au Parlement de Toulouse à Monseigneur le Garde des Sceaux sur les nouveaux édits* . . . (n.p., n.d.), pp. 5, 9.

[45]Scholars like Mornet ("L'enseignement," p. 466) and Bouchard (*De l'humanisme*, p. 612) have denied the appeal of Rousseau to legal men, but his was not the case at the Toulousan bar.

[46]Espic, "Discours," p. 16; Jean Baptiste Mailhe, "Mes chimères, ou les prestiges de l'illusion. Ode," *Recueil de l'Académie des Jeux Floraux*, 1781. Espic's appreciation of Rousseau came quite early; Rousseau did not find his warmest audiences until the 1780s.

tended to provide free legal counsel to the poor.[47] When the Academy of Floral Games made a eulogy of Rousseau its contest subject in 1786, it was no wonder that two Toulousan advocates, Bertrand Barère and Antoine Chas, captured the prizes.[48]

The expanding cultural horizons of the Toulousan barristers did not lead inevitably to a deep appreciation of the philosophes. Philippe Poitevin, for example, was an outstanding proponent of literary studies for advocates, but he had some occasional harsh words for the great names of the Enlightenment.[49] However, the barristers' cultural redefinition had its roots in the Enlightenment. The same spirit of the age that made traditional attitudes unacceptable also made the barristers' traditional cultural interests inadequate.[50] This did not mean that the men at the Toulousan bar abandoned their own legal studies. The advocates remained immersed in jurisprudence, and they found in enlightened opinion new perspectives from which to examine the law.

LAW AND LEGAL REFORM

Jurists and social reformers of the eighteenth century were critical of established law, both civil and criminal. Turning from questions of classification and past application, legal thinkers began to measure law by new standards of justice, equity, efficiency, and humanity; by each standard, established law was frequently found wanting.[51] As the Toulousan barristers redefined their cultural goals and range of pursuits, they, too, became more critical of existing legislation and adopted new standards by which to measure it. This was especially the case for criminal justice. The Toulousan barristers became vocal proponents of change in criminal legislation.

Dissatisfaction with the existing criminal laws was widespread in Toulouse by the late eighteenth century. Even so traditional and narrow-minded a figure as Pierre Barthès, a minor official and chronicler of the city, began to criticize the criminal justice system. For years he had attended and duly reported each public hanging or torture, evincing absolutely no sympathy for the criminal and seeming certain

---

[47] Jean Joseph Gez, *Discours addressé à une société d'avocats . . . sur son projet d'une Conférence de Charité* (n.p., 1783).

[48] See *Recueil de l'Académie des Jeux Floraux*, 1786. pp. 170-205 for the prize-winning essays.

[49] "Sémonce," *Recueil de l'Académie des Jeux Floraux*, 1786, p. 138.

[50] For the "spirit of the age," see Peter Gay, *The Enlightenment: An Interpretation*, 2 vols. (New York, 1967-69), 2: 3-55.

[51] I know of no general works on eighteenth-century legal thought, aside from studies of the criminal reform movement. For an important introduction to legal thought, see William F. Church, "The Decline of the French Jurists as Political Theorists," *French Historical Studies* 5 (1967): 1-40.

that this punishment alone prevented anarchy. In the 1770s, however, Barthès first expressed some doubts about the efficacy of harsh punishment in deterring crime: year after year he had seen the guilty tortured, mutilated, or killed, but crime continued. He had even read some pamphlets from Paris on the subject.[52] Like Barthès, the barristers were disturbed about the ineffectiveness of the established criminal laws. But an even greater impetus for reform, as far as they were concerned, was the need to curb the brutality and inhumanity of the criminal code.

French criminal law was based on the harsh Ordinance of 1670, whose purpose was to ensure that punishment inevitably followed crime.[53] The procedure it established gave no advantage to the accused and no aid to the establishment of his innocence, the tacit assumption being that it was preferable to punish an innocent person from time to time than to give a criminal the chance to deceive the court. The entire procedure took place in secrecy, and the accused was not necessarily informed of the charges against him. No counsel was permitted in the trial of first instance, and this rule extended to the appeal in cases involving serious crimes. One judge had complete power over the case: it was left to him both to defend and prosecute the accused. The magistrates who decided the case saw and questioned the accused only once before passing sentence. If the judges believed that the proof of guilt was considerable but not complete, they could arrange for torture—the preparatory question—to extract a confession. Even after being found guilty, the criminal's torture was not at an end, for the judges could seek the names of accomplices through the preliminary question.[54]

The first public criticism of criminal procedure from the Toulousan bar came in a brief signed by Joseph Marie Duroux in 1762, four years before Beccaria's influential work, *Dei delitti e delle pene*, appeared in French. Duroux questioned the effectiveness of torture, though, only in moderate language: "It has been shown a thousand times that the Question can lose the innocent and save the guilty . . . it's more an ordeal of patience than of truth."[55] But he went beyond this in his criticism of criminal law. Duroux was very much aware that other countries

---

[52]*B.M.T.*, MS. 706, fol. 25–26. For the conservatism of Barthès, see Edmond Lamouzèle, *Toulouse au XVIIIe siècle* . . . (Toulouse, 1914), introduction.

[53]The following paragraph is based on Adhémar Esmein, *Histoire de la procédure criminelle en France* (Paris, 1882).

[54]For a description of the forms of judicial torture in Toulouse, see Paul de Casteras, *La société toulousaine à la fin du XVIIIe siècle* (Toulouse, 1891), pp. 104–6.

[55]Duroux fils, *Observations pour le sieur Jean Calas* (n.p., 1762), p. 58. David Bien, in *The Calas Affair* (Princeton, 1960), p. 11, n. 8, claims that Duroux only signed this brief, and it was written by counselor Lasalle. Even if this was the case, Duroux must have agreed with the principles expressed in it, and he must have been willing to have his name publicly associated with it.

had much milder criminal procedures. That France, otherwise the most cultured and humane of nations, had such a severe criminal code seemed intolerable to Duroux. He believed that the abolition of judicial torture would render criminal justice infinitely more humane, and more effective, too.

Public appeals for the reform of criminal justice multiplied after 1770. The *cause célèbre* of Catherine Estinès, a young girl accused of poisoning her father, provided Pierre Fermin de Lacroix with the opportunity for requesting changes in the criminal code beyond the abolition of torture. His widely read mémoire expressed the hope that Louis XVI would hear of this case "and hasten the reform of our criminal laws, so ardently desired by all right-thinking men." Lacroix offered no specific proposals, but he did identify himself with a powerful nationwide current of opinion.[56] So did the thirty-two barristers who formed the Conference of Charity, that humanitarian association to provide legal defense for the poor. They aspired, by their example, "to render our criminal laws more gentle and more humane."[57]

The unpublished notes of Bertrand Barère, then a young, rising barrister, indicate that he thought long and systematically about criminal reform.[58] Like Duroux, Barère bemoaned the fact that France, the greatest and most enlightened nation, had a criminal code suited "for Iroquois or cannibals." Barère desired numerous changes in criminal procedure, including counsel for the accused and public interrogation. But what makes Barère's reform proposals especially noteworthy and significant is his special interest in penal legislation, a much neglected aspect of French criminal administration.[59] He called for the abolition of corporal punishment in most instances, the prohibition of imprisonment for debt, and the improvement of prison conditions. Although English criminal law was superficially known and much admired at the Toulousan bar, Barère discerned its major fault: the harsh punishments meted out. The young barrister called upon Louis XVI to promulgate a penal code—but one that was more humane than the English one. Finally, Barère carefully considered the arguments for and against the abolition of capital punishment but expressed no definite stand in these notes, perhaps because he was

---

[56]Pierre Fermin de Lacroix, *Mémoire pour Catherine Estinès* (Toulouse, 1786), p. 54. (The printed brief is itself undated.)

[57]Gez, *Discours*, p. 18.

[58]*A.D.*, Hautes-Pyrénées, Fonds Barère, *laisse* 31. This is a collection of notes on his reading and personal thoughts, written both before and during the Revolution. Since there is no pagination, I will not cite each quotation from it separately.

[59]For a discussion of Old Regime penal law, see Carl Ludwig von Bar, *A History of Continental Criminal Law* (Boston, 1916), pp. 259-64. Almost all writings on criminal law concerned procedure.

unable to make up his mind on this issue.[60] It is clear that Barère shared the humanitarian concern for the accused which his colleagues felt and extended this to the convicted criminal.

No doubt Barère's opinions on criminal reform were more concrete and more advanced than most others at the Toulousan bar, but there was still a very widespread desire for changes in the criminal code. Amid the chorus of speeches celebrating the reestablishment of the Parlement in 1775, the elderly barrister Jean Besaucelle delivered a harangue to the Criminal Chamber (*Tournelle*) that included a strong plea for reform:

The most enlightened part of the Nation desires a reform of our criminal laws. These terrible buttresses that have so often retained frightening maxims no longer listen to the lessons of humanity. Our century waits for the boon of a Legislator whom providence destines for great things. It is worthy of you magistrates to accelerate the moment of this so-much-desired reform by your representations [to the king].[61]

It is inconceivable that Besaucelle would have made such a bold public appeal in the name of the Order of Barristers if he had not had widespread support from his colleagues. This desire for more humane criminal laws was an important indicator of a new social attitude. A greater sensitivity to the plight of the unfortunate was replacing fear and the impulse to repress as basic responses to deviancy.[62]

In comparison to the urgent and deeply-felt criminal reform movement among the Toulousan barristers, demands to alter civil legislation were hardly voiced. Perhaps civil laws themselves are more protected from currents of changing opinion because they are often social norms stated in juridical language.[63] But the barristers had other reasons for not favoring civil reform. As students and masters of Roman law, they identified with it, and they saw the jurisprudence of the Parlement as partly their own work. When changes in civil law were attempted, they were often seen as royal interference with provincial customs and prerogatives, so opposition to reform engaged the barristers' sense of localism and attachment to the Parlement. This suspicion of civil law reform can best be seen in the barristers' response

[60]For a review of eighteenth-century works on capital punishment, including the works Barère consulted, see Dominique Muller, "Les magistrats et la peine de mort au 18e siècle," *Dix-huitième siècle* 4 (1972): 79-107.

[61]Jean Besaucelle, in *Journal de ce qui s'est passé à l'occasion du rétablissement du Parlement de Toulouse dans ses functions* (n.p., n.d.), pp. 148-49.

[62]As Peter Gay has written, ". . . humanity was acquiring the status of a practical virtue" (*Enlightenment*, p. 36).

[63]Jean Imbert, *Histoire du droit privé* (Paris, 1966), p. 5.

to codification, which had had the support of celebrated jurists since the sixteenth century, at least, and was being effected by royal officers in the early eighteenth century.[64]

The resistance of the Parlement to royal initiatives at private law reform, especially codification, was hardly new by the mid-eighteenth century. Louis XIV's Ordinance of 1667, which attempted to unify civil procedure only, had met with open hostility from the Sovereign Court of Toulouse.[65] Of course, the court was unsympathetic to the moderate efforts of Chancellor d'Aguesseau to unify civil law in the first half of the century. The chancellor intended to respect the basic differences between Roman and customary law and limit unification to "what is most essential for public order."[66] His work, embodied in several royal ordinances dealing with donations (1731), testaments (1735), entails (1747), and other subjects, encountered resistance at the Sovereign Court of Languedoc. In their remonstrance against the Ordinance of 1735 on testaments, the Toulousan parlementaires were more consistent than all other sovereign court magistrates in advancing their own jurisprudence as superior to royal legislation.[67] The Toulousan magistrates even added a general statement to their remonstrance declaring their unwillingness to see "pure Roman principles" replaced by legislative text.[68]

At least until the 1770s, the bar seemed to be as much in opposition to legal unification as the magistrates were. This is the conclusion one must draw from the barristers' ostracism of the one proponent of codification among them, Jean Baptiste Furgole. He was the most highly-regarded jurist of Toulouse at mid-century, so respected, in fact, that the chancellor d'Aguesseau had corresponded with him about legal questions and sought his advice in preparing ordinances.[69] Much of Furgole's professional work consisted of treatises that commented on these ordinances and advanced their provisions over previous jurisprudence.[70] As if responding to the Parlement's remonstrance of 1735, Furgole wrote that "the Ordinances of our King are the laws we ought

[64]Henri Cauvière, L'idée de codification en France avant la rédaction du code civil (Paris, 1910) discusses legal unification before the French Revolution.
[65]Pierre Timbal, "L'esprit du droit privé au XVIIᵉ siècle," Dix-septième siècle, no. 58 (1963), p. 33. In fact, the Parlement was emerging victorious in some of its long-term battles with the crown over civil law reform. See Pierre Timbal, Droit Romain et ancien droit français (Paris, 1960), p. 167.
[66]Cauvière, Codification, p. 46.
[67]Henri Regnault, Les ordonnances civiles du Chancelier D'Aguesseau (Paris, 1938), p. 31.
[68]Ibid., p. 243.
[69]Animé Rodière, Les grands jurisconsultes (Toulouse, 1874), p. 379.
[70]Among Furgole's works were the Commentaires sur l'ordonnance de Louis XV sur . . . les substitutions (Paris, 1767); Ordonnance . . . de donations (Toulouse, 1733); Traité des testamens . . . , 3 vols. (Paris, 1769).

to regard as the first and principal [ones] to which the dispositions of Roman law ought to be subordinated."[71] His commentaries occasionally expressed the hope that the royal acts would "correct" the jurisprudence of the Parlement.[72] Furgole's colleagues did not approve of his positions, especially because Roman law was declining in prestige and needed defenders, not critics.[73] The jurist's local reputation and career suffered accordingly.

Furgole never received from the Toulousan bar the respect due to a jurist of his stature. He had an international reputation and his scholarly works were widely consulted, but Furgole was rarely praised in his home city.[74] And though jurists of such importance usually became capitouls, Furgole was never even nominated. In fact, when the king placed him on the *norme*, there was apparently some attempt to reject his candidacy, followed by an unusual protest against the "irregularity" of the procedure—though irregularity of many sorts had long been a normal part of the selection process.[75] The barristers did not even select Furgole, their most renowned colleague, *batonnier* of their Order.[76] Proponents of codification were evidently not highly regarded—or lightly excused—at the Toulousan bar, at least before the last decades of the Old Regime.

Furgole's position never gained widespread acceptance among Toulousan advocates, but his ideas did become more respectable in the twenty years following his death in 1761. A few of the more advanced thinkers at the bar were converted to legal unification, and they spoke openly in favor of it in the Floral Games. One such convert was the distinguished pleader Jamme. His eulogy of Louis XV in 1775 lavished praise on the ordinances of d'Aguesseau, which Jamme saw as the first strike against a legal structure in which "the law . . . floated at the mercy of opinions, according to the times and places where it is examined." The existing state of the law was, for him, a "monstrous deformity" which reason could not accept.[77] How far Jamme wished codification to proceed is unclear, but he did praise Louis XV for attempting to establish a "perfect uniformity."

[71]Furgole, *Traité des testamens*, 1: iv.

[72]See, for example, *ibid.*, 1: 39, on proof by witnesses for military testaments; p. 430, for Furgole's criticism of d'Olive and the jurisprudence of the Parlement on the legal disabilities in second marriages for women; p. 453, for his comments on Catellan.

[73]Philippe Sagnac, *La législation civile de la Révolution française* (Paris, 1898), pp. 15-16.

[74]Armand-Gaston Camus, *Lettres sur la profession d'avocat* (Paris, 1777), p. 99.

[75]J. B. A. d'Aldeguier, *Histoire de la ville de Toulouse depuis la conquête des Romans . . .*, 4 vols. (Toulouse, 1835), 4: 284.

[76]Bertrand Barère, *Eloge de Jean-Baptiste Furgole, avocat au Parlement de Toulouse* (n.p., n.d.), p. 19.

[77]Alexandre Jamme, "Eloge de Louis XV, Roi de France . . . ," *Recueil de l'Académie des Jeux Floraux*, 1775, pp. 98-99.

For Jamme, the criterion of uniformity was all-important as a standard by which to judge established law. He might well have accepted the *content* of Roman law as enforced by the Parlement of Toulouse. Two other, more radical thinkers saw codification as only the beginning of civil law reform, because uniformity was, for them, only one criterion among many. In the name of reason, utility, and "legal nationalism" (an insistence on French laws for Frenchmen) they rejected the very principles on which the established civil law of Toulouse was based. In his Discourse of 1784, celebrating the American Revolution, Mailhe called established law "an inextricable labyrinth in which are confused successively and by chance customs of the conqueror and the conquered, of barbarian nations and well-governed ones, centuries of ignorance and enlightened centuries."[78] This confused mass of laws, so difficult to comphrehend or to justify, was for him "the source of most of the evils that afflict humanity." Mailhe proposed that Frenchmen "reject this mass of foreign laws and substitute for them new ones which are proper."[79] This barrister obviously had no reverence whatsoever for the "pure principles of Roman law" so hallowed by the Parlement.

Once again, Bertrand Barère pursued the criticism of established law further and more systematically than anyone else at the bar. Applying the criteria of reason and utility to law, Barère adopted an extremely anti-Romanist position and found in the customary law of northern France the principles by which civil law should be altered.[80] A fundamental tenet of Roman law was absolute paternal authority over the family and its property.[81] In Toulouse, a son of any age remained under the control of his father until emancipated. To Barère, this principle did not meet the test of reason; when a son ceased to need his father's protection, paternal authority should cease. Barère wanted the law to emancipate the son at a fixed age. This barrister struck even closer to the heart of Roman law when he attacked the right to dispose of property at death through a testament. This right was a fundamental principle of Roman law, distinguishing it from the customary laws of northern France, which regulated the devolution of property in the interest of the family.[82] Barère argued that a man had no right over

---

[78]Jean Baptiste Mailhe, "Discours sur la grandeur et l'importance de la révolution qui vient de s'opérer dans l'Amérique septentrionale," *Recueil de l'Académie des Jeux Floraux*, 1784, p. 22.

[79]*Ibid.*

[80]The following discussion is based on Barère's manuscript notes, *A.D.*, Hautes-Pyrénées, Fonds Barère, *laisse* 31. For a much earlier "reformer" who found support in customary law, see Donald Kelly, *"Fides Historiae*: Charles Dumoulin and the Gallican View of History," *Traditio* 22 (1966): 347–402. Dumoulin was held in very high regard in Barère's time.

[81]Imbert, *Droit privé*, pp. 13, 30.

[82]*Ibid.*, p. 30.

property after his death, and the law ought to prevent fathers from disinheriting their "natural" heirs, their children. This preference for customary over Roman principles would triumph in the Revolution. In fact, Barère's colleague, Mailhe, proposed to the National Convention the abolition of the right to will one's property in direct succession (7 March 1793), effectively ending Roman law in France.[83] It is tempting to believe that he first discussed the desirability of this change with Barère, years before the Revolution, in Toulouse.

Barère employed reason and utility not only to measure the merit of certain laws, but also to suggest desirable social goals. He implicitly arrived at the conception of law as a mechanism to improve society. Like Rousseau, he wished to use laws to reduce the extremes of wealth, and he found Roman law and the jurisprudence of the Parlement unacceptable for this purpose. Barère believed that the laws governing the disposal of property should divide successions as equally as possible among the children,[84] thus mitigating against the concentration of wealth in one hand. That was also the goal of another of Barère's proposals, the abolition of entails (substitutions). Royal attempts to limit entails had been resisted by the Parlement for centuries, and Barère deplored this.[85] He argued that entails allowed the testator to designate the recipient of his property for several generations, thereby preserving great families but harming society in general by restricting the circulation of wealth.

These two anti-aristocratic reforms were realized during the Revolution, but another of Barère's proposals went beyond even the Jacobins of 1793. Barère argued for the abolition of dowries. With these suppressed, "virtue, beauty, and finally the good qualities would be recompensed by marriage." Not only was this intended to improve the education of women, but it would also have established a society in which marriageability depended on personal virtue rather than on family status. For its time, this was egalitarian thought pushed to an extreme.

It was not fortuitous that Barère attempted to resurrect the reputation of Furgole by eulogizing him before the Conference of Charity in 1783. The young social critic had long recognized his intellectual kinship and indebtedness to the jurist: it was not the work of a philosophe but rather Furgole's treatise on testaments that had first

---

[83]Sagnac, Législation civile, p. 225.

[84]Barère was willing to allow a small portion of the estate to be at the father's free disposal.

[85]The "rights of the eldest" were not usually recognized in the south, so entail was used to keep family fortunes together. This explains why the Parlements of the south resisted attempts to limit substitution. See Paul Viollet, Histoire du droit civil français (Paris, 1893), pp. 879–80.

brought Barère to question the right to dispose of property by will.[86] Furgole had pointed the way toward a critical examination of civil law and the application of external standards to measure its reasonableness and equity. Several barristers of the next generation carried this approach well beyond the jurist's intentions, a few to genuinely radical positions. Most Toulousan advocates, though, were hostile or indifferent to this questioning of established civil law. They believed in the need for substantial variations to meet local conditions,[87] and they could not regard the Roman principles in which they were trained, and of which they were masters, as "foreign" or unreasonable. Any minor adjustments that were required could be made by the Parlement itself through its own jurisprudence.

Thus, enlightened attitudes had an important, but limited, impact on legal thought at the Toulousan bar. The barristers felt the new demands of humanity quite deeply, and they dismissed the social fear expressed in existing laws. Yet, even the most ardent criminal reformers remained insensitive to, or unconcerned about, many other failings of the judicial system.[88] The barristers' briefs almost never contained appeals to "reason" or to "nature." These enlightened standards lacked the force of the humanitarian impulse, and only a few pleaders applied them to civil law. Far from replacing their traditional authorities and standards with new ones, the barristers mixed the two and often held enlightened notions in subordination to their older authorities and loyalties.

ECONOMICS, POLITICS, AND RELIGION

The barristers could claim a special authority in legal questions, but they also took an interest in a wide range of public affairs. In writings and speeches the barristers freely addressed themselves to matters of public import. One academician wrote of an informal group composed largely of young barristers which he disparagingly called the "newsmongers" because they discussed the latest events and considered it their business to spread the news about town.[89] The expansion of

[86]Barère, *Eloge de Furgole*, p. 14. Barère may also have been influenced by Furgole's work on entails, but he did not mention this in the eulogy.

[87]The barristers had very respectable authorities for this position. No less than Montesquieu was one of them.

[88]The barristers never spoke out against the excessive costs of justice, the excessive duration of cases, and many other problems. Seigneurial justice escaped their criticism, too. On this, see John Mackrell, "Criticism of Seigneurial Justice in Eighteenth-Century France," in *French Government and Society, 1500-1850*, ed. John F. Bosher (London, 1973), pp. 123-44.

[89]Darquier, "Eloge de M. de Garipuy," in *Histoire et mémoires de l'Académie royale des sciences, inscriptions et belles lettres de Toulouse* (Toulouse, 1784), pp. 134-35.

cultural horizons resulted in a heightened interest in matters not directly related to law.

A number of Toulousan advocates had a lively interest in economic reform. The barrister-academician Guillaume Martel first introduced physiocratic doctrine into the Floral Games, and when he published his poem "Political Economy" in 1770, he had to provide extensive notes, references, and definitions for the uninformed reader.[90] Martel used the royal edict of July 1764, which allowed some freedom of trade in grain, as an occasion to extol physiocratic reforms.[91] He affirmed the existence of a hidden, harmonious order in nature and defined government as "the observation of natural laws, which assure to nations and to each man in particular the property of his being and the right to pursue his needs through his work."[92] It was the duty of states to let this natural order operate without restraint. Martel believed that the edict of 1764 foretold the eventual realization of this hope, and he was enthusiastic enough to expect "a new world" to follow from his economics.[93]

Like many physiocrats, Martel was uninterested in manufacturing and looked upon it with disfavor. For him, France was an agricultural nation. Rejecting an essential tenet of mercantilism, Martel believed that the interests of the artisan, manufacturer and urban worker could easily be sacrificed to those of the cultivator. He hoped that the liberation of the grain trade would draw some of the urban masses to agricultural labor where "work, exalting your soul, will console humanity."[94]

Martel's optimism and distaste for manufacturing were shared by Jean Baptiste Mailhe. Mailhe's remarkable discourse on the American Revolution allowed him to combine two passions: physiocratic economics and Anglophobia.[95] He glorified the Americans for ending the English domination of the seas, a development which promised to open commerce to all, enrich the world (since trade was infinitely expandable), and engender thousands of material and moral improvements. Mailhe had a firm faith in the benefits of material progress. Trade and communication would extinguish national differences and

[90]Pierre-Jean Monbrun, "La lutte philosophique en province: les Jeux Floraux de Toulouse," *Bulletin de littérature ecclésiastique* 23 (1922): 169.

[91]Guillaume Martel, "L'économie politique. Ode à Louis XV," *Recueil de l'Académie des Jeux Floraux*, 1770, pp. 1-3. For the background to this edict, see Georges Weulersse, *Les physiocrats* (Paris, 1931), p. 153.

[92]Guillaume Martel, "Eloge de Clemence Isaure," *Recueil de l'Académie des Jeux Floraux*, 1772, p. 42.

[93]Martel, "L'économie politique," p. 2.

[94]*Ibid.*, p. 6. This was a common attitude among physiocrats. See Weulersse, *Physiocrats*, pp. 159-60.

[95]Physiocrats were frequently Anglophobes. See Francis Acomb, *Anglophobia in France, 1763-1789* (Durham, 1950), p. 42.

religious prejudices, thereby ending wars and despotism. The human mind, thus liberated from all artificial restraints, would become infinitely creative. Mailhe even speculated on the possibility of inventing an "areostatic machine" as long as superstition did not fetter human reason.[96] Neither Turgot nor Condorcet surpassed Mailhe in creating a euphoric picture of continuous social progress based ultimately on physiocratic reform.

No other barrister possessed Mailhe's fertile imagination and sweep of vision, but physiocratic ideas and a faith in man's ability both to alter existing institutions for the better and to improve the quality of life were widespread at the Toulousan bar. Just as Besaucelle used the public celebration at the reestablishment of the Parlement to champion criminal reform, so Pierre Alexandre Gary harangued the court in praise of Turgot's economic reforms:

Here in rendering foodstuffs free, he [Louis XVI] annihilated frauds and favored production; in freeing importation, he called forth abundance . . . one law which devastated our countryside in subjugating our cultivators—already the *corvée* exists no more.[97]

It was unlikely that Gary, speaking as a representative of the Order, would have been so bold to praise Turgot if the minister's work did not have the support of many barristers. A belief in the material progress to be achieved by uprooting old institutions and following the natural laws of freedom and pursuit of interests had captured opinion at the bar. On this topic, Gary and many other advocates were no less advanced than the more radical thinker, Mailhe.

Though the barristers were hardly practitioners of the physiocratic virtues of careful land management, they, along with the parlementaires, were the most ardent proponents of free trade in Toulouse.[98] A letter from the Sovereign Court to the king in 1769 protested against the reversal of a free-trade policy: ". . . the least suspension of liberty of the grain commerce would [be] the most deadly blow, the most terrible punishment."[99] The magistrates' adherence to physiocratic reforms, a matter which touched them deeply as landlords, probably explains the prestige of these ideas at the bar.

---

[96]Mailhe, "Discours sur la grandeur," pp. 9–36.
[97]Pierre Gary, in *Journal de ce qui s'est passé* . . . , p. 133. See also *Lettre des avocats à Monseigneur le Garde des Sceaux*, p. 16, where it was claimed that commerce "should be free like air and water."
[98]G. Marinière, in "Les marchands d'étoffes de Toulouse à la fin du XVIIIe siècle," *Annales du midi* 70 (1958): 275, claims that the textile merchants were uninterested in physiocratic reform.
[99]*A.D.*, 51 B–29.

The speculative and reforming approach with which barristers considered economic relations did not extend into politics. For the advocates, students of law and history, political relations were fixed by constitutional principles acting through institutions; as political theorists they were jurists. They stressed constitutional theories that favored the Parlement in its struggle with the crown. If their constitutional thought had any single inspiration, it was the work of the Toulousan magistrate La Roche-Flavin, who published his *Thirteen Books of the Parlements of France* in 1617. This book was in most barristers' libraries, and its content was repeated, refined, or strengthened by the decrees of the Parlements during the eighteenth century.[100] The letter sent by the barristers to the Keeper of the Seals (1788) emphasized the original election of the king in a general Parlement and implied that the sovereign courts descended from the "nation assembled." Moreover, the letter claimed that the Parlements represented the Estates-General when the latter was not convoked. All this was to be found in La Roche-Flavin. The letter also implied a contractual relationship as the basis of authority, but the contract was feudal rather than Lockean in inspiration. It was between the monarch and the province, not between king and people, and it hardly formed the basis for a theory of state. Like the Parlements themselves in the second half of the century, the barristers placed the law above royal authority—with varying degrees of boldness and consistency. The letter to the Keeper of the Seals denounced the "deadly maxim" that the king's power had no limits. The king ought to govern according to the law, though the barristers ultimately admitted only self-imposed restraints on his power. They declared that the king had "an absolute power to do good" and quoted Fénelon's *Telemachus* in support of this.[101] Pierre Gary went much further in his speech at the recall of the Parlement. His formula, "One King, One Law, One Parlement: eternal and immutable relations," seemed to establish the courts and the law as sources of authority separate from and equal to the king.[102] Thus, the barristers drew their political theories from traditional sources, sometimes bending their authorities to defend the Parlement against royal power.

In view of the barristers' juridical approach to political relations, it is interesting to examine their reading of a theoretical work like Rousseau's *Social Contract*. Two Toulousan barristers, Bertrand Bar-

[100]William F. Church, *Constitutional Thought in Sixteenth Century France* (Cambridge, Mass., 1941), pp. 133, 147. On the Parlements, see Roger Bickart, *Les Parlements et la notion de souveraineté nationale au XVIIIe siècle* (Paris, 1932) and Henri Sée, "La doctrine politique des Parlements au XVIIIe siècle," *Revue historique de droit français et étranger* 3 (1924): 287–306.

[101]*Lettre des avocats . . . à Monseigneur le Garde des Sceaux*, pp. 3, 5-6, 9, 11.

[102]Pierre Gary, in *Journal de ce qui s'est passé*, p. 131.

ère and Antoine Chas, commented on this treatise in their prize-winning eulogies of Rousseau.[103] Neither admired the work deeply or seemed conscious of its political relevance, though there were Frenchmen who did both.[104] Both Barère and Chas appreciated *Emile* and the *Discourse on the Origins of Inequality* more than they did the political treatise. Barère considered the *Social Contract* only briefly and called its ideas "those ravishing chimeras of human society." Though the book contained "primitive truths," Barère apparently did not consider it pertinent to concrete situations. Chas, too, displayed an inability to treat the *Social Contract* as a politically relevant document. He did apprehend the "daring" balance which Rousseau established between the king and the people and the notion of legitimacy arising from the contract itself. But he could not identify these with existing public law, however much he approved of them:

Happy the People who could be governed by these principles. But how reduce them to practice? If it is not possible to change entirely the constitution of a state without shaking it to its foundations, it is not, without doubt, the same, relatively speaking, with individuals, in which reform ought to operate with the greatest benefits.[105]

Chas could take the *Social Contract* seriously only by transforming it into a *moral* argument; even advanced thinkers like he and Barère could not easily integrate such speculative theory into their political notions.[106] Their thinking about political arrangements was guided by public law and constitutional arguments.

If the barristers' constitutional approach to politics precluded an interest in speculative thought, it did not completely block innovation. The public law they cited allowed for no popular participation in government outside the Estates-General. Nevertheless, the barristers im-

---

[103]Antoine Chas, "Eloge de Jean-Jacques Rousseau," and Bertrand Barère, "Eloge de Jean-Jacques Rousseau, citoyen de Genève," in *Recueil de l'Académie des Jeux Floraux*, 1786.

[104]Several historians have treated the question of how much and how the *Contrat Social* was read: Joan McDonald, *Rousseau and the French Revolution, 1762-1791* (London, 1965), chap. 4; Wallace Katz, "Le Rousseauism avant la Révolution," *Dix-huitième siècle* 3 (1971): 205-222. Arguing that the work was read as a politically-relevant document is Durand Echeverria, "The Pre-Revolutionary Influence of Rousseau's *Contrat Social*," *Journal of the History of Ideas* 33 (1972): 543-60.

[105]Antoine Chas, "Eloge de Rousseau," pp. 179-80.

[106]Echeverria (in "The Pre-Revolutionary Influence") has argued that Rousseau's notions of popular sovereignty and contract theory were being used to justify the limitation of monarchical authority. This may have been true in some circles, but Barère and Chas did not see the *Social Contract* as relevant to this debate, and the *Lettre des avocats à Monseigneur le Garde des Sceaux*, concerning the May Edicts of 1788, did not use arguments borrowed from Rousseau; it argued along the lines of traditional constitutional theory.

plicitly assigned an important extraconstitutional role to the governed
—or at least to the propertied, educated subjects. That role involved
the formation of an intelligent and informed public opinion to which
those in power had a duty to listen. The barristers saw this extraconstitutional source of governmental direction as crucial to progress and to
social improvements. But if public opinion was to be useful, it had to
be critical and unrestrained. Mailhe praised the new American government—and implicitly criticized his own—for its "civil, moral, and
political liberty: [there are] no barriers to inhibit thought [or] the
enlightening of government. . . ."[107] Martel emphasized the need for
philosophers to explore all mysteries,[108] and Barère's eulogy of Louis
XII delicately reminded kings that they ought to encourage talented
men to speak openly and consider their judgments.[109] Rejecting the
idea of passive acceptance as a subject's duty, the barristers hoped for a
public opinion that would be critical and independent. Espic's ode to
"beneficent princes" pictured monarchs as no more than supreme
administrators who had to earn, not expect, the good will of their
subjects.[110] And Jamme implied that the public had a right to review
the legitimacy of wars waged by kings. This belief in the importance
of, and necessity for, an independent public opinion was the most
significant innovation in the barristers' political thought.

One barrister who did think about large and sudden changes in
political relations was Mailhe. Rebellion against royal authority was a
constant theme in his poems and discourses. But far from advancing
radical proposals on this subject—as he did on civil law—Mailhe was
always strongly hostile to rebellion and rebels, at least until 1784. In his
poem "Charles II, or the Reestablishment of the English Monarchy"
(1777), Mailhe declared in absolutist terms:

De revolutions toujours insatiables
Toujours impatients contre le joug des loix
Apprenne que Dieu seul est le Juge des Rois.[111]

Cromwell, for him, was an "abominable monster." Two years later,
Mailhe won another prize for his poem about Lisimon, the peasant
who raised Henry IV and taught him the wisdom and virtue to rule

[107]Mailhe, "Discours sur la grandeur," p. 22.
[108]Guillaume Martel, "Sémonce," *Recueil de l'Académie des Jeux Floraux*, 1771,
p. 88.
[109]Leo Gershoy, *Bertrand Barère, A Reluctant Terrorist* (Princeton, 1962), pp. 25–26.
[110]Espic, "Les princes bienfaisans," *Recueil de l'Académie des Jeux Floraux*, 1764,
pp. 4–8.
[111]Mailhe, "Charles II," *Recueil de l'Académie des Jeux Floraux*, 1777, p. 10.

with mercy after a period of great turmoil and rebellion.[112] In the same year, Mailhe published his poem about "The Taking of La Rochelle" in revolt against Louis XIII.[113] He later wrote an ode to Maria Theresa, another monarch who, like Henry IV and Charles II, came to the throne after a period of rebellion.[114] In each case, the monarch in question was a benevolent figure who restored order and humanity after rebellious confusion. Mailhe's discourse on the American Revolution was the last in a series of works about rebellions, but it marks an important transition in his conception of revolts. The American Revolution seemed to teach Mailhe that rebellions could have a positive, desirable consequence: liberty. His poem went beyond a mere glorification of a French victory to a celebration of liberty itself.[115] Thus, in the last years of the Old Regime, Mailhe departed from his blanket condemnation of armed resistance to authority, but his new attitude toward revolts was clearly more a reaction to concrete events than a result of theoretical political thought.

Despite their demands for complete freedom of thought, the barristers were not boldly speculative in their political ideas; and they were even less so in their religious thinking. Barère, so daring in his legal and social reform schemes, strongly disapproved of religious controversy. He had to curb his enthusiasm for Rousseau when the citizen of Geneva attacked established religion. Referring to *The Faith of the Savoyard Vicar*, Barère asked, "Why must genius always please itself by touching sacred objects? Would that the talented could exercize themselves in this sphere without incursions on respected truths."[116] The barrister-academician Philippe Poitevin, who had the delicate task of writing a eulogy for Abbé Prades, denied the controversial religious views attributed to the abbé and described him as a devout and orthodox Catholic.[117] To act in outward conformity to Catholic

[112]Mailhe, "Lisimon, ou le père nourricier de Henri IV," *Recueil de l'Académie des Jeux Floraux*, 1779, pp. 6-7.

[113]Mailhe, "Prise de la Rochelle. Poème," *Recueil de l'Académie des Jeux Floraux*, 1779, pp. 6-7.

[114]Mailhe, "Marie-Thérèse. Ode," *Recueil de l'Académie des Jeux Foraux*, 1781, pp. 48-50.

[115]Thoumas, "Jeunesse de Mailhe," pp. 233-40. For the defense of a much less abstract notion of "liberty," see Jean-Baptiste Furgole, *Traité de la seigneurie féodale et du franc alleu naturel* (Paris, 1767).

[116]Barère, "Eloge de Rousseau," p. 205. It is interesting to compare Barère's reaction to that of a future associate, Jean-Pierre Brissot, who "had his eyes opened" by the work. See Brissot's *Mémoires*, 4 vols. (Paris, 1830), 1:50-54.

[117]Poitevin, *Mémoire pour servir*, 2:146. Prades' controversial religious notions are discussed in Robert R. Palmer, *Catholics and Unbelievers in Eighteenth-Century France* (New York, 1961), pp. 117-31.

doctrine was the first rule of public decorum for all barristers, regardless of their personal persuasion. The *Protestant* barrister Jacob Londois, author of the constitution for a Masonic lodge, stipulated that members must attend a mass after each yearly election.[118] Barristers strongly believed in the need to preserve and respect Catholic forms.

Despite this absence of religious questioning, the place of religion in the barristers' lives and their understanding of Christian morality were undergoing profound changes. By mid-century, barristers seemed incapable of comprehending religious fervor. Passionate behavior inspired by religion was "fanaticism" to them. The advocate Jean Raynal wrote a history of Toulouse that concentrated on the Wars of Religion, and he treated both Catholics and Protestants as fanatics worthy only of disdain. Indeed, Raynal could not accept religion as their basic motivation for action; he viewed the war as a struggle for power among the great nobles.[119] Another advocate, Ponsard, echoed Raynal's denunciation of fanaticism in his poem about President Duranti, a leader of the Catholic League in Toulouse. Ponsard portrayed Duranti as a good man ruined by his failure to let reason conquer his religious fanaticism.[120]

This insensitivity to the demands of orthodox religion led to a radical, if unconscious, reassessment of Christian morality. The barrister Joseph Faure thought of himself as an orthodox Catholic, but he nonetheless believed that God demanded only what was reasonable.[121] And the barristers' conception of "reasonableness" increasingly excluded austerity and included worldly pleasures. Monasticism seemed irrelevant, even dangerous, to them. In 1770, Martel published a poem addressed to mothers, in which he advised them, without qualification or hesitancy, not to have their daughters raised in convents. Martel saw religious vows as an encouragement to laziness and uselessness and convents as establishments where vices and crimes were hidden by an unnatural lugubriousness. The feigned austerity of these houses shut out love and laughter, which the barrister considered innocent and natural pleasures.[122] Jamme, too, disapproved of religious orders and praised a new law inhibiting legacies to monasteries. He believed that religious houses weakened the state by preventing funds from flowing into commerce, and he lamented the fact that families lost their children to "a passing inspiration [which] often threw them into a

[118]*B.M.T.*, MS. 1184, fol. 4.

[119]Jean Raynal, *Histoire de la ville de Toulouse* (Toulouse, 1759), pp. 200-260.

[120]Ponsard, "Eloge historique de Jean-Etienne Duranti, premier président au Parlement de Toulouse," *Recueil de l'Académie des Jeux Floraux*, 1770, pp. 5-25.

[121]Félix Pasquier, ed., *Notes et réflections d'un bourgeois de Toulouse . . . d'après des lettres intimes* (Toulouse, 1917), p. 8.

[122]Guillaume Martel, "Les dangers du cloître. Epitre aux mères," *Recueil de l'Académie des Jeux Floraux*, 1770, pp. 20-25.

cloister to be the sad victims of penitence and despair."[123] Like many other barristers, Jamme could not comprehend religiously-motivated behavior, whether it was fighting heretics or devoting one's life to prayer. Worldly pursuits, like love or even commerce now seemed much more important than the contemplative life of traditional Christian morality.

The barristers' imperviousness to religious fervor engendered a spirit of tolerance, a principle underscored and made more conscious by the Calas affair in the 1760s. Not surprisingly, the bar as a whole failed to take a public stand on this famous case, in which a Protestant father was accused of killing his son for converting to Catholicism. For the bar to have done so would have been quite extraordinary, and, moreover, bigotry was not the only reason for accepting the sentence against Calas.[124] Scholars have sifted the evidence until the present without arriving at a definitive assessment of the verdict. At any rate, individual barristers did emerge as defenders of Calas. Théodore Sudre won the lasting admiration of Voltaire for his well-argued defense of the Protestant and his family. Joseph Marie Duroux was no less adamant than Sudre in combating the myth that Protestants punished converts with death. It is difficult to believe that these barristers were alone in rejecting the prejudices concerning Protestants that flourished in Toulouse immediately after the crime. Indeed, the advocate Carbonel, assessor of the city, asserted Calas's innocence, and Monyer protested against the cruel treatment given to the accused.[125] From the little evidence we have, there seems to have been much more debate about the case among the advocates than among the parlementaires who made the decision, and certainly more than among the populace at large.

Ultimately, the Calas affair served to impress upon educated Toulousans the importance of religious tolerance, and the bar was ready and willing to accept this new spirit. In the early 1750s, even before the affair, the barrister Brun de Rostang had argued against the stereotype of Jews as covetous and dishonest.[126] Barristers like Lacroix, Laviguerie, and Gary later argued for and applauded the Parlement's decision to recognize Protestant marriages and grant other civil liberties.[127] The tragic fate of Jean Calas did not truly create new religious attitudes, but

---

[123]Jamme, "Eloge de Louis XV," p. 100.
[124]See Bien, *Calas Affair*, pp. 7–24.
[125]Jean-Baptiste Dubédat, *Histoire du Parlement de Toulouse*, 2 vols. (Paris, 1885), 1: 382–85.
[126]Brun de Rostang, *Réponse au mémoire pour Abraham Roger et autres marchands juifs . . .* (n.p., n.d.), pp. 5–6.
[127]Jean-Baptiste Laviguerie, *Arrêts inédits du Parlement de Toulouse*, 2 vols. (Toulouse, 1831), 2: 92–93; Aldeguier, *Histoire*, 4: 379; Lacroix, "Pierre Fermin de Lacroix," p. 108.

it made an older spirit of open-mindedness more conscious.[128] The case undoubtedly added prestige and urgency to the "enlightened" attitudes appearing at the bar by mid-century.

BIRTH, TALENT, AND SOCIAL STATUS

The social relations of the Toulousan barristers demonstrated a deep status-consciousness, an acute awareness of the inequalities among men. At this point, we wish to explore more closely the barristers' thoughts and assumptions about the determinants of social status. The philosophes were, of course, questioning traditional notions of hierarchy; "equality" was becoming a frequently-voiced slogan, whether it had much meaning or not.[129] What theories, assumptions, justifications, and criticisms did the Toulousan barristers have about the inequalities that characterized their society in this Age of Enlightenment?

It is informative to compare the barristers' social attitudes to an "enlightened" analysis of social structure. Jean d'Alembert provides a coherent discussion of the determinants of social position in his "Essay on the Society of Literary Men and the Great."[130] Though his opinion takes into account many of the enlightened assumptions about human nature and treats traditional views critically, d'Alembert did not want to undermine the existing social order, and most philosophes would have accepted his position. Thus, d'Alembert's analysis provides a convenient point of departure for studying the barristers' social attitudes.

For d'Alembert, all distinctions among men were to some extent artificial, for there was a natural human equality which required implicit recognition. Yet d'Alembert admitted that a hierarchy was necessary; he demanded only that the inequalities be as reasonable as possible. He saw three determinants of status: birth, wealth, and talent. The "real" differences between men involved talent alone. Deference to birth and wealth were a matter of social convention; one gave "exterior consideration" to people of high birth or great fortune and reserved "inner esteem" for the talented.[131] But d'Alembert did insist that this outward regard for ancestry and fortune—and he considered both of equal social significance—was reasonable and obligatory.[132] Ulti-

---

[128]Bien, *Calas Affair*, p. 148 and chap. 7.

[129]Aristocrats of Burgundy, for example, used the rhetoric of equality freely. See Regime Robin-Aizertin, "Franc-Maçonnerie et lumières à Semur-en-Aurois en 1789," *Revue d'histoire économique et sociale* 43 (1965): 236.

[130]Jean d'Alembert, "Essai sur la société des gens de lettres et des grands," in *Mélanges de littérature, d'histoire et de philosophie*, 5 vols. (Amsterdam, 1760-68), vol. 1.

[131]*Ibid.*, p. 361.

[132]*Ibid.*, pp. 361-64.

mately, he sought a social order that accepted the social reality of birth while honoring men of merit.

No Toulousan barrister left so systematic a discussion of social structure, but numerous informal remarks on the subject make it possible to explore their social attitudes. Like d'Alembert, the Toulousan barristers clearly valued talent and saw it as a meaningful distinction among men. They believed that talent conferred an important dignity on a man and thought it urgent that merit be recompensed. Such recognition of talent was not only just but useful: the commendation given to men of talent inspired others to emulate their efforts.[133] Indeed, barristers berated the "vulgar minds" who could recognize only ancestry and not talent.[134] To value merit was a mark of discernment and enlightenment.

In other important ways, the barristers' social thinking diverged from that of d'Alembert. The men of the Toulousan bar did not think in terms of "natural equality"; in fact, they never used the term themselves. Though they occasionally alluded to bold, unorthodox subjects like "original goodness," even theoretical "equality" was not part of their framework of ideas.[135] Furthermore, the barristers did not acknowledge wealth (theoretically, that is) as an independent determinant of status. For d'Alembert, "opulence and independence" were just as significant as "high birth," but the barristers never considered that notion, which might well have been distasteful to them. Their social conceptions conformed much more to a "society of orders," in which birth and function determined status, and wealth accompanied this standing.

The barristers' social attitudes diverged most profoundly and most tellingly from those of d'Alembert on the subject of birth. Ancestry and inherited status were not mere social conventions to the men of the Toulousan bar; these were identifiable social realities. Indeed, in 1789 the barrister Poitevin compared "the virtues and titles of glory which are transmitted from father to son" with the distinctions "that merit alone extracts from chance," and he found the former to be "more interesting."[136] These barristers saw no conflict at all between personal merit and inherited virtue as sources of distinction; one erred only in considering birth the *sole* source of respectability. The barristers would have found nothing incongruous in one legal brief that simultaneously

[133]See, for example, Jamme, "Eloge de Louis XV," p. 91 and various other eulogies in the *Recueil de l'Académie des Jeux Floraux*.

[134]Guillaume Martel, "Complément fait au nom de l'Académie des Jeux Floraux à M. de Niquet," *Recueil de l'Académie des Jeux Floraux*, 1772, p. 30.

[135]See Espic, "Discours," p. 16, for the concept of "original virtue."

[136]Philippe Poitevin, "Eloge de M. de Senaux, président à mortier au Parlement de Toulouse," *Recueil de l'Académie des Jeux Floraux*, 1789, p. 80.

defended a client's right to a university chair because of his merit and referred to another party as being "recommended by his birth and the thousand hereditary virtues in his family."[137] It was only the most radical barrister, Barère, who saw the respect attributed to high birth as little more than social convention, unrelated to virtue itself.[138]

The barristers' acceptance of birth and inherited status was sincere but uncritical. They made no attempt to define the virtues inherited or to determine whether these were transmitted by upbringing or through the blood.[139] Moreover, the advocates seemed entirely unaware of a very important nuance in their own social thought: the inherited stains that they conceived to be the inevitable result of lowly extraction seemed more real and meaningful to them than the virtues transmitted through noble ancestry. In this sense, the social division that seemed to matter most to the barristers was not between nobles and commoners, but rather between those of respectable origins and those of "vile" birth.[140]

In recognizing "birth" as a mere convention, d'Alembert implicitly removed the social stigma from lowly extraction. But the barristers profoundly acknowledged the indelible mark that unrespectable birth left on a person, regardless of his individual accomplishments. This notion of inherited "vileness" was so much a part of their mental framework that it inevitably entered their legal arguments. To bring discredit upon the opposing party in a case, Mousinat, a future member of the National Assembly, pointed out that she was the daughter of a domestic servant, and he berated her for "always [having] the deadly ambition of appearing above her state."[141] The distinguished barrister Faget lauded the son of a baker who had risen, through effort and talent, to an important army post for "never forgetting the lowliness of his extraction. . . . Flattered by his distinctions, he never lost sight of his birth." The opposing party, however, though a military officer, was worthy only of contempt, for "he offers on all sides of his genealogy nothing but vile artisans, village tailors, butchers, and a domestic for a paternal grandfather."[142] Conversely, a

[137]Jean Boubée, *Factum pour Dome Laume, professeur de l'Université de Toulouse* . . . (n.p., n.d.), pp. 2, 9, and *passim*.

[138]Barère, "Eloge de Furgole," p. 7.

[139]For contemporary opinions on these matters, see Marcel Reinhard, "Elite et noblesse dans la seconde moitié du XVIIIe siècle," *Revue d'histoire moderne et contemporaine* 3 (1956): 5–6.

[140]The prerevolutionary Robespierre manifested the same social attitudes. See Joseph I. Shulim, "The Youthful Robespierre and His Ambivalence Toward the Ancien Régime," *Eighteenth-Century Studies* 5 (1972): 410.

[141]Jean Jacques Mousinat, *Réponse aux griefs pour le sieur Dupau . . . contre Melle. Millet-Lagardette* (n.p., n.d.), pp. 3, 10.

[142]Jean Pierre Faget, *Mémoire servant de réponse pour Demoiselle Anne Huc . . .* (Toulouse, n.d.).

respectable ancestry was a point in favor of a client. Lacroix, for example, reminded the court of the ancient "bourgeois" status of his client's family, implying that this extraction marked him as incapable of committing a crime.[143]

In contrast to their notions about inherited stigma, the virtues of high birth were vague and qualified, even if their existence was sincerely accepted. The prestige bestowed by noble birth was frequently contrasted unfavorably with the distinction derived from talent. Even Poitevin, who consciously defended traditional positions, believed that the virtues of "high birth" had "less *éclat*" than those of talent. And to "the man of merit whom Heaven had born in an obscure state," Poitevin could only counsel humility; he did not defend the virtues and prerogatives of noble extraction.[144] The barristers rendered deference to high birth because it was tied to a social system and an entire pattern of relationships that they did not question.

When, on the eve of the Revolution, the barristers were confronted with demands for a new social hierarchy based on wealth, talent, and education, one that denied the inherent virtue of high birth, they would be only partially prepared to recognize its validity. Before they could do so, they would have to clear away many unconscious assumptions and hitherto uncritically accepted attitudes.

In 1768, Abbé Audra wrote to Voltaire:

I now know Toulouse well enough to assure you that there is not, perhaps, another city in the Kingdom with so many enlightened men. As for the Parlement and the barristers . . . practically all under 35 are full of zeal and light . . . .[145]

The cultural expansion at the Toulousan bar had born fruit in a noticeable intellectual vitality and a sensitivity to the new currents of thought. Indeed, the barristers were "enlightened" in any contemporary sense of the word. Open to the essential innocence of worldly pleasures, aware of the importance of tolerance, the drama of salvation no longer dominated their outlooks. Material progress fostered by rational changes in legislation was widely accepted. Talent was viewed as an important distinction that demanded recognition and reward. Above all, the barristers were sensitive to the plight of the unfortunate, and the demands of "humanity" inspired a critical attitude toward established institutions.

[143]Pierre Lacroix, *Observations pour sieur Veyrenc contre le Marquis de Pierre-Bernis* (Toulouse, 1769), p. 6.
[144]Poitevin, "Eloge de M. de Senaux," p. 80.
[145]Voltaire, *Correspondence*, vol. 70, letter 14365.

But the intellectual ferment at the Toulousan bar had its limits. The Enlightenment failed to teach the barristers how to ask intricate and sophisticated questions about their place in society, about social organization, and about patterns of authority. Only a very few advocates, like Barère, and perhaps Mailhe, developed a comprehensive critique of society. The others championed limited reforms or single causes, many of which were effected during the Old Regime.[146] To be "enlightened" was to participate in a pervasive cultural movement that interested and influenced many parlementaires in the same way that it touched the Toulousan barristers. Far from finding in the philosophes' works and in enlightened ideas an ideology with which to challenge the existing order at crucial points, the barristers assimilated, applied, or ignored the new opinions within the confines of their traditional perspective.

[146]The preparatory question was abolished in 1780, and in 1788 the crown announced its intentions to reform criminal justice.

V

THE BARRISTERS
IN TOULOUSAN SOCIETY
AND POLITICS

THE BARRISTERS' SOCIABILITY

Barristers cultivated an image of seriousness, diligence, and devotion to legal studies. One would have thought they had little time for a private life. But it is important to look behind this facade and examine the barristers' sociability—the purposes, range, and context of their social relations.[1] Such a study provides significant insights into the informal structure of the barristers' social relations.

Despite the somber image they sought, the barristers seem to have been gregarious. They frequently joined voluntary associations with serious, usually charitable, purposes. Such was the Conference of Charity, to which thirty-two barristers belonged in the 1780s. This, however, was a quasi-professional group and was limited in membership. A much better notion of the barristers' social tastes and values comes from an analysis of their participation in Freemasonry and the brotherhoods of Penitents. The barristers were very active in both, and, regardless of the very different ideological orientations of the two, they seemed to derive the same satisfactions from each.

Freemasonry was a widespread movement in Toulouse, attracting 500 to 600 members in twelve lodges by the eve of the Revolution.[2] The barristers' participation may be studied through the surviving membership tables, which provide the names of about 460 Freemasons, 75 to 90 percent of the total.[3] Nearly a fourth of the Toulousan Masons, 114 of them, entitled themselves *avocat*. Many of these were simply law school graduates, but the *practicing* barristers were still numerous: they

---

[1]The seminal work on sociability is Maurice Agulhon, *Pénitents et Francs-Maçons de l'ancienne Provence (Essai sur la sociabilité méridionale)* (Paris, 1968). I have drawn extensively from this book at many points in this chapter.

[2]J. Gros, "Les loges maçonniques à Toulouse," *La Révolution française* 40 (1901): 254.

[3]Bibliothèque nationale, fonds maçonnique. I have deposited a microfilm of these membership lists at the Departmental Archives in Toulouse.

amounted to 15 percent of the total lodge membership (70 of the 460). With such weight in the ranks of Masonry, the barristers must have been able to stamp their values and attitudes on the movement.

Barristers entered the Masonic lodges especially in the decade 1773 to 1783, and those who joined were primarily the young. A sample of 38 barrister-Freemasons for whom age data exist indicates that the average barrister first entered a lodge in his twenty-eighth year. There were numerous Freemasons who were still only law students, and only two in the sample were over forty years old. The impulse to join a lodge had its most profound impact upon the advocates who began their practices between 1760 and 1770; 34 percent of them became Masons. The attraction of the lodges continued during the next two decades, when 30 percent of the new barristers entered Freemasonry. In comparison, the barristers who started practicing before 1760 were hardly attracted to the movement at all.[4] As we shall see, their sociability had other outlets.

For what purpose did all these barristers come together in Masonic lodges? Both pro-Mason historians of the Left and their conservative opponents have viewed Masonry as an ideological movement. A belief in social reform, progress, and even equality supposedly brought men into the lodges, where these ideals were discussed and practiced.[5] More recently, Maurice Agulhon has suggested that Freemasons were much more conscious of the sociable aspects of the movement—gathering, banqueting, toasting, and talking—than of the serious ideological content of the meetings; if, indeed, there was one.[6] In Toulouse, documentary and circumstantial evidence seems to support the sociable view of Freemasonry. Only one register of lodge deliberations has survived, and it contains very little ideological content. The Masons in this lodge, United Hearts, composed of merchants, barristers, and liberal professionals, deliberated almost exclusively about trivial matters or procedural formalities.[7] The constitution of the lodge Peace (*De*

----

[4]The various local almanacs list the dates at which advocates first entered the bar. See table V-1, below, for an analysis of the attraction which different age groups felt for Freemasonry.

[5]For a review of the literature on Freemasonry, see Daniel Ligou, "La Franc-Maçonnerie française au XVIIIe siècle," *L'information historique*, Mai-Juin, 1964, pp. 98–110. For the pro-Masonic view, see Gaston Martin, *La Franc-Maçonnerie française et la préparation de la Révolution* (Paris, n.d.); for the anti-Masonic view, see Gustave Bord, *La Franc-Maçonnerie en France* (Paris, 1908). There have been recent studies of Masonry on a local level: André Bouton, *Les Francs-Maçons Mançeaux et la Révolution française* (Le Mans, 1958); Pierre Barral, "Un siècle de maçonnerie grenobloise (1750–1850)," *Cahiers d'histoire* 2 (1957): 373–94, and volume 41 (1969), a special issue devoted to Freemasonry, of the *Annales historiques de la Révolution française*. Despite these works, the meaning and significance of Masonry remains uncertain.

[6]Agulhon, *Pénitents et Francs-Maçons*, pp. 203–10.

[7]*B.M.T.*, MS. 1182.

la Paix), dominated by barristers, specifically excluded discussions of religion or of the state.[8] Moreover, the one lodge that definitely had a dynamic social commitment, the *Encyclopédique*, founded in 1787, did not remain within the Freemason movement.[9] By 1789, it had become an "Encyclopedic Society" which held weekly public meetings to debate "the most interesting question to humanity, the support of the poor."[10] On the eve of the Revolution, Toulousan Freemasonry was being mocked for its mysterious and empty rituals. Several Masons created a scandal when they parodied the initiation of a naive peasant into the rites of the lodges.[11] Freemasonry was worthy of such jest in their eyes.

Focusing on the Toulousans in greatest contact with enlightened ideas confirms the essentially sociable nature of Freemasonry. Of the sixty-eight individuals in scientific and literary academies of Toulouse in 1789, only eleven seemed to have been Freemasons, and they were not always the academicians most in tune with new attitudes. The Advocate-General Lecomte, for example, had been criticized for his severe application of the criminal laws; yet he became a member of the lodge Perfect Friendship in 1782.[12] Only three of the nine barrister-academicians were Masons, and they had displayed no particular eagerness to enter a lodge.[13] Indeed, the radical Barère did not become a Freemason until 1788.[14] Barristers like Rouzet, who wrote plays; Espic, whose poems showed him to be an early disciple of Rousseau; Gez, and Sudre, both socially-conscious members of the Conference of Charity, were not Freemasons. All these men, familiar with new ideas and sensitive to the demands of humanity, felt no impulse to enter a lodge.

Only the registers of deliberations, which are nearly all missing, could provide conclusive insights into the ideological content of Masonry. Certainly, we would wish to deny neither the possibility of differences among lodges on this point nor the usefulness of Masonry in diffusing the vocabulary and slogans of the Enlightenment.[15]

[8]*B.M.T.*, MS. 1184, fol. 4, article 2. This provision was probably quite common in Toulousan Freemasonry.

[9]See F. P. Calas, *Histoire de la loge l'Encyclopédique de Toulouse, depuis sa création en 1787 jusqu'à ce jour* (Toulouse, 1887). Its members were divided into committees in which they studied questions of public usefulness and made concrete suggestions.

[10]*Affiches, annonces, et avis divers ou Feuille hebdomadaire de Toulouse*, 20 mai 1789, p. 85. See also the statement of its founder, *A.D.*, L-302, dossier of Delherm.

[11]Gros, "Loges maçonniques," pp. 252–53.

[12]Fonds maçonnique, table of "La Parfaite Amitié" (1782); for criticism of Lecomte see Gillaume Martel, "Eloge de M. Lecomte," *Recueil de l'Académie des Jeux Floraux*, 1787, p. 223.

[13]These were Jamme, Mailhe, and Barère.

[14]He joined the lodge "Encyclopédique." Jamme did not become a Freemason until 1778.

[15]Freemasons used the vocabulary of the Enlightenment without having any real commitment to its meaning. See Régime Robin-Aizertin, "La loge La Concorde à l'orient

However, the indirect evidence strongly suggests that men entered lodges for social contact, not for serious discussion of ideas and reforms among like-minded men.[16]

If a sociable impulse brought barristers into the lodges, it becomes important to ascertain with whom they wished to associate. All but three lodges had a distinct social identity, their memberships dominated by one occupational group or social stratum.[17] Two lodges were essentially groups of barristers, and two-thirds of the advocates in Masonry belonged to these. In the True Friends United, twenty-five of the forty-eight Freemasons were barristers, and five others were law students. Twenty-two of the thirty-two members of the lodge Peace in 1782 came from the bar. Barristers also aspired to enter the aristocratic Perfect Friendship lodge, with its twenty-five parlementaires and sixteen *gentilhommes*. Only very rich or noble barristers, like Jean Baptiste Viguier, Michel Malpel, or Jean Desirat, entered this exclusive circle. Moreover, the social composition of these lodges underscores an important informal cleavage in the social world of the Toulousan courts: the division between the Parlement and the lesser tribunals. Barristers of the Seneschal Court or Merchants' Court were nearly excluded from the lodges of their colleagues at the Parlement. The pleaders at the lower tribunals entered Masonic lodges that were dominated by merchants, artisans, or shopkeepers. Apparently, the barristers' social contacts divided along corporate lines.

The barristers at the Parlement openly expressed their exclusive socializing principles. "No one," declared the constitution of the Peace lodge, written by barrister Londois, "may be received as a Mason or an officiate who is not of a profession nearly equal to that of most brothers in the lodge."[18] The membership of Peace is, therefore, an indicator of the groups that barristers accepted as their social equals. In 1782, there were six large-scale merchants, one *écuyer*, a doctor, a "bourgeois," and a musician, in addition to twenty-two barristers.[19] Thus, the Freemasons of this lodge were from that intermediate stratum just below the aristocracy. The True Friends United lodge was a little more varied in composition, but it too, drew most of its members from the same

---

de Dijon," *Annales historiques de la Révolution française* 41 (1969): 433–46; and "Franc-Maçonnerie et lumières à Semur-en-Auxois en 1789," *Revue d' histoire économique et sociale* 43 (1965): 234–41.

[16]These were also the preliminary conclusions of Michel Taillfer, who is currently studying the Enlightenment in Toulouse.

[17]The socially-mixed lodges, "Arts et Sciences liberaux," "St. Joseph des Arts," and "Encyclopédique," recruited members on the basis of professional specialty. The objective was to have all branches of human endeavor represented. Hence, artisans mixed with liberal professionals.

[18]*B.M.T.*, MS. 1184, fol. 24.

[19]Bibliothèque nationale, fonds maçonnique, Toulouse, table for *De la Paix*, 1782.

intermediate stratum. Only a few middling professionals gained admittance.[20] The barristers consciously rejected wide social contacts for a self-imposed social isolation based on a finely-developed sense of exclusiveness.

Ostensibly, the Penitent brotherhoods were very different kinds of associations. But if we take into account that these were older, larger, and less intimate groups, we can observe the same social values and preferences that shaped lodge memberships influencing the social structure of these religious fraternities. The Blue Penitents, known since the early seventeenth century as the aristocratic brotherhood, preserved this social character until the Revolution.[21] In 1778, over 100 robe nobles were members.[22] Barristers, of course, wished to be Blue Penitents, and many were admitted. There were sixty-one of them, a fifth of the bar, in this brotherhood by 1780. This included most of the rich, noble, or distinguished barristers, like Gary, Laporte, Desirat, and Dirat.[23] The brothers of the Black Penitents were somewhat less socially distinguished. Much of their membership came from the intermediate social stratum of large-scale merchants, barristers, and civil officers, and from the middling professions. In this brotherhood were a few important barristers along with their less distinguished colleagues.[24] The Grey and White Penitents were more popular in composition, though men of higher rank were sometimes present as officers. It was to these confraternities, dominated by shopkeepers and artisans, that barristers of the lesser tribunals belonged, just as they entered the more popular Masonic lodges.[25] Whether as Penitents or as Freemasons, barristers at the Parlement behaved similarly. They associated whenever possible with the parlementaires; otherwise, they sought their own intermediate stratum. Above all, they avoided contact with the artisans, shopkeepers, and all below the level of the middling professions, leaving these strata to the barristers of the lower courts.

[20]In 1775, this lodge included twenty-five barristers, five law students, two attorneys, three *greffiers*, two officers of the Parlement, a military noble, a canon, three *écuyers*, two *négociants*, and a watchmaker.

[21]There was a popular saying, originating in the early seventeenth century: "Noblesse des Bleus, Richesses des Noirs, Antiquité des Gris, Pauvreté des Blancs." See Abbé P. E. Ousset, *La Confrérie des Pénitents Bleus de Toulouse* (Toulouse, 1927), p. 80, n. 3.

[22]P. Barranguet, "Les confréries dans le diocèse de Toulouse au milieu et à la fin du XVIII siècle," *10ᵉ Congrès d'études de la fédération des sociétés académiques et savantes, Languedoc-Pyrénées-Gascogne* (Montauban, 1956), p. 297.

[23]*A.D.*, E-922. This is a complete list of members, probably from the early 1780s.

[24]*A.D.*, E-941-954, *Cérémonial que Messieurs les Pénitents Noirs de la ville de Toulouse doivent observer* . . . (Toulouse, n.d.). At a general assembly in 1782, there were nine *négociants*, six barristers, four *gentilhommes*, three civil officers, three *bourgeois*, one attorney, and an artist. The corporation of attorneys may have had an official affiliation with this brotherhood.

[25]For the Grey Penitents, see *A.D.*, E-936-938; for the Whites, E-927-933.

Such affinities between Penitents and Freemasons have led to the suggestion that contemporaries were more aware of the similarities between the two associations than of the differences. Maurice Agulhon has argued that the Penitents' original purpose of mutual emulation in piety and contrition had been subordinated to socializing, and, under these circumstances, simultaneous membership in both fraternities would not have been incongruous.[26] Certainly, the Toulousan Penitents were no longer animated by a deep sense of piety and Christian devotion.[27] Nevertheless, the barristers were not usually *both* Penitents and Freemasons. The lists of Penitents, which are far from complete, yield the names of ninety-five barristers, only thirteen of whom were members of Masonic lodges. These two fraternal associations were alternative, not complementary, forms of socializing for the barristers. Whether a barrister became a Freemason or Penitent, however, was not a matter of his spiritual condition; the distinct membership of the two associations did not signify a division of the bar into the pious and the freethinkers. Rather, membership in one or the other association depended largely on age. If we examine the bar in 1785 (a convenient year for our data), we find a third of the older advocates—those practicing at least since 1770—to have been Penitents, while less than a tenth of the younger barristers belonged to the order. The proportions were reversed for the Masonic movement (see table V-1). Apparently the barristers were attracted to the penitential groups until the 1770s, when Masonic lodges began to grow. Younger barristers then found the lodges much more appealing forums for their fellowship: meetings were more frequent and intimate, the occasion more conducive to conviviality. It may have been, too, that these younger barristers had a clearer or stronger sense that spiritual matters were less central to their lives. But the older barristers were touched by the new religious attitudes too. As Penitents, they concentrated increasingly on secular, charitable functions. They stayed out of Masonry, not because the lodges were too *mondain*, but because this was a movement of the young.[28]

If new religious attitudes pervaded both groups, both retained the same social values, prejudices, and patterns. The younger barristers may have found a secular context more suitable to their socializing, but they did not seek a new range of social contacts. The fraternal habits of

[26]Agulhon, *Pénitents et Francs-Maçons*, pp. 203–10.
[27]Barranquet, "Confréries," p. 301. In 1778, the Blue Penitents decided to wear shoes during their processions because the cobbles hurt their feet!
[28]Such divisions might be useful in studying generational continuities and disconti-nuities. See Alan B. Spitzer, "The Historical Problem of Generations," *American Historical Review* 78 (1973): 1353–85.

TABLE V-1.   Age and Socializing Preferences of Barristers (1785)

Year Entered Profession	Total Entrants	Penitents		Freemasons	
		No.	%	No.	%
Before 1750	22	11	50.0	0	0
1750–59	31	10	32.2	4	12.9
1760–69	44	15	34.1	15	34.1
1770–79	85	7	8.2	25	29.3
1780–85	39	2	5.1	11	28.2

Sources: Bibliothèque nationale, fonds maçonnique; *A.D.*, E-922-954; *Almanach historique de la province de Languedoc* (Toulouse, 1885).

Note: The percentages columns are to be read as percentage of all entrants who joined the respective fraternal associations.

both young and old proved more enduring than their spiritual commitment.[29]

Barristers undoubtedly spent much more of their nonoccupational time socializing among family, friends, and relatives than in voluntary fraternal associations. Unfortunately, the documentary material on this aspect of their social lives is particularly weak, so we must rely heavily on inference and on speculation. The evidence that does exist points to an intense intertwining of family, neighbor, and colleague in the barristers' social relationships. With residences so highly segregated along professional lines and with the strong tendency of colleagues' families to intermarry, the barristers' circles of friends, relatives, and colleagues must have been nearly coterminous. Even though many of the barristers were not natives of Toulouse, they settled in the legal quarter and soon became integrated into this milieu, which apparently had a considerable capacity for absorption.

Lists of witnesses to the signing of marriage contracts provide some opportunity to test this speculation about the barristers' social contacts. These lists (see table V-2) indicate the professions of those with whom barristers had meaningful—though not necessarily genial—relations. Nobles were probably disproportionately represented by this source because families prevailed upon their most distinguished contacts to attend the ceremony. Interesting, too, is the near-absence of parlementaires. They no longer took the trouble to favor a promising barrister with attendance at his wedding, as they had done in the previous century. By and large, the witness lists attest to the same

---

[29]Voluntary associations in France have supposedly reinforced social divisions, rather than breached them, down to the present day. See O. R. Gallagher, "Voluntary Associations in France," *Social Forces* 36 (1957): 153–60.

TABLE V-2.   Witnesses to Marriage Contracts

Occupation	Number	Percent
Non-noble barristers	57	24.2
Noble barristers	32	14.3
Négociants	23	9.8
Clergy	22	9.0
Simple noble	21	8.9
Attorney	21	8.9
Praticien	12	6.0
Civil officer	10	5.2
Marchand	8	3.3
Physician	8	3.3
Greffier	6	2.3
Artisan	3	1.2
Parlementaire	3	1.2
Other	6	2.4
Total	232	100.0

Source: A.D., 3E, marriage contracts of 87 barristers, 1740-1790.

pattern of sociality observed in the penitential and Masonic brother-hoods. The barristers' interaction with their colleagues was intense; with others in their intermediate stratum, frequent; and with groups below the middling professions, rare.

It is important, at this point, to examine more closely the extent and quality of relations which barristers had with the aristocracy and the *peuple.* Such contacts might have had important formative influences on their social and political attitudes. For example, the ties of loyalty and respect between parlementaires and barristers were tested several times during the last decades of the Old Regime. Were professional bonds between the two groups supplemented by personal ties of friendship and familiarity? This question is difficult to answer in view of the dearth of documents. It seems unlikely, however, that barristers, especially non-noble ones, would have been invited to the salons of Mesdames du Bourg, de Cambon, de Resseguier, or Mengaud de Lahage.[30] The parlementaire d'Aldeguier noted in his contemporary history of Toulouse that Bertrand Barère was "living in rather great intimacy with a number of parlementaires."[31] The very fact that d'Aldeguier mentioned this in his history of Toulouse indicates the singularity of the situation. Barère's familiarity with the aristocracy was based not on his position as a barrister of importance but on his

[30]On these salons, see Roger de Vives de Regie, *Les Femmes dans la société de nos derniers parlementaires toulousains* (Toulouse, 1901), p. 60.

[31]J.-B.-A. d'Aldeguier, *Histoire de la ville de Toulouse depuis la conquête des Romans . . .* , 4 vols. (Paris, 1835), 4: 390. I have also examined the correspondence and family papers of Riquet de Bonrepos, *A.D.,* 4-J. There were no references to barristers, suggesting little social contact.

reputation as a man of letters, of wit, and of "bons mots." It was for this reason, too, that the academician Jean Baptiste Mailhe was received in aristocratic salons.[32] A barrister who was simply erudite carried no weight in the social world of the parlementaires.

The barrister who integrated himself most fully into parlementaire circles was Philippe Vincent Poitevin. Born near Montpellier in 1742, he taught *lettres* in a *collège* before entering the Toulousan bar in 1769.[33] He soon established contacts in high robe circles. Poitevin became the legal tutor of the future Advocate-General Resseguier and was familiar enough with President du Bourg to participate in his family festivities.[34] Poitevin was well-received in the salons, appreciated there for his "piquant couplets" and, curiously enough, for his ability to make geography humorous.[35] Whether or not these aristocrats viewed this barrister as an "equal," they did demonstrate some affection and concern for him. In return, Poitevin gave them his complete loyalty.

Poitevin's social situation, however, was unique. His acceptance into aristocratic circles placed him in such a rarefied atmosphere that he hardly knew his colleague and fellow academician, Jean Joseph Gez.[36] Nothing could have demonstrated more completely how narrow and stratified the different social spheres within the Toulousan legal world really were. The barristers' identification with parlementaires was not based on familiarity with them. Their most meaningful ties to the magistrates were, as we shall see, professional ones.

The barristers' nonprofessional contacts with the *peuple* may well have been as limited as their contacts with the aristocracy. Barristers thought of the lower social groups as being disorderly and dangerous by nature. The advocate Soulé, for example, wrote in a brief that police officers deserve sympathy "for their daily exposure to the hatred and resentment of the populace due to its antipathy for discipline and order."[37] Contact between members of the lower strata and barristers occurred smoothly and without discomfort only when each assumed clearly-defined superior-inferior roles (for example, landlord-tenant, *maître*-sharecropper, lawyer-accused). One petty trial of offended honor illustrates the tensions and formalities that structured the

---

[32]Vives de Regie, *Les femmes*, p. 82.

[33]*Biographie toulousaine, ou Dictionnaire historique*, 2 vols. (Paris, 1823), 2: 187.

[34]Clément Tournier, ed., *Le Mésmerisme à Toulouse, suivi de lettres sur le XVIIIe siècle d'après les archives de l'hôtel du Bourg* (Toulouse, 1911), pp. 69–70, 90. Philippe Poitevin-Peitari, *Mémoire pour servir à l'histoire des Jeux Floraux*, 2 vols. (Toulouse, 1815), 2: 353.

[35]*Biographie toulousaine*, 2: 187.

[36]Poitevin-Peitari, *Mémoire*, 2: 372–76.

[37]Guillaume Soulé, *Mémoire pour les maires, consuls . . . de Lunel . . .* (n.p., n.d.), p. 10.

barristers' relations with the *peuple*.[38] Advocate Louis Auguste de la Mothe was engaged to settle a debt owed by a fisherman from a nearby village. The barrister decided to visit the fisherman and urge him to pay the debt rather than have his property seized. De la Mothe wore his professional robes to the fisherman's residence, apparently to inspire fear and respect. When he addressed the debtor, de la Mothe noted that the miscreant failed to remove his hat. This act of disrespect angered the barrister, and he knocked the hat off the fisherman's head. The debtor, enraged by both the attack and the demand for money, declared that he had seen men in robes before and was not awed. He called de la Mothe a "f—— trickster" and threatened to throw him in the river. This incident illustrates, on the one hand, popular hostility to legal men, and on the other, the unwillingness of the well-situated to treat the laboring poor as beings worthy of dignity and respect.

Ultimately, the barristers formed a rather isolated social group. This gave the bar a great deal of cohesiveness, but it also inhibited the development of wider frames of reference and obscured the distinction between corporate and individual interests. The consequences of this position for the barristers' political outlook can be seen through their participation in local and national conflicts.

PUBLIC SERVICE AND MUNICIPAL REFORM

Men of high social standing and legal expertise, barristers were frequent participants in local government. Indeed, men from the bar were crucial to the administration of the city, for they nearly monopolized the offices of greatest responsibility and power. The leading capitoul, called the *chef de consistoire*, was always an advocate.[39] So was the syndic, whose duties included the supervision of all legal disputes involving the city. This was a permanent office, and most administrative matters passed through his hands. The four assessors of the city were also important public functionaries, aiding the capitouls in their judicial and police duties.[40] Among the assessors were generally one or two barristers of some professional importance. Since the other assessors were chosen more for their connections than for their qualifications, most of their responsibilities must have devolved upon the barristers.[41] The Treasurer of Toulouse, a venal officer, was the barrister-capitoul Prévost during the last decade of the Old Regime, while the Clausolles, a family of barristers, had held the post of *greffier*

---

[38]*A.D.*, B—seigneurial justice, Fenouillet. Case of 16 October 1771.
[39]Léon Dutil, "La réforme du capitoul toulousain," *Annales du midi* 19 (1907): 305–6.
[40]Roger Sicard, *L'administration capitulaire sous l'ancien régime* (Toulouse, 1952), pp. 39–40.
[41]Dutil, "La réforme," p. 320.

since at least 1770.[42] In addition, three advocates served as officers in the Municipal Tribunal. Thus, with the exception of tax collectors and minor clerks, barristers held nearly every important office at the Hôtel de Ville.

Until the municipal reorganization of 1778, these officers shared their power and burdens with a series of councils and commissions composed mainly of former capitouls.[43] Since barristers were a large component of the former capitouls living in the city (fifteen of fifty-three in 1789),[44] they were prominent in these councils. The Bourgeois Council was the most influential organ of administration; in 1775, the only year for which data exist, barristers held six of the twenty-four regular positions on the Council.[45] All legal problems and conflicts involving the city were considered by the "Council of the Long Robe," composed of six distinguished barristers. One or two more might have served on the financial commissions, but merchants usually dominated these.

The reform of 1778 created two new administrative councils with considerable power, and barristers occupied numerous places on both. On the Political Council, charged with reviewing all matters of pure administration and approving expenses above 100 livres, there were eight advocates among the twenty-eight selected members in 1780.[46] When the royal government reorganized this council once again in 1781—with the express purpose of reducing the barristers' participation—there were still five advocates out of thirty-two members.[47] The General Council, convoked only in unusual circumstances, had fifteen appointed members, and advocates held an average of four of these posts in the last decade of the Old Regime.[48] Service in the Hôtel de Ville was, thus, a very common activity for Toulousan barristers before and after the reform.

The advocates' participation in public affairs extended beyond the municipal government. Their legal expertise and social prominence made them suitable administrators for various quasi-public institu-

---

[42]*Almanach de la ville de Toulouse*, 1780-1790. See sections on municipal administration.

[43]For details on these councils, see Sicard, *L'administration capitulaire*, and Edmond Lamouzèle, *Essai sur l'administration de la ville de Toulouse à la fin de l'ancien régime* (Paris, 1910).

[44]*Almanach historique de la province de Languedoc* (Toulouse, 1790), pp. 213-16.

[45]*A.D.*, C-279, list of members of Conseil des Bourgeois.

[46]*Almanach de la ville de Toulouse*, 1780. See the section on "administration municipale." The figures cited here include only the regularly selected members. There were others who held honorary positions on the council by virtue of their rank or position in Toulousan society.

[47]*Almanach de la ville de Toulouse*, 1782.

[48]*Almanach de la ville de Toulouse*, 1780-1790. This, again, includes only the regularly-selected members.

tions. One or two barristers regularly sat on the board of the Royal *Collège* (formerly the Jesuit school). Others served as legal counsel to the Order of Malta, to which the most important Toulousan aristocrats belonged. As important men in their neighborhoods and parishes, barristers, along with parlementaires and large merchants, were to be found as officers of the hospitals or directors of the parochial charity house.[49]

Public assistance and care for the unfortunate claimed the time, attention, and sense of paternal obligation of several barristers. Toulouse had two major institutions for the poor, the Hôtel-Dieu St. Jacques and the Hôpital général de la Grave, and the barristers served both. The Hôtel-Dieu had a board of directors whose occupational composition was partially fixed by edict; at least eight, and later, six of the twenty-four directors had to be barristers.[50] During the 1780s an average of seven barristers administered the Hôtel-Dieu each year. The General Hospital had a governing board of thirty, and barristers composed nearly a third of it for the last decade of the Old Regime.[51] These administrators performed a task of great responsibility and difficulty, given the perennial shortage of funds to care for a growing number of poor. The monthly or biweekly meetings were only the beginning of their work on behalf of the destitute. Barristers also served as syndic of the General Hospital and counsels for the poor of the Hôtel-Dieu. The amount of time and energy that advocates devoted to the poor through these two institutions, the Conference of Charity, and the religious brotherhoods was considerable.

The barristers who assumed public responsibilities and became local notables formed a restricted, but by no means closed, group. Entry came with wealth or professional distinction. During the last twenty years of the Old Regime, about fifty barristers—one out of six or seven—assumed some public office. Most of these had been ennobled through the *capitoulat*; until 1778, royal legislation placed most public institutions under the direction of former capitouls. The reform of 1778, however, admitted men to the municipal councils before they became capitouls so they might gain experience in public affairs.[52] The Political Council, for example, selected talented *roturier* barristers of the Parlement for a role in local administration. Seven such commoners entered the Council prior to the Revolution. Public offices were nearly closed to barristers at the nonsovereign court and to the less

[49]*Ibid.*

[50]See François Buchalet, *L'assistance publique à Toulouse au dix-huitième siècle* (Toulouse, 1904), for the administration of the charitable institutions.

[51]There were usually nine barristers among the administrators of the General Hospital. See *Almanach de la ville de Toulouse*, 1780–1790.

[52]Dutil, "La réforme," pp. 328–29.

important *avocats* at the Parlement. By and large, participation in local administration reflected and enhanced the position of leading barristers as the most distinguished nonaristocrats in Toulouse.

The extensive involvement of the barristers in public administration gave them an interest in any effort to alter the municipal government. When the crown instituted reforms in the 1770s, barristers became actively embroiled in the controversies that ensued. The concerns of the royal government were, at various times, to make the administration of Toulouse more efficient and to reduce the influence of the Parlement. Barristers, however, perceived the reform as an attack on their corporate privileges. Throughout the long dispute, the barristers' concern was to preserve as many ennobling offices and honors as possible for themselves and their colleagues. Their approach to public affairs was, thus, a narrow, corporate one.

Before examining the municipal reform, it is necessary to discuss briefly the barristers' corporate organization and habits of association. Strictly speaking, the barristers had no corporate organization at all, for their Order had no letters patent that conferred this legal status. Moreover, the barristers preferred to think of the Order as an association based on honor, mutual respect, and common concerns.[53] Such a conception complemented their claims to independence and high status. They refused even to keep minutes of their deliberations. Nonetheless, the Order did perform the functions of a professional corps. There are indications, too, that corporate attachments were becoming weaker in the context of everyday life.[54] The barristers seemed concerned with separating their family and professional lives, and their expanding cultural horizons brought them a new range of interests beyond the law. Diminishing participation in corporate processions suggests that the barristers' sense of collective identity was declining.[55] However, advocates continued to relate to political institutions and authorities as members of a corporate body. And when the honors and privileges of this body were in question, barristers were capable of vigorous collective action. The reform of the municipal government elicited just such a response from the barristers.

---

[53]*A.M.*, AA-100, *Principes, progrès, et suite de la scission formée par 26 avocats au Parlement de Toulouse*, pp. 2, 9.

[54]This point is made by Philippe Ariès in *Centuries of Childhood: A Social History of Family Life*, trans. Robert Baldick (New York, 1962), pp. 365–405. My findings tend to support his claim.

[55]Immediately after the Maupeou coup, fewer than a hundred barristers marched with their Order to congratulate the eldest magistrate on the reestablishment of the Court. See *Journal de ce qui s'est passé à l'occasion du rétablissement du Parlement . . .* (n.p., n.d.), pp. 7–8.

In the mid-1760s, the royal government began to discuss changes in the municipal administration, a move urged by intendants since the beginning of the century. The Estates of Languedoc precipitated a serious pamphlet war in 1775 by suggesting that Toulouse be given the same form of government as the other cities of the province.[56] Barristers were active pamphleteers, and they became the chief defenders of the existing administration. The distinguished barrister and former capitoul Jean Carrière wrote a very factual, straightforward memoir which attempted to defend the administration by describing it in detail and by praising the integrity of its personnel. He noted, for example, that the commissions were composed of barrister-capitouls, and these were "almost always among the most celebrated of the Parlement."[57] Jean Castillon, the barrister, academician, and librarian, offered a more elaborate apologia for the municipal government. His general contention was that existing abuses were inevitable, and no reform could change certain, possibly undesirable, situations. For example, critics of the existing regime blamed the ennoblement of capitouls for the deterioration of Toulousan commerce: children of ennobled merchants abandoned trade, it was claimed, for professions suitable to their new status. Castillon answered these critics by pointing out that the local economy lacked vitality for other reasons: its inland position and its lack of raw materials, to name only two.[58] The most uncompromising defense of the administration came from Jean Claude Deadde. His was a panegyric on the municipal government, lauding its ancient privileges and respectable origins. For Deadde, the administration was just what it ought to have been.[59]

The terms upon which the barristers defended the municipal status quo merit further attention. Their criteria for evaluating the government were ancient privilege, previous existence, and convenience. The barristers did not consider efficiency, equity, or usefulness. Their memoirs never conceded the need to correct obvious abuses, such as the selection of "foreigners" for capitouls. Apparently, they acquiesced in the process that made the Toulousan municipal government a pawn in a game of influence among Parisian courtiers. In the end, the barristers' defense of the municipal government was a corporate defense of their benefits and privileges. Deadde, Castillon, and Carrière were not defending the capitoul system out of personal interest; the first two were minor barristers and unlikely to become capitouls, while Carrière was already ennobled. As barristers, though, they wanted to retain for their profession and their colleagues as many honors, dignities, and

[56]Dutil, "La réforme," p. 313.
[57]*A.D.*, C-284, "Mémoire concernant l'administration de la ville de Toulouse."
[58]*A.D.*, C-285.
[59]*Ibid.*

privileges as possible, and this required the preservation of the existing municipal structure. Hence, they argued forcefully for the continuance of the ennobling powers of the *capitoulat* but did not discuss its abuses. The narrow, corporate viewpoint of the barristers in this dispute over municipal reform continued into other phases of the controversy as well.

The first phase of dispute ended with the royal reform edict of 1778. Despite the opposition of the barristers, the structure of the administration underwent substantial changes. The incumbency of the capitouls was extended a year to provide for greater experience and expertise. The actual selection of the capitouls was returned to local bodies, and fixed social requirements were placed on the nominees. Of the eight capitouls, two were to be nobles, two, former capitouls, and only four places were open to commoners of distinction. These commoners had to serve two to four years in administrative councils before they would be eligible for higher office.[60] A further provision that was to have some importance in the subsequent disputes was the suppression of the *chef de consistoire*. Now that there were gentlemen-capitouls, there was no need for one alderman to lead all the others. Instead, one capitoul, called the "First of Justice," was placed in charge of the municipal tribunal.

The controversies and reexamination engendered by the reform concerned two different issues. The first involved a squabble over precedence between the gentlemen-capitouls, already nobles of long standing, and the First of Justice, always an ennobled barrister. Which one would have the honor of receiving commissions from the Parlement? Who would be an honorary member of the Floral Games? The First of Justice claimed these distinctions because he replaced the *chef de consistoire*, who had previously held the honors, and the gentlemen-capitouls claimed them on the basis of social rank. The barristers in the municipal administration took this issue very seriously. Pierre Gary and Jean Gouazé, both of whom had devoted many years to public service, wanted to resign rather than submit to the gentlemen-capitouls. They believed this dispute was important enough to merit the renunciation of honorable positions and the disruption of the city government.[61]

The second, and much more significant, dispute arising from the reform of 1778 concerned the number of barristers serving in the municipal government. The barristers, as we have seen, were always careful to protect or expand their share of ennobling positions; but their very prominence in public councils aroused the jealousy of other

---

[60]Dutil, "La réforme," pp. 326–30.
[61]*Ibid.*, pp. 330–39; *A.D.*-287, letter of Gary to Intendant (no date).

occupational groups. Soon after the reform, the Order of Barristers tried to increase their avenues to ennoblement. The Order, together with the large-scale merchants (*négociants*), claimed that half of the new capitouls had to be chosen among their colleagues alone.[62] This claim was enough to arouse the attorney and former capitoul, Chauliac, to protest to the intendant. He seemed to lead the opposition in the municipal councils to this offensive by the Order of Barristers.[63]

The controversy over the barristers' participation in municipal government easily became enmeshed in a still more serious problem: the subjection of the city administration to the Parlement. The Sovereign Court had long had a "party" among the members of the municipal councils and had strongly influenced the city through its representatives to those bodies. The royal government, on the other hand, had always tried to reduce the influence of the Parlement by selecting capitouls who would not necessarily support the court.[64] In 1782, a trivial incident involving the firing of a city jailor by the capitouls began a series of run-ins between the municipal corps and the Parlement.[65] The Parlement then began to apply stronger pressure to subordinate the city government to its will, and the barristers in the Hôtel de Ville were the main agents of its control.[66] To counteract the influence of the Sovereign Court, the crown once again reorganized the city government in October of 1783. This time, the seats on the council were apportioned to numerous professional groups. The Political Council was to have among its non-noble members two barristers, but also four merchants, three *bourgeois*, one surgeon, one notary, and so on. The General Council would have only one barrister among its *roturier* members.[67] Both councils, however, might have—and certainly did have—more advocates, who were former capitouls, so that in the end this aspect of the reform was ineffective. Nonetheless, both the Parlement and the Order of Barristers perceived the threat and reacted accordingly. The Parlement forbade the application of the edict and sent a remonstrance to the king.[68] Individual barristers in the councils, like the former capitoul Pierre Albaret, protested against the new edict. Incited by the Parlement, several barristers demanded a meeting of the

[62]*A.D.*, C-287, "Observation sur l'élection des capitouls de Toulouse."

[63]*A.D.*, C-287, letter of Chauliac to Intendant, 31 December 1783; Dutil, "La réforme," pp. 340-50.

[64]See, for example, *A.D.*, C-278, "Etat des avocats, ancien capitouls . . ." (1767-1768), especially the comments on Gouazé and Pons. Also, *A.D.*, C-287, letter of Marquis de Belesta to Intendant, 29 November 1783.

[65]Henri Rozy, "Un conflict en 1782 entre le capitoulat de Toulouse et le Parlement . . . ," *Mémoires de l'Académie des sciences . . . de Toulouse*, 7ᵉ série, 7 (1875): 479-82.

[66]*A.D.*, C-287, letter of Marquis de Belesta to Intendant, 29 November 1783.

[67]Dutil, "La réforme," p. 344.

[68]*A.D.*, C-287, *arrêt* of Parlement, 9 December 1783.

Order to issue an official protest. The *batonnier*, forewarned by the subdelegate, tried to prevent such a meeting, only to have the younger hotheads threaten to hold a session without him.[69] When the Order assembled, the barristers sent a deputation to the Parlement to express their gratitude for its defense of "the interests of the Order and for having rendered witness to the preference which the Order [of Barristers] merits by its knowledge over all the other corps of the city." Then they voted to present a memoir to the Keeper of the Seals

to represent to him the injustices done to the place of First of Justice and the prejudice resulting from the suppression of the second of justice, and at the same time the wrong done to the Order of Barristers in designating such a small number to the Council.[70]

Throughout this five-year controversy, the barristers had regarded public offices as corporate "property" which they had to protect. Wider questions of justice, equity, or efficiency received scant attention. The Toulousan barristers were still too enmeshed in corporate attachments to act as individual citizens, concerned with the public interest. Their intense social interaction and isolation from other groups undoubtedly reinforced this tendency to view public matters from a corporate point of view.

BARRISTERS AND THE PARLEMENT IN POLITICAL CRISES

The municipal councils and commissions provided a forum for the barristers to play an important role in local politics. Conflicts between the crown and the parlementaires, increasingly intense in the second half of the century, placed the barristers in a much wider political context. These conflicts not only tested the barristers' willingness to act in political crises but also tried their loyalty to the magistrates.

These crises repeatedly demonstrated the fidelity of the barristers to the parlementaires. To be sure, the magistrates received wide support as defenders of provincial liberties against royal "despotism," but the bonds which tied the barristers to their superiors were of a special nature and strength, and they deserve careful examination. Rarely was this fidelity based on familiarity; as we have seen, few barristers made their way into aristocratic circles or even aspired to do so. Rather, the barristers were tied to the magistrates by a complex relationship involving respect, fear, deference, and dependence. The aloofness of the parlementaires did not prevent the barristers from identifying with

---

[69]*A.D.*, C-287, letter of subdelegate Ginisty to Intendant, 24 December 1783.
[70]*Ibid.*

them. The diligent, sober, and serious life style of the significant minority of magistrates who kept the court functioning smoothly won the barristers' deep respect.[71] Mutual interest in the law and in the study of jurisprudence created cultural bonds between the two groups. The barrister Jean de Poisson, for example, exchanged rare legal manuscripts with Counselor Aiguesvives.[72] The bench and the bar shared more tangible interests, as well. Maintaining the full authority, prestige, and jurisdiction of the Parlement concerned them both; a diminution of any of these might have reduced the barristers' clientele or professional status. Thus, they welcomed the parlementaires' staunch defense of their court.

Professional activities placed barristers in a special patron-client relationship with individual magistrates. To have the favor and "protection" of a powerful officer of the court led to many victorious cases and a successful career. Moreover, prevailing judicial practices and morality permitted the direct solicitation of the magistrate in favor of a client. The evidence suggests that barristers availed themselves of this practice frequently and built up a personal indebtedness to the parlementaires. The barrister Chas, for example, wrote to Counselor d'Albis thanking him for "so many proofs of kindness" in the past and requesting him to take an interest in his client's case.[73] The advocate Boyer implored Madame d'Albis to influence her husband in his client's affairs. She, in turn, requested her husband to treat the client "as favorably as your equity and insight will permit."[74] Thus, ties of dependence and patronage united the bar and the bench.

The magistrates, for their part, insisted upon loyalty and support from the bar. When it was not forthcoming voluntarily—as it usually was—they could resort to fines, the threat of suspension, withdrawal of favor, or intimidation. Fines were probably rather common.[75] The case of a young barrister in the Political Council, François Besaucelle, provides an interesting example of intimidation. As a relative of the capitoul Chauliac, leader of the anti-parlementaire faction in the council, Besaucelle had divided obligations and loyalties. He tried to

[71]See François Bluche, *Les magistrats du Parlement de Paris au XVIIIᵉ siècle (1715-1771)* (Paris, 1960), pp. 280-83 for the functioning of a Sovereign Court. More research needs to be done on provincial courts. For the parlementaires' image, see Pierre Nicolas Berryer, *Souvenirs*, 2 vols. (Paris, 1839), 1: 34. This Parisian barrister remembered the magistrates as rich men who, in spite of their wealth, rose at 4:00 A.M. to read legal cases, so great was their devotion to public duty.

[72]*A.D.*, 3E-1157, fol. 185, testament of Poisson.

[73]Auguste Puis, ed., *Une famille de parlementaires toulousains à la fin de l'Ancien Régime. Correspondance du Conseiller d'Albis de Belbèze* (Paris, 1913), p. 132.

[74]*Ibid.*, p. 238.

[75]Two very prominent barristers received fines. For Duroux, see B-1681, fol. 333; for Jamme, see his pamphlet, *Aux maire et officiers municipaux . . .* (n.p., n.d.), p. 5, in the *B.M.T.* revolutionary pamphlet collection.

resolve these by ceasing to attend the meetings. However, the Advocate-General told him that "not to be for the Parlement was to be against it." With this warning, the young barrister sided with the court.[76] Usually, however, the ties binding barristers to the magistrates made such intimidation unnecessary.

Until the attack on the Parlement by Chancellor Maupeou in 1771, the Sovereign Court had not been threatened with fundamental changes in its organization or jurisdiction. Until then, the conflicts between the court and the crown concerned the registration of specific laws. Individual barristers may have had important behind-the-scenes roles as legal advisors or as pamphleteers, but there was no collective activity by the bar. Such was the case in 1763, when the Parlement refused to register a fiscal edict and suddenly recessed without royal permission. A barrister defended the court with legal arguments and precedents justifying its action.[77] With the Maupeou coup, however, the power of the Parlement was threatened in such a fundamental manner that collective action was a possible response for the barristers.

After Maupeou's attack on the Parisian Parlement in February of 1771, the personnel of the Toulousan Sovereign Court were insecure and uncertain. Rumors of Maupeou's intention to strike in Toulouse circulated, even though this Parlement was not so vigorous as others in protesting his policies.[78] The Toulousan parlementaires apparently feared that Maupeou would expel some magistrates and replace them with barristers and non-noble judges, who would be more readily under his control. Early in May, the court issued a decision that "no one, be he magistrate, barrister, or other, may contradict his oath by taking over the office and functions of magistrates who were not removed from their functions by the proper forms of law."[79] This declaration was immediately nullified by the Royal Council, but its sense was probably not lost on the bar.

For all the warning they had, the court personnel showed no evidence of having planned decisive action when the coup came. On 2 September 1771 the intendant, St-Priest and the governor, the count

---

[76]Dutil, "La réforme," p. 360. Voltaire accused the Parlement of intimidating one barrister so much that he refused to defend his own son against accusations in the Calas affair. See François Marie Voltaire, Correspondence, ed. Theodore Besterman (Geneva, 1959), vol. 49, letter 9775.

[77]Lettre d'un avocat au Parlement de Toulouse à un avocat au Parlement de Paris au sujet de l'arrêt par lequel le Parlement a prorogé sa séance (n.p., n.d.).

[78]G. Crebassol, "Le Parlement Maupeou à Toulouse" (D.E.S., University of Toulouse, 1949), p. 28; Jules Flammermont, Le Chancelier Maupeou et les Parlements (Paris, 1883), p. 264.

[79]Cited in Flammermont, Chancelier Maupeou, pp. 387-88. This may have been aimed more at the Seneschal Court officers than at the barristers.

of Périgord, a known opponent of the Parlements, forced the registration of the edict suppressing the Parlement of Languedoc. The magistrates were ordered to return immediately to their homes and not to receive visitors.[80] At the same time a new tribunal, the Superior Council, was created at Nîmes, and this new court seriously cut into the jurisdiction of the Parlement. President d'Aguin, a leader of the magisterial opposition, claimed that the new council reduced the jurisdiction of the Parlement by two-thirds and removed the wealthiest areas,[81] but his estimate was undoubtedly exaggerated. A few days later, seventy magistrates were exiled by *lettres de cachet*, while the intendant permitted fifty parlementaires to remain in Toulouse so that he might persuade them to join the new court. In the end, thirty-seven counselors consented to take seats in the Maupeou Parlement.[82] These judges came largely from the families who were relatively new to the Parlement, while the older magisterial families, like Resseguier, Senaux, and du Bourg, were adamant in their opposition to the new court.

The barristers were no more organized in their resistance to Maupeou than were the magistrates. If there was any attempt to organize a "strike" at the bar, as was done at other Parlements, there is no evidence for it. On 5 September, when the Maupeou court began its first session, the barristers pleaded as usual, and they continued to appear with the same frequency as before. No pleading advocate retired voluntarily to protest the Maupeou coup.[83] Even when the Parlement was reestablished in 1775, the barristers never claimed more than to have "made the most fervent wishes for this happy revolution" while continuing to serve the Maupeou court.[84] Only Philippe Poitevin, the personal friend of parlementaires, may have actively resisted the coup; Attorney-General Resseguier worried that Poitevin had been exiled by a *lettre de cachet*.[85]

The barristers' failure to defend the Parlement and their own interests more actively was not the result of any basic disloyalty; rather, it was a bow to necessity, confusion, and fear. The barristers were unaccustomed to taking vigorous and independent political stands. They were under pressure from clients to plead their cases. They feared

---

[80]*Ibid.*, p. 450.

[81]Edmond Lamouzèle, "Le Parlement Maupeou à Toulouse . . . d'après une correspondance inédite," *Revue des pyrénées* 19 (1907): 240.

[82]Flammermont, *Chancelier Maupeou*, pp. 450–51.

[83]*A.D.*, B–registers of *Grand' Chambre*, 1771–1772. One local historian, Joseph Soulié (*Le coup d'état judiciaire du Chancelier Maupeou . . .* [Toulouse, 1896], p. 40, n. 14) claims that barristers retired from the bar in protest. The registers of the Parlement refute this assertion.

[84]See the speeches made by the barristers in *Journal de ce qui s'est passé à l'occasion du rétablissement du Parlement . . .* (n.p., n.d.).

[85]Tournier, *Le Mesmérisme à Toulouse*, p. 70.

the crown's anger against resisting barristers: in Paris, a strike at the bar had been met by allowing attorneys to assume the title and functions of the advocates.[86] Finally, and most important, thirty-seven magistrates had capitulated and were serving the Chancellor. With the magistrates weak and divided, the barristers could hardly have offered effective resistance. They were not daring enough, at this point, to act alone.

The absence of organized resistance did not preclude subtle friction between the bar and the new court. Outwardly, the Maupeou court functioned smoothly. Under the surface, however, there were indications of tensions and anxieties about the loyalty of court personnel. The barristers and attorneys refused to maintain their usual formal discipline in the new court; they stopped wearing their professional robes until they were ordered to do so by the Parlement.[87] Moreover, the court seemed particularly active in attempting to win the favor of the bar—as if it were insecure about the barristers' support. It vigorously suppressed an anonymous pamphlet that mocked the barristers.[88] The First President, hoping to win the favor of the younger pleaders—who tended to be the fomenters of resistance—requested attorneys to give them cases.[89] Finally, the Parlement admitted two practicing advocates to the bench. The admission of two wealthy and noble barristers, Pierre Théodore Delort and Jean Baptiste Lapomerède de Laviguerie,[90] hardly signaled a profound change in the recruitment policy, but it did indicate a limited receptivity to talent. This came in the fourth year in the court's existence and may have represented the ultimate concession to the barristers in an attempt to secure their loyalty.[91]

The evident insecurity of the Maupeou parlement indicates that the barristers accepted the Maupeou coup with resignation, just as they later claimed. They displayed their loyalty to the old Parlement even more forcefully by not taking up practice at the new Superior Council at Nîmes. This court, with its large jurisdiction, might have been attractive to Toulousan barristers, especially with the over-crowding at the bar in Toulouse. Yet, only three young barristers, Claude Castor Bragouse, Joseph Monyer, and Antoine Chas, associated themselves

[86]Jean Fournel, *Histoire des avocats au Parlement et du barreau de Paris*, 2 vols. (Paris, 1813), 2: 479-81.

[87]Soulié, *Coup judiciaire*, p. 73.

[88]Florentin Astre, *Les procureurs près le Parlement de Toulouse* (Toulouse, 1858), p. 25.

[89]Soulié, *Coup judiciaire*, p. 69.

[90]Robert de Roton, *Les arrêts du Grand Conseil portant dispense du marc d'or de noblesse* (Paris, 1951), p. 76.

[91]In Grenoble, the barristers pressured the Parlement to admit some of their colleagues. See Jean Egret, *Le Parlement de Daupiné et les affaires publiques . . .* , 2 vols. (Grenoble, 1942), 1: 293. There is no evidence that Toulousan barristers made the same demands.

with the new Council.[92] The attorneys' rate of defection was much higher: twelve of the hundred or so went to practice in Nîmes.[93] Thus, the fervent claims of fidelity which barristers made when the old Parlement was restored were sincere.

At the very end of the Old Regime, the barristers' loyalty was tested once again, this time under circumstances that bolstered their courage and audacity. Royal authority had been seriously shaken by the Assembly of Notables and by the exposure of the crown's financial difficulties. Just then, the Parlements faced the most serious threat to their autonomy and status from the Lamoignon Edict.[94] On 8 May 1788 the count of Périgord constrained the Toulousan Parlement to register this edict, which transferred the right to remonstrate to a single Plenary Court in Paris, drastically reduced the jurisdiction of the Parlements, and created new, rival tribunals, the *Grands Bailliages*. This law understandably caused great consternation among the Sovereign Court personnel. Some magistrates tried to protest, and the parlementaires were soon exiled.

The atmosphere of political crisis and the ferocity of the attack on their court united the Toulousan bar in militant defense of the Parlement: the barristers took decisive action. On 17 May, the *batonnier* of the Order visited the First President to promise him the fidelity of the bar. The barristers took an oath to reject all offers of places in the Grand Bailliage and to expel from the Order any barrister who disobeyed "as having broken the links that attach him to an association the essence of which consists of . . . delicacy and honor."[95] The Order then sent a protest to Lamoignon, Keeper of the Seals.[96] Such action was bold and self-sacrificing. Not only did the barristers carry out the protest without the organized support of the parlementaires, but the oath they took excluded them from ennobling offices in the Grand Bailliage. This was a considerable sacrifice to make and attests to the depths of their devotion to the Parlement in this crisis.

Individual barristers took the protest against the May Edict much further. Three in particular, Joseph Marie Duroux, Alexandre Jamme, and Jean Baptiste Lafage, assumed the lead in organizing public opinion against the judicial coup and against the Grand Bailliage. These distinguished advocates edited a newspaper (*Nouvelles affiches*

[92]*A.D.*, B–registre d'enregistrement des lettres patents (especially fol. 65); B–plumitif civil des audiences du Conseil de Nîmes (1771–1775). Bragouse became Substitute to the Attorney-General at this court. The other two were barristers.

[93]Astre, *Procureurs*, p. 34.

[94]On the background to the May Edict, see Jean Egret, *La Pré-Révolution française (1787–1788)* (Paris, 1962).

[95]Cited in Axel Duboul, *La fin du Parlement de Toulouse* (Toulouse, 1890), p. 29.

[96]*Lettre des avocats au Parlement de Toulouse, à Monseigneur le Garde des Sceaux . . .* , (n.p., n.d.).

et courier récréatif) which violently attacked the new tribunal and the ministers. So furious was their rhetoric that they were summoned to Paris where, presumably, the Bastille awaited them.[97] However, the crown was forced to revoke the May Edict before the barristers were punished, and they returned to Toulouse in triumph. Their entry into the city was the occasion for public celebration, and a medal was struck declaring them "defenders of the *Patrie*." A "patriotic feast" was held in their honor at the home of Count Jean Dubarry, and poems glorified their names and deeds.[98] In the celebration and excitement, the political significance of the event was lost. For the first time, barristers emerged as the most articulate and forceful defenders of the Parlement and constitutional forms. They no longer hid behind the magistrates.[99] In political crisis, the barristers finally found the courage and independence to act as boldly as the magistrates. From then on, barristers intervened forcefully in national political struggles.

The entire Toulousan legal world was not, however, united in the defense of the Parlement. Even among the barristers there was not complete fidelity: three advocates were suspected of betraying the Sovereign Court. Bertrand Merle and François Senovert, as capitouls, allegedly tried to dissuade the Municipal Council from protesting against the Lamoignon Edict.[100] Michel Malpel supposedly aided the count of Périgord in the forced registration of the Edict. Malpel and Senovert were placed on trial before their peers, but lack of evidence or the unwillingness of a majority of barristers to attack their colleagues —especially since the Parlement had been restored—secured them acquittal.[101] However, so emotional was this issue of loyalty for a number of barristers that they broke with their Order and campaigned for the punishment of Malpel. Ultimately, forty-eight barristers joined this vehemently pro-parlementaire faction, including Duroux, Jamme, Lafage, and many of the younger pleaders.[102] The schism was a serious matter that generated a great deal of hostility.[103] The bar—this cohesive group of colleagues, friends, and relatives—had rarely been so divided.

[97]Jean-Baptiste Dubédat, *Histoire du Parlement de Toulouse*, 2 vols. (Paris, 1885), 2: 676; Duboul, *Fin du Parlement*, p. 35. No copies of the newspaper have survived.

[98]*Couplets à l'occasion de la fête patriotique donnée par M. le Comte J. Dubarry . . . ;* Duboul, *Fin du Parlement*, p. 39.

[99]This was the case in Grenoble, too. See Egret, *Le Parlement de Dauphiné*, 2: 360.

[100]Gustave Baudens, "Les brochures et l'état des esprits à la veille de la Révolution," *Recueil de législation de Toulouse* 6 (1910): 344.

[101]*A.M.*, AA-100, *Principes, progrès et suite de scission* . . . , pp. 2-3; Baudens, "Les brochures," p. 345.

[102]*A.M.*, AA-100. For a list of barristers who joined this faction, see *A.D.*, E-26542, deliberations of the Order of Barristers (8 mars 1789).

[103]For example, Duroux expelled the barrister Chas from his private law conferences because he joined the opposing faction. See *A.M.*, AA-100, *Principes, progrès* . . . , p. 4.

If, in this controversy, the bar displayed varying degrees of loyalty to the Parlement, none of the barristers (except, perhaps, Malpel, Senovert, or Merle) made any attempt to gain personally from the May Edict. Not one practicing barrister even solicited a magistracy in the Grand Bailliage, though barristers would have been obvious candidates,[104] nor did any barrister plead before the new tribunal.[105] The veritable "traitors" to the Parlement were the members of the Seneschal Court of Toulouse. The judges of this court registered the Lamoignon Edict with hardly a word of protest[106] and then accepted places on the bench of the Grand Bailliage. The barristers and attorneys of the Seneschal Court became the practitioners at the new tribunal.[107] No barrister of the Parlement did anything comparable to support the enemies of the Sovereign Court.

The May Edict revealed a deep rift in the Toulousan legal world, between the personnel of the Parlement and that of the Seneschal Court. This antagonism was a long-standing one, based on rivalries and tensions of several kinds.[108] The Parlement had always opposed royal edicts which expanded the competence of the Seneschal Court and had never favored the *sénéchausée* in jurisdictional disputes. Moreover, the personnel of the lesser tribunal suffered constant humiliation at the hands of those attached to the Parlement. Magistrates and barristers at the *Palais* did not hide their contempt for the men of the Seneschal Court. Pleaders at the Parlement did not even recognize the barristers of the *sénéchausée* as colleagues and social equals, and they excluded them from their Order and from their Masonic lodges. Furthermore, advocates of these two courts competed for clients, public dignities, and prestige. The events of 1788 offered the Seneschal Court personnel an opportunity to settle old grievances.

The developments following the Lamoignon Edict marked an important stage in the political history of the Toulousan legal world. In the face of catastrophe for the Parlement, barristers became forceful and visible leaders of public protest. Though there were a few defections, most advocates refused to consider their personal advantages

---

[104]*A.D.*, C-62, letter of Subdelegate Ginisty to Intendant, 10 August 1788; letter of 20 August 1788. Jean Alayrac, a former barrister at the Seneschal Court, then a subdelegate, requested a magistracy.

[105]*A.D.*, B–registers of Grand Bailliage.

[106]Duboul, *Fin du Parlement*, pp. 30–31. For the reaction of the other Seneschal Courts of the region, see *Recueil de toutes les pièces qui constatent ce qui s'est passé au Parlement de Toulouse le 3 mai jusqu'au 20 octobre*, (n.p., 1789).

[107]*A.D.*, B–registers of the Grand Bailliage.

[108]The Seneschal Court had been disloyal to the Parlement at the time of the Maupeou coup. See Dubédat, *Histoire du Parlement*, 2: 605.

and, instead, championed the Sovereign Court. On the other hand, the Seneschal Court personnel emerged as the leading opponents of the Parlement. Such was the alignment of forces in 1788. It remains to be seen whether the same loyalties and rivalries prevailed as France prepared for its "regeneration" in 1789.

VI

THE TOULOUSAN BARRISTERS
IN THE REVOLUTION
(1788-1793)

Debate over the identity and motivations of the "revolutionary bourgeoisie" has been intense since Alfred Cobban attacked the "orthodox" interpretation nearly twenty years ago. Nevertheless, scholars on all sides of this debate have assumed that barristers and other legal men played an important revolutionary role—though their views vary in emphasis and shading, to be sure. For Georges Lefebvre, these men "laid the intellectual foundations of, and then guided, the Revolution."[1] Cobban described the cataclysm of 1789 as an upheaval created by "lawyers," landowners, and civil servants.[2] Prompting this agreement was the preponderance of barristers in the national leadership of the Revolution. Nearly a fourth of the Constituent Assembly and a similar proportion of "patriot" deputies in 1791, the men who gave the new France its basic direction, were *avocats*.[3] A quarter of the National Convention, too, and outstanding figures in both the Constituent and the Convention, had served the bars of France during the Old Regime.[4] However, it remains for us to question just how representative these national leaders actually were and to examine, on a local level, the behavior of the barristers in face of revolutionary change.

[1]Georges Lefebvre, *The French Revolution*, trans. E. M. Evanson, 2 vols. (New York, 1962), 1:45. The quotation refers broadly to all legal professionals, including *avocats*.
[2]Alfred Cobban, *The Social Interpretation of the French Revolution* (Cambridge, 1964), chap. 6. J. M. Thompson, Albert Goodwin, and François Furet also stress the role of "lawyers." Alison Patrick has recently emphasized the need to study lawyers in *The Men of the First French Republic* (Baltimore, 1972), pp. 261, 273.
[3]Philip Dawson, *Provincial Magistrates and Revolutionary Politics in France, 1789-1795* (Cambridge, Mass., 1972), p. 238; Robert R. Palmer, "Sur la composition sociale de la Gauche à la Constituante," *Annales historiques de la Révolution française* 31 (1959): 154-56.
[4]Alfred Cobban, *The Myth of the French Revolution* (London, 1955), appendix.

THE PRE-REVOLUTION IN TOULOUSE

The most significant phenomenon in France from September 1788 to the Revolution itself was the rise of the political struggle between the Third Estate and the nobility. By the winter of 1788-89, the controversies over representation to the Estates-General and to the provincial Estates had engendered a consciousness of the separate—if not conflicting—interests of nobles and commoners.[5] The violence that erupted in Rennes between law students and supporters of the nobles electrified public opinion, and the general resistance to vote by head mounted by the nobility hardened commoners in their determination to gain greater voice in public affairs.[6] In January 1789, Abbé Sieyès proclaimed to France that the Third Estate was "everything" while the nobles alone were "nothing."

In Toulouse, as elsewhere, the barristers played an active and visible role in prerevolutionary events.[7] Ultimately, most of them would support the rising demands of the Third Estate and many would welcome the events of July 1789. But they did so quietly, sometimes timidly, acting more as "barristers" than as "commoners." There were important reasons why the advocates were not among the vociferous challengers of the "privileged" orders, who had appeared elsewhere in France that winter. One reason was the local political context created by the struggle to reform the Estates of Languedoc.[8] Here, the reform movement was a cooperative effort among the orders, so it did not engender conflict and distrust between commoners and nobles. But even more fundamental in shaping the politics and attitudes of the Toulousan barristers were their persistent ties of loyalty to the Parlement and their identification with its magistrates. Neither the prerevolutionary political situation nor the political mentality of the advocates was conducive to the development of an aggressive "patriot" movement at the Toulousan bar.

Languedoc possessed the most active provincial Estates in France. They were composed not of elected representatives but of men who had

---

[5] Jean Egret, *La Pré-Révolution française (1787-1788)* (Paris, 1962), pp. 338-51.

[6] Jean Egret, "Les origines de la Révolution en Bretagne (1788-1789)," *Revue historique* 213 (1955): 189-215.

[7] Jean Egret has provided several local studies of the pre-Revolution: "La Révolution aristocratique en Franche-Comté et son échec," *Revue d'histoire moderne et contemporaine* 1 (1954): 245-71; "La pré-révolution en Provence," *Annales historiques de la Révolution française* 26 (1954): 97-126; see, too, Egret's article (cited above) on Brittany.

[8] This reform movement has been treated by Pierre-Henri Thore "L'union dans la lutte contre les Etats de Languedoc," in *Congrès régional des Fédérations historiques de Languedoc. Carcassonne* (1952), pp. 225-42. Thore has not examined this movement in a comparative framework.

a right to attend the Estates by virtue of their rank. Included in them were three archbishops, the bishops of twenty designated sees, and twenty-three barons, while commoners were represented by sixty-eight deputies from specified cities, which usually sent their municipal officers.[9] The Estates of Languedoc differed from their counterparts in other provinces in that they were not patently dominated by the nobility. The commoners outnumbered the privileged orders and, in fact, proponents elsewhere of the doubling of the Third Estate in the Estates-General cited the Languedoc assembly as a precedent.[10] The structure of this organization precluded struggles between commoners and nobles for control of the provincial bodies like those that had occurred in Brittany and Provence. Demands for reorganization came from the privileged orders in Languedoc, who argued that the existing Estates represented no one well, and the Third Estate merely cooperated with them.

Dissatisfaction with the provincial assembly crystallized after the royal announcement of an Estates-General in September (1788). The claim of the Estates of Languedoc to select deputies to Versailles provoked the attack.[11] The Parlement of Toulouse, hostile to the Estates in any case, was among the first to protest.[12] By a decree of 24 October, the parlementaires declared that "the first two orders are without true representatives at the Estates" and, therefore, assemblies of the *sénéchausée* ought to select the deputies to Versailles.[13] In January the Parlement repeated its plea and, this time, requested the king to call a special assembly of the three orders to reorganize the Estates.[14] Soon afterward, the nobles of Toulouse assembled and made a similar request for an extraordinary assembly.[15] The *Cour des Comptes* of Montpellier and the nobles of Béziers and Carcassonne joined the attack.[16] Thus, in Languedoc, nobles led the move to reform the provincial Estates.

The argument that no order was properly represented in the Estates drew commoners into the reform movement—but as associates, not opponents, of the privileged orders. The merchants of Toulouse were

---

[9]Maurice Chauvet, *Pages d'histoire du Languedoc* (Nice, 1967), pp. 266–67.

[10]Georges Lefebvre, *The Coming of the French Revolution*, trans R. R. Palmer (Princeton, 1947), p. 55.

[11]Thore, "L'union dans la lutte," pp. 225–26.

[12]The "barons" of the Estates attempted to exclude parlementaires from their assembly.

[13]Armand Brette, ed., *Recueil de documents relatifs à la convocation des Etats Généraux de 1789*, 4 vols. (Paris, 1894–1915), 1:164.

[14]*Ibid.*

[15]*A.M.*, AA-318, *Arrêtés de l'Assemblée de la Noblesse du diocèse de Toulouse (du 13 janvier, 1789).*

[16]Brette, *Recueil de documents*, 1:166–68.

among the first to protest.[17] In late January, and again in February, the various corporate bodies of Toulouse sent representatives to an assembly of the Third Estate. Just as in the struggle against the May Edict, barristers played an extremely prominent role in forming public opinion and directing public action. The advocate and law professor Jean Laurens Rigaud was elected president of the assembly, and Jamme, already a hero for his defense of the Parlement, became "Orator of the People."[18] In this capacity he was the principal speaker at the assembly and, more importantly, he expressed the official opinions of the Third Estate of Toulouse during the following crucial months. When a special deputy was needed to represent the assembly at Versailles, Jean Baptiste Viguier, the leading Toulousan barrister, was selected as "an unequivocal mark of the confidence which we have in his patriotic zeal."[19] The assembly also established an intermediary commission to carry on its battle against the Estates; on this committee were Jamme, Viguier, Rigaud, Jean Jacques Mousinat, and Claude Castor Bragouse. In the end, all but one advocate at the assembly served in some official capacity.

This general absence of antagonism among orders was important in forming the political atmosphere. Elsewhere, the attempt to reform the provincial Estates reinforced and intensified local conflict over the organization of the Estates-General, but this was not the case in Toulouse. At any rate, the effort lost its force when, in mid-February, the king decreed that the general assembly of the sénéchausée would select deputies to the Estates-General.[20] Public attention now turned to the problems of choosing deputies for Versailles and drafting grievance lists (*cahiers de doléances*).

In this phase of the pre-Revolution, too, the barristers were hardly audacious champions of the Third Estate against the privileged orders. Most barristers desired conciliation and concession from all sides, and some even defended the parlementaires against attacks from other commoners. It was not surprising that the magistrates themselves pressed for the selection of three advocates, Jamme, Duroux, and Lafage, as deputies to Versailles.[21] These men, noted for their heroic

---

[17]Thore, "L'union dans la lutte," p. 227.

[18]*Procès-verbal de l'Assemblée générale de tous les ordres et corporations formant le Tiers Etat* . . . *(19 janvier, 1789); A.D.*, L-2155, *Procès-verbal de l'Assemblée générale* . . . *(6 février, 1789).*

[19]*A.D.*, L-2155, *Procès-verbal de l'Assemblée générale de l'Ordre du Tiers Etat* . . . *(17 février, 1789),* p. 14.

[20]Brette, *Recueil de documents*, 1:162.

[21]See the pamphlet, signed by Veritas, entitled *Lettre d'un habitant de Toulouse à un habitant de Rabasten, du 30 mars, 1789*, pp. 2, 6.

defense of the Parlement in May, could be relied upon to protect the interests of the Sovereign Court. Duroux and two other prominent pleaders, Roucoule and Savy, may have reflected the opinion of a sizeable number of colleagues when they recommended a parlementaire as deputy for the Third Estate of Toulouse, arguing in a pamphlet that the magistrates had always served commoners well by opposing unjust taxes.[22] Thus, the local aristocracy found useful allies among the barristers. No other commoners seemed to speak in their favor.

Resistance to the influence of parlementaires over the selection of deputies came not from barristers but from the officers of the Seneschal Court.[23] Their traditional hostility to the Parlement extended into this prerevolutionary period. These officers wrote pamphlets that attacked the court and encouraged commoners to see the magistrates as their enemies. They also circulated handbills denouncing the favorites of the Parlement, Duroux, Jamme, and Lafage, as unsuitable deputies.[24] As we shall see, the Seneschal Court officers were largely successful in arousing resistance to the will of the Parlement.

Despite the intensity of the debate between commoners and nobles all over France concerning the reform of the provincial Estates and representation in the Estates-General, this class conflict was *not* the dominant issue at the Toulousan bar. This was demonstrated by the rift in the Order of Barristers that occurred in March.[25] With the sovereign courts of France under attack as the defenders of the privileged orders, we might have supposed that this schism occurred between the supporters of the Parlement and its newly-declared enemies: an "aristocrat-patriot" struggle in microcosm. Instead, it was a manifestation of traditional issues and attitudes: corporate solidarity, fidelity to the magistrates, and disagreement over the legal nature of the Order of Barristers itself. The basis of the dispute concerned Michel Malpel's exoneration from the charge of "treason" to the Parlement.[26] The barristers favorable to Malpel were not enemies of the parlementaires, even in this period of interorder confrontation. They opposed the May Edict, calling it an "unhappy revolution," and praised the magistrates' "courage and patriotic virtues."[27] Théodore Sudre and Jean Bernard Bellomaire, both ardent supporters of the parlementaires

---

[22]Baron R. de Bouglon, *Les reclus de Toulouse sous la Terreur*, 3 vols. (Toulouse, 1912), 3:20. The pamphlet itself is lost.
[23]Veritas, *Lettre d'un habitant de Toulouse*, p. 2. In the Franche-Comté, too, the Seneschal Court officers led the attack on the Parlement. See Egret, "La Révolution aristocratique," p. 264.
[24]Veritas, *Lettre d'un habitant de Toulouse*, p. 6.
[25]See pp. 145–47 for the origins of this schism.
[26]*A.M.*, AA–100, *Principe, progrès, et suite de la scission. . . .*
[27]*Ibid.*, pp. 1–2.

on the municipal councils, joined the side of the "traitor" Malpel.[28] Sudre would later unite with the magistrates in opposing the Revolution. So would Jean Joseph Berger, Jean Baptiste Estingoy, Jean Raymond Bastoulh, and Jean Joseph Tremolières; yet, in the spring of 1789, they all defended Malpel.[29] On the other hand, the anti-Malpel group included a number of future revolutionaries, who would soon favor the suppression of the Parlement and even the persecution of the magistrates. Jean Baptiste Mailhe, the rising barrister, academician, and progressive thinker, was among the enemies of Malpel. In 1790, however, Mailhe would be the first to denounce the parlementaires as public enemies.[30] Among the defenders of the Parlement were also François Beral, Jacques Floret, Jean Joseph Janole, Jean Jacques Mousinat, and Bernard Etienne Arbanere, all of whom supported a Revolution that attacked the Sovereign Court.[31] This alignment is inexplicable if seen in terms of an interorder conflict. The sides which barristers chose had more to do with protecting the "independence" of the profession, solidarity with a colleague, or belief in Malpel's innocence. Traditional loyalties and issues were still important to them. They did not see the political world as divided into friends and enemies of the Third Estate.

When the assemblies of the Third Estate met in early March, they were subjected to the subtle and not-so-subtle pressures of interested persons and groups. The Parlement, so influential in the city, had its three favorites, Jamme, Duroux, and Lafage selected as deputies.[32] In the larger assembly for the sénéchausée, however, the magistrates had much less power; none of these three was selected to represent Toulouse in the Estates-General. Both Jamme and Duroux had been among the most prominent Toulousans during the prerevolutionary period, and the inhabitants were accustomed to looking to them for leadership. Undoubtedly, each had a right to expect that the Third Estate would again turn to him for direction. The failure to select either one as a deputy to Versailles was probably a conscious effort on the part of the Third Estate to avoid men who were too closely allied to the parlementaires. The campaign of the Seneschal Court officers and other opponents of the Sovereign Court had prevailed. Barristers did figure prominently on the list of eight deputies from the sénéchausée of

[28]See *A.D.*, C-287, letter of Marquis de Belesta to Intendant, 29 November 1783. Both barristers are named as supporters of the Parlement in the Municipal Council.

[29]For a list of barristers in the pro-Malpel faction, see *A.D.*, L-223, "Délégués désignés par plusieurs avocats. . . ."

[30]*Journal universel et affiches de Toulouse et du Languedoc*, no 41 (13 October 1790).

[31]For a list of anti-Malpel barristers, see, A.D., 3E-26542, *Délibérations de l'Ordre des avocats* (8 mars, 1789).

[32]See *A.D.*, L-223, "Protestation de plusieurs députés. . . ."

Toulouse, but these were not the ones who were particularly associated with the magistrates. Two of the three Toulousan residents sent to Versailles were barristers: Jean Jacques Mousinat and Jean Baptiste Viguier.[33] Both had gained some public attention in the movement to reform the Estates of Languedoc. In addition, the advocate Jean Hebrard was the alternate deputy. The Third Estate as a whole was more conscious of conflict with the privileged orders than were the barristers alone, so the sénéchausée assembly rejected the favorites of the Parlement.

This affront to the Sovereign Court did not go unchallenged, however. The capitouls, probably led by Duroux himself, charged that there were "irregularities" in the selection of deputies. The case came quickly before the Parlement, which would have harassed its enemies had not the king called the case to the Royal Council.[34] The Sovereign Court of Languedoc was apparently ready to assert its traditional authority, even in a rapidly changing political context.

If the magistrates failed to prevail in the selection of the deputies, at least they had some influence over the drafting of the cahier. The agent of the parlementaires in this matter was the barrister Jamme. As Orator of the People, he wrote the cahier for the city of Toulouse.[35] Well-disposed toward the magistrates, he penned proposals that were conciliatory to the Second Estate.[36] Two weeks later, the Third Estate of the sénéchausée wrote its cahier, and Jamme, along with Duroux, Lafage, and other barristers, served on the commission charged with this task.[37] It is not surprising that this second cahier resembled Jamme's work very closely. Thirty-five of the forty-five grievances in the sénéchausée cahier were the same as, or similar to, the ones penned by Jamme.[38] The other commissioners altered or amended Jamme's cahier somewhat—often to the disadvantage of the magistrates—but his essentially conciliatory tone and demands remained. The magistrates' influence was great enough to provoke complaints from their opponents. One anonymous pamphlet charged that the magistrates, capitouls, barristers, clergy, and nobles prevented the Third Estate from expressing its true views,[39] and the former Seneschal Court officer

---

[33]Viguier was most probably selected because he was already in Paris. It is not clear whether or not Toulousans understood his views on the public issues.

[34]Brette, Recueil de documents, 1:175–76.

[35]See his claim in his open letter, Aux maire et officiers municipaux, aux autorités constitués . . . , found in the B.M.T. pamphlet collection.

[36]His cahier will receive greater attention later in this chapter.

[37]A.M., AA–318, Cahiers des plaintes et doléances de la sénéchausée de Toulouse.

[38]For Jamme's cahier, see A.M., AA–95, Cahier des plaintes et doléances de la ville et banlieu de Toulouse.

[39]Le Toulousain à Versailles, chargé de présenter au Roi . . . doléances de ses concitoyens. This is in the B.M.T. pamphlet collection.

François Corail (de St. Foi) later claimed to have led commoners in the struggle to reveal their true grievances against the wishes of the Parlement.[40]

Thus, throughout the prerevolutionary period, the barristers had not broken with the Parlement. Bertrand Barère, it is true, had decided by the summer of 1788 that the Sovereign Courts must be undermined;[41] but he—the most radical thinker at the Toulousan bar, then in the thick of Parisian politics—was the exception. In Toulouse, aggressive attempts to limit the influence of the parlementaires could not be expected from the bar; these efforts had to come from elsewhere, especially from the Seneschal Court. If there were some advocates of the Parlement who sided with the Seneschal Court officers, their role was very obscure. Most barristers desired, above all else, cooperation from all groups as France began the momentous task of social and political reorganization.

THE BARRISTERS' PROGRAM FOR SOCIAL AND POLITICAL CHANGE

There were few moments in French history when so many men deliberated on public affairs and possible reforms as in the spring of 1789. The pamphlet war and the need to draft cahiers compelled men to think systematically about national needs. The convocation of the Estates-General opened entirely unprecedented possibilities for redistributing taxes and public responsibilities. Understandably, latent issues and demands now came to the surface. Unfortunately, we possess few direct expressions of the barristers' opinions at this crucial time. The cahier of the Order of Advocates is missing, as are the grievance lists which advocates may have written as seigneurial officers for villages.[42] Still, we do have the writings of three influential barristers, Jamme, Duroux, and Rouzet, each of whom took a very different political stance after July 1789. Together, they permit us to assess the quality of changes deemed desirable or acceptable at the bar as a whole.

The surviving documents demonstrate that the barristers were in essential agreement about the social and political changes that France required. All three barristers recognized the need to abolish hereditary privileges and to give greater dignity and opportunity to commoners.

[40]*A.D.*, L-298, dossier of Corail.

[41]Leo Gershoy, *Bertrand Barère, A Reluctant Terrorist* (Princeton, 1962), p. 55. Barère had left Toulouse for Paris, and this undoubtedly gave him a different perspective on events.

[42]The surviving cahiers from the parishes in the region have been compiled in Félix Pasquier and François Galabert, eds., *Cahiers paroissiaux des sénéchausées de Toulouse et de Comminges en 1789* (Toulouse, 1928) and Daniel Ligou, ed., *Cahiers de doléances du Tiers Etat du pays et jugerie du Rivère-Verdun* (Paris, 1961).

At the same time, these advocates remained friendly toward the parlementaires, mindful of their interests and careful not to undermine their pre-eminence. Any disagreement among barristers involved tactics rather than substance. How aggressive did commoners have to be to assure the needed reforms? Was "vote by head" necessary? Barristers had different answers to these matters of strategy, but there seemed to be a consensus on what the Estates-General needed to accomplish.

Jamme's cahier was an amalgam of his hopes for substantial change and also for the protection of vested interests,[43] and his recommendations were always moderate and conciliatory. In view of his previously-stated skepticism about the benefits of religious orders, one might have expected Jamme to demand their suppression.[44] But it was typical of his approach to reform that he desired the coming Estates only to "render religion more useful to the State." He had also expressed discontent with civil and criminal laws in the past, but his language in 1789 was moderate and vague. Jamme asked only that these laws be "rectified." Was his reticence on this issue an attempt to avoid offending the parlementaires, who did not include a demand for law reform in the noble cahier? Jamme also lamented the degradation of the Church, and he called for an end to plurality of benefices, huge court pensions, and harsh military discipline.

This barrister's treatment of privilege illustrated both his concern for reform and his consideration of established interests. Jamme recognized that privileges of all kinds were both unjust and deleterious to society, but he applied this principle in a tactful and conciliatory manner where the parlementaires were concerned. He did demand equality of taxation, but it was already clear that the Toulousan nobles would concede this. In fact, Jamme led the commoners' delegation to the assembly of nobles to thank them for "the sacrifices they were willing to make of their fiscal privileges."[45] Though Jamme wanted royal *collèges* open to commoners, he would still leave half the places in these schools to nobles. He avoided conflict with noble opinion about seigneurial reforms by not mentioning the subject. Jamme's dual—indeed, contradictory—concern for a more open society *and* for the magistrates' interests appears most clearly in his treatment of venality. Jamme demanded that all public positions be accessible to persons of merit, but he made no general attack on venal offices. His cahier specifically requested that prelatures and church benefices be

---

[43]*A.M.*, AA–95, *Cahier des plaintes . . . de la ville et banlieu de Toulouse* (17 mars, 1789). All quotes come from this cahier.

[44]See chap. 4 for Jamme's religious opinions.

[45]*A.D.*, L–223, *Procès-verbal, mandat, et cahier des doléances de la Noblesse de la sénéchausée de Toulouse*, p. 2.

opened to all, but he did not refer to judicial positions.[46] Evidently, Jamme was attempting to steer an uneasy course between the condemnation of exclusive privilege and the safeguarding of the parlementaires' position.[47]

This friend of the magistrates undoubtedly found it easier to reconcile his dual concerns when he turned to constitutional questions. Jamme did not request the vote by head at the Estates-General, a demand which the nobility had firmly rejected. But he did want a doubling of the Third Estate representation (and he had earlier specified that the provincial Estates should be modeled on those of Dauphiné, where vote by head prevailed). Consent by the "nation" for taxation, freedom of the press, and the abolition of the *lettre de cachet* were reforms Jamme expressed along with the nobility. Following the nobles' cahier, he wanted the Parlement affirmed as part of the constitution and the magistracies declared irremovable. To further safeguard the Sovereign Court, he desired that the right of Toulouse to have a Parlement be confirmed.[48] Jamme evidently believed that commoners and nobles were ready to cooperate in effecting the reforms France most needed.

The social and political views of Joseph Marie Duroux differed from those of Jamme in some important ways, but always on matters of strategy, not substance.[49] Their disagreement arose from differences in temperament, not from divergencies in social outlook and "class consciousness." Duroux was bolder and more independent than his colleague Jamme. Duroux had twice been reprimanded and fined by the Parlement, once for opposing the court in the Municipal Council and once for slanderous language in a legal brief. He had even been daring enough to oppose royal nominations for capitoul. Yet he was, like Jamme, conciliatory to the nobility even when he claimed to identify with the Third Estate and support its interests.

As a capitoul and a *seigneur*, Duroux might have attended the noble assembly—his son sat there—but he chose to be among the commoners, probably expecting to be their leader.[50] Duroux went beyond Jamme by advocating voting by head at the Estates-General. He also expressed the

---

[46]*A.M.*, AA–95, *Cahier des plaintes* . . . , p. 6.

[47]The commoners in the *sénéchausée* assembly used Jamme's cahier as a base, but they rejected his ambivalence toward privilege. Not only did they demand the abolition of certain seigneurial rights, but they wanted "to admit all citizens to military and civil places, *notably to the offices of the magistrature*" (italics mine). See *A.D.* L–318, *Cahier des plaintes et doléances de la sénéchausée de Toulouse* . . . , p. 10.

[48]*A.M.*, AA–95, *Cahier des plaintes*, pp. 3, 4, 7–10.

[49]His proposals can be found in the *Discours prononcé par M. Duroux, avocat au Parlement et capitoul, dans l'assemblée tenue par le Tiers Etat de la Ville de Toulouse, le 10 mars, 1789.*

[50]For those who attended the assembly of nobles, see *A.D.*, L–223.

hope that new laws would remove from commoners "the discouraging and degrading stain which centuries of barbarism imprinted on the Third Estate."[51] He demanded that all public offices be open to the qualified and that fiscal exemptions be abolished. For all his concern that commoners receive greater respect and opportunity, however, Duroux did not want to undermine the nobility. He addressed the Second Estate as the "ancient nobility accustomed to devoting your lives to the support of the Throne and to the well-being of the State." He assured nobles that his attack on fiscal privileges "should carry no danger to those of dignity" and affirmed that the vote by head "was not contrary to the reciprocal rights of the three orders."[52] Ultimately, Duroux seemed to desire the preservation of honorific privileges within a society that was open to the talent of commoners.

Though Duroux and Jamme were to turn against the Revolution by the winter of 1789, their general social outlook, reforms, and tone were still similar to those of one advocate who became a very active revolutionary. This was Jacques Marie Rouzet, who produced a pamphlet offering advice to the Third Estate on the eve of the Revolution.[53] Rouzet's career demonstrated that he possessed uncommon talent, ambition, and resourcefulness.[54] The son of a tailor, he rose to an important place at the bar, with a large practice in Toulouse and distinguished clients in Paris. Using his contacts in Paris and Versailles, he became involved in a lucrative financial venture at the end of the Old Regime. Rouzet's career after 1789 was equally impressive. Judge at the Civil Tribunal of Foix and professor of law at Toulouse, he also served as president of the District and was a deputy to the National Convention. When he was imprisoned during the Terror, Rouzet's resourcefulness and ability aided him once again. He used his incarceration to make important contacts: with the patronage of the Orléans family, Rouzet ended his life as the count de Folmont. Certainly, Rouzet knew how to seize upon events and turn the vicissitudes of politics to his advantage. Yet, his pamphlet displayed none of the angry attacks on privilege that we might have expected from a "self-made" man born of the *peuple*. Instead, Rouzet's work was a sober and serious analysis of privileges based on law and history. His learned tone accompanied modest proposals shaped by law and

[51]Duroux, *Discours*, p. 4.
[52]*Ibid.*, pp. 4–5.
[53]The pamphlet, entitled *Etrenne pour l'année 1789, ou Almanach historique à l'usage du Tiers Etat*, was published anonymously. I have not been able to locate the pamphlet either in Toulouse or Paris. Fortunately, the Toulousan *érudit*, Dr. Louis de Santi, left notes on this work: see *B.M.T.*, MS. 1324. Quotations in the following paragraph are from Dr. de Santi's notes.
[54]See Pierre Archès, "Les origines du conventionnel toulousain Jacques-Marie Rouzet," *Annales du midi* 83 (1971): 431–39.

precedent, not abstract reason. Rouzet recognized privileges as "political absurdities," but unreasonableness was not sufficient grounds for suppression. His approach is best illustrated by the treatment of ecclesiastical taxation, an important problem in this pamphlet. Rouzet examined the historical basis for clerical exemption from taxation and concluded that the Romans recognized no such privilege.[55] He then turned to canon law to show that it did not recognize fiscal exemption, but even this did not settle the question for him. Adhering strictly to the law, he recognized that privileges were granted by the king and could only be revoked by him. He therefore counseled the Third Estate to

respect the work of our sovereign in privileges and, while waiting for the king himself to carry the flame of wisdom to abuses, let us remind the *privilégiés* that . . . history offers us . . . perfect equality of all citizens.

Thus, Rouzet denied the right of the nation assembled to suppress privileges on its own authority. Moreover, he supplemented these legal arguments with a social argument that demonstrates his essentially conservative intentions: "The *menu peuple* is more easily retained in dependence when it sees itself treated as well as the great."

A second issue treated in Rouzet's pamphlet was the position of the Third Estate in the body politic. The barrister's ire had been aroused by aristocratic pamphleteers who insisted that commoners were descendants of slaves. This claim, however, did not convert Rouzet to the position of Sieyès. Rouzet remained moderate in his aims and legalistic in his approach. Using law instead of reason, he attempted to show, not that commoners were "everything," but that they were worthy of respect.

That each of these barristers—so different in personality, family background, and later involvement in the Revolution—had such similar views strongly implies a consensus on moderate reform at the Toulousan bar. Without question, the barristers' thought on public issues had evolved rapidly since the summer of 1788. In response to the unprecedented opportunities for reordering state and society presented by the Estates-General, the barristers must have reexamined the notions they had accepted so uncritically for so long. Inherited virtue, for example, no longer seemed to justify an aristocratic monopoly of high offices. There was no single source of ideological inspiration for their

---

[55]Rouzet was not alone in taking this approach. See Boyd Schafer, "Quelques jugements de pamphlétaires sur le clergé à la veille de la Révolution," *Annales historiques de la Révolution française* 16 (1939):120.

program; all their proposals had been considered and discussed well before 1788.[56] On some points, Enlightenment thought reinforced the barristers' everyday experience: the emphasis on the importance and dignity of personal merit is one example. The language of national consent in which the barristers couched their political demands probably derived from the aristocratic resistance to royal "despotism" since the Assembly of Notables. Certainly, the barristers' social and political expectations had been fundamentally altered by the calling of the Estates-General, but always along lines that had been familiar to them during the Old Regime.

Thus, the advocates in the pre-Revolution were much as they had been in the last decades of the Old Regime: highminded, enlightened, and deferential. They anticipated the Estates-General with the hope that reform and regeneration could occur in a manner acceptable to nobles and commoners alike. By the time they realized that harmony, conciliation, and moderation could not prevail, it was too late: the Old Regime had already fallen.

REVOLUTION AND COUNTERREVOLUTION

Toulousans might have congratulated themselves on the public harmony and order that reigned in their city during the summer and fall of 1789. On the surface, at least, the events of July were accepted by everyone.[57] Toulouse was one of the few large cities not to experience even a partial municipal revolution.[58] Duroux, as first capitoul, spoke officially for the city when he applauded the events of 14 July in Paris. He had been shocked by the dismissal of Necker (on 12 July) and now hoped that "the diverse Orders that compose the nation . . . are going to work in concert and without respite toward the restoration of the State, the perfection of the Constitution. . . ."[59] On hearing the news of the Parisian insurrection, a group of young men rushed to the First President of the Parlement to present him with a tricolored cockade; the head magistrate graciously accepted the offering.[60] By September the patriotic militia had been formed, and its officers were noblemen,

---

[56]On this last point, see the remarks by Colin Lucas in his suggestive article "Nobles, Bourgeois and the Origins of the French Revolution," *Past and Present*, no. 60 (Aug., 1973), pp. 118-19.

[57]Philippe Wolff, *Histoire de Toulouse* (Toulouse, 1961), p. 295.

[58]Daniel Ligou, "A propos de la Révolution municipale," *Revue d'histoire économique et sociale* 38 (1960): 166-75. Ligou is incorrect in stating (on p. 166) that the capitouls were elected municipal officers in 1790.

[59]*A.M.*, AA-318, *Délibérations du Tiers Etat de la ville de Toulouse . . . (26 juillet, 1789)*.

[60]Félix Pasquier, ed., *Notes et réflections d'un bourgeois de Toulouse au début de la Révolution d'après les lettres intimes* (Toulouse, 1917), p. 26.

often scions of parlementaire families.[61] But this public harmony could not prevail despite the high hopes for national regeneration.

As the National Assembly began to dismember the Old Regime, barristers found that not all the changes were acceptable to them, and they would have to make important, even agonizing, decisions about their relation to the new order. The Revolution began to touch their own lives in important ways, and most men at the Toulousan bar seemed to oppose it or withdraw in confusion; only a minority stood with the new order and served it. Faced with entirely new possibilities for themselves and for the state, the barristers were split as never before.

By the early winter of 1789, the public harmony was rapidly disintegrating. In public, Duroux continued his prorevolutionary rhetoric, expressing his "admiration [for] the stunning revolution" at a meeting of the city council in November.[62] At the same time, he, Pierre Roucoule, and Mathieu Lespinasse, all important barristers, were involved in one of the first openly counterrevolutionary acts in Toulouse. The clergy and nobility of Toulouse had written protests against the destruction of the provinces by the Constituent Assembly, and these three barristers wrote "approbative consultations" to accompany them. This was a condemnation of the Revolution itself, and the National Guard legions denounced it as such.[63] Barristers had struck their first blow at the Revolution, and it would not be their last.

At the same time, some enthusiastically prorevolutionary barristers were coming to public attention. The home of Jean Antoine Romiguières, a rich barrister at the Seneschal Court, became a center for receiving letters from Paris and discussing the news.[64] Jacques Marie Rouzet, Raymond Marie Loubers, Guillaume Dorliac, and Guillaume Bordes were well enough known for their patriotic zeal to be chosen as special commissioners by their National Guard legions.[65] Claude Castor Bragouse, Bernard Pons de Vier, and Jean François Clausolles spoke out for prorevolutionary measures at the municipal council meetings.[66] At the same time, the advocates who had grave reservations about the Revolution were becoming known. Rumors circulated that Jamme "had talent and probity, but he was too much attached to the Parlement, which made his fortune. . . ."[67] When the electors met early in 1790 to select officers for the newly created ad-

---

[61]*Affiches, annonces et avis divers de Toulouse et de Haut-Languedoc*, no. 37 (16 septembre, 1789), p. 153.
[62]*A.M.*, AA-95, *Délibérations prises par le Conseil général renforcé . . . le 26 novembre, 1789*, p. 7.
[63]*Affiches, annonces, et avis . . .* , no. 47 (25 novembre, 1789), p. 191.
[64]*A.D.*, L-335, dossier of Romiguières.
[65]*Affiches, annonces, et avis . . .* , no. 47 (25 novembre, 1789), p. 193.
[66]*A.M.*, AA-95, *Délibérations . . .* , p. 2.
[67]Jamme, *Aux maire et officiers municipaux . . .* , p. 4.

ministrative bodies, they eschewed the barristers like Jamme, Duroux, Sudre, and Albaret, who had formerly been active in public life but whose patriotism was now suspect. Revolutionary barristers captured all the leading local offices: mayor, attorney-general-syndic of the Department, attorney-syndic of the District, president of the Civil Tribunal. This attested to the talent and patriotic reputation of some barristers.[68] But the electors knew that many at the Toulousan bar were not friends of the new order.

The year 1790 witnessed not only the establishment of the new institutions and constituted authorities created by the National Assembly but also the beginning of the counterrevolutionary offensive. The opponents of the new order used both militant and peaceful collective methods to arouse public opposition to liquidation of the Old Regime. As a result, by the fall of 1790 Toulouse had gained a reputation for being a center for counterrevolutionary agitation. Barristers were frequent leaders or supporters of this movement. As early as January 1790, the local patriotic journal reported that the barristers were angered by recent legislation of the National Assembly: they were said to "complain that they will no longer be permitted to interpret the law, too clear not to be understood by all citizens; the attorneys [complain] that their clientele . . . will not even furnish water to drink."[69] It was, in fact, among the personnel of the Parlement that the most virulent counterrevolutionary force in Toulouse was to be felt. These men were conveniently organized into the Second National Guard Legion of St. Barthélemy (a quarter of the city near the *Palais de Justice*) and were ready to make trouble for the new regime. The leader of St. Barthélemy was the President d'Aspe. In April, the group began to interfere with the municipal government and later demanded the suppression of all popular clubs.[70] Still worse, it paraded with arms and clashed with the patriotic legions. In one skirmish, barrister Etienne Dominique Taverne, recently elected judge of the Civil Tribunal, was attacked.[71] The St. Barthélemy Legion had several barristers in it. Pierre Bruno Roucoule was apparently the right-hand man of President d'Aspe. Among the many former legal men of the Parlement in the legion were barristers Jean Joseph Gez, Jean François Bergez, Philippe Jacques Guizet, Jean (?) Moulin, and Duroux.[72] In the end, the authorities could do nothing but suppress

---

[68]See the appendix for a full list of barristers in public office.

[69]*Journal universel et affiches de Toulouse et de Languedoc*, no. 3 (20 janvier, 1790), p. 11.

[70]*Ibid.*, no. 15 (14 avril, 1790); no. 33 (21 août, 1790).

[71]Emile Connac, *La Révolution à Toulouse et dans le département de la Haute-Garonne* (Toulouse, n.d.), pp. 11–16.

[72]*A.D.*, L–312, dossier of Gez; L–283, dossier of Giles François Astre; L–310, dossier of Pierre François Furgole; *Affiches, annonces, et avis . . .*, no. 47 (25 novembre, 1789); *A.M.*, AA–95, *Délibérations . . . par le Conseil . . .*, pp. 2–3 (see list of deputies).

this group and disarm the inhabitants of the quarter. Even two years later, the city government would not reestablish a legion there, "in view of the danger of putting arms into the hands of the enemies of the public order."[73]

Barristers who disapproved of the violent approach of the legion took part in other aspects of the 1790 counterrevolutionary offensive. In April, several large-scale assemblies of active citizens were held, ostensibly to protest specific events, but in reality to arouse and focus opinion hostile to the Revolution. On 12 April 1790, about 150 "active citizens" united to protest an injustice done to Duroux: he had received a commission from Versailles to organize the Department, but Rouzet had seen to it that the commission was revoked. The leaders of this assembly were the barrister Gez and the attorney Arbanere.[74] In attendance at the meeting were at least sixteen barristers, including Jamme, Jouve, Furgole (junior), Ardenne, and Mayniel.[75] The assembly sent its petition to the advocate Viguier, who had been elected deputy to Versailles. Viguier apparently sympathized with them, for he later left the National Assembly without taking leave or asking permission of his constituents, obviously in protest against its work.[76]

The religious legislation of the National Assembly in the spring of 1790 provided the counterrevolutionaries with a more powerful rallying point for opinion hostile to the Revolution. In mid-April, active citizens assembled "to deliberate on the interests of the Catholic, Apostolic, and Roman religion." This assembly declared itself alarmed by the law suppressing religious orders and demanded their retention in Toulouse. The president of this meeting was the noble barrister Théodore Cucsac and the secretary was attorney Pierre Barada; on the executive commission was Mitou, a barrister at the Merchants' Court. At least forty-three advocates, many of whom had protested in favor of Duroux, attended these counterrevolutionary deliberations.[77] Many barristers must have signed a proclamation against the religious policies of the new government.[78] We cannot identify them because the document is missing, but we do know that barristers who supported the counterrevolutionary Catholics of Nîmes were numerous. Faced with the zealously patriotic stance of the Protestants, Catholics at Nîmes declared "their fears of the dangers that menace religion and the monarchy."[79] Toulousan counterrevolutionaries circulated a peti-

---

[73]*A.M.*, 1D-1, fol. 149.

[74]*A.M.*, 2 I-50 (entry of 12 April 1790).

[75]*Délibérations des citoyens actifs de Toulouse assemblés au nombre de plus de 150 . . . .* This is in the *B.M.T.* pamphlet collection.

[76]*Ibid.*, p. 18; Brette, *Recueil de documents*, 2:571.

[77]*Procès-verbal de l'assemblée des citoyens actifs de la ville de Toulouse . . . (18–20 avril, 1790)*, in *B.M.T.* pamphlet collection.

[78]This proclamation is mentioned in Connac, *La Révolution à Toulouse*, p. 14.

[79]*Délibérations . . . des citoyens Catholiques de la ville de Nîmes . . . (20 avril, 1790)*.

tion in their support, and seventy barristers signed it.[80] This was a fourth of the bar, and a third of the advocates at the Parlement. If such a high percentage of barristers publicly manifested their opposition to the Revolution, there were certainly many others who were too cautious to do so but had serious objections to the new order. And so strong was the antipathy of some barristers for the Revolution that they renounced honored positions rather than profess loyalty to the new government. At least four members of the Law Faculty (Gouazé, Daram, Delort, and Ruffat) forfeited their chairs by refusing to take the loyalty oath.[81] It was no wonder that the advocate Rouzet disassociated himself from his former colleagues and classified them in a pamphlet along with nobles, seigneurs, priests, and monks, as enemies of the Revolution.[82]

The counterrevolutionary barristers and magistrates attempted to stir up public opinion not only through petitions and assemblies but also through the press. Three parlementaires, d'Aguin, Cambon, and Tristan d'Escalonne, and two barristers, Duroux and Jean François Bergez, edited a journal, the Quatre Evangélistes.[83] Internal evidence shows that barristers were meant to be an important audience for the newspapers. References to advocates were frequent: Malpel's "treason" to the Parlement was recalled; Bragouse, an active revolutionary, was dubbed "Iscariot"; Rouzet was a primary target of the invective. The journal demonstrated the considerable talents of Duroux and Bergez in using biting satire to defend the Old Regime.

The last move in the counterrevolutionary agitation of 1790 came from the Parlement itself. On the eve of its abolition in late September, the Parlement issued a decree against the work of the Constituent Assembly. The decree stated that the deputies had gone far beyond their powers in giving France a new constitution and declared the innovations void.[84] This protest was the work of two magistrates (de Montegut, de Resseguier) and barrister Jamme.[85] The immediate purpose of the decree was to arouse, by example, all the Parlements of France to a last-chance resistance. In the end, it had no positive results for the parlementaires. The local authorities denounced the decree

[80]Tableau par lettre . . . des citoyens prétendus actifs, qui ont signés dans Toulouse l'adhésion aux protestations . . . à la fanatique et incendiaire délibération des soidisans Catholiques de Nîmes, in B.M.T. pamphlet collection.

[81]Louis Vié, L'Université de Toulouse pendant la Révolution, 1789-1793 (Toulouse, 1905), pp. 14, 28. Gouazé tried to foment trouble among the poor by encouraging the Sisters of Charity, who worked at the Hôtel-Dieu, to refuse the oath. See A.D., L-313, dossier of Gouazé.

[82]The pamphlet itself is lost, but portions of it are quoted in the journal Les Quatre Evangélistes, ou Supplément aux actes des apôtres, no. 4 (n.d.), p. 41.

[83]For the editors of the journal, see Journal universel . . . , no. 33 (21 août, 1790), and Bouglon, Les reclus, 3: 30, n. 3. Copies of this newspaper are in the Bibliothèque nationale.

[84]A.D., L-2577, Arrêtés du Parlement de Toulouse . . . des 25 et 27 septembre, 1790.

[85]Axel Duboul, La fin du Parlement de Toulouse (Toulouse, 1890), p. 63.

vigorously and the National Assembly ordered the municipal government to arrest the magistrates, who eventually fled to Spain.[86] Until then, hopes of reversing the revolutionary tide had been strong, and the sense that reaction was inevitable had animated the protests from the legal quarter. With the collapse of expectations in the fall of 1790, enemies of the Revolution became resigned to events or withdrew to contemplate future revolt. Opposition to the new order would not emerge so openly again until the last years of the Directory.[87]

If the counterrevolutionary agitation of 1790 received support, leadership, and publicity from barristers, there was also a significant group at the Toulousan bar who took an active part in the Revolution. Altogether, twenty-six barristers assumed a public office in 1790.[88] With Mailhe at the head of the Department, Malpel at the head of the District, and Rigaud leading the Municipality, the barristers seemed to have preserved and extended their prerevolutionary public prominence. And, in this new regime, barristers were also able to attain the most important magisterial positions. The judicial institutions created by the Constitutent Assembly represented a reaction against permanent, professional, aristocratic magistrates in favor of temporary ones called to the bench by popular will.[89] The elections in Toulouse produced a bench of capable judges who had been promising or leading barristers in the Old Regime. Serving the District Civil Tribunal were the barristers Bragouse, Arbanere, Romiguières, Verieu, Taverne (until his death in 1791), and Boubée. Later, Arbanere became the president of the new criminal court. A few Toulousan barristers were even elected to magistracies in other districts.[90]

In the first year of the Revolution, half the barristers who were to serve in the new regime were already doing so. Throughout the revolutionary period (up to 1799), only fifty-four barristers out of 276 held a public office at any level.[91] This includes such minor positions as Justice of the Peace, held by Antoine Chabaton in the rural canton of

[86]The barrister Mailhe was one of the first to denounce the Parlement. See *Journal universel . . .* , no. 41 (13 octobre, 1790).
[87]For the barristers' participation in the royalist insurrection of the Year VIII, see *A.D.*, L-2268, -2240, -2285, -2276, -2269, and -2282; *A.M.*, 2H-39-40. See also Joseph Lacouture, *Le mouvement royaliste dans le Sud-Ouest, 1797-1800* (Toulouse, 1932).
[88]See the appendix.
[89]For the reorganization of the courts, see Jacques Godechot, *Les institutions de la France sous la Révolution et l'Empire* (Paris, 1951); Edmond Seligman, *La justice en France pendant la Révolution*, 2 vols. (Paris, 1901), vol. 1; Emile Giraud, *L'oeuvre d'organisation judicaire de l'Assemblée nationale constituante* (Paris, 1921).
[90]*Journal universel . . .* (16 octobre, 1790). Rouzet became judge at Foix, and Mouysset, at Villneuve d'Agens. See *Journal universel . . .* (27 octobre, 1790). Barristers were elected to administrative bodies outside Toulouse, too.
[91]The reader should be warned that lists of office holders were often inaccurate or incomplete. Hence, a few omissions are possible.

Hauterive. Considering the possibilities for public service that the Revolution opened to men of legal training and skills in public speaking, fifty-four was not a very large number. Forty of these held more than one public position. Jean Joseph Janole, for example, was a municipal notable in 1791 and 1792, *agrégé* at the Law Faculty, and judge at the Civil Tribunal. Jean Romiguières was a municipal officer, president of the Department, civil judge, and royal commissioner. Only fourteen advocates held just one position. If prorevolutionary barristers figured prominently in local administration, it may have been due more to their multiple office holding than to their total numbers.

Between the seventy barristers who publicly opposed the Revolution in 1790 and the fifty-four advocates who served in the new order, somewhat less than half the barristers openly manifested their attitude toward the Revolution. This brings us to an important question: were there many among the others who favored the Revolution but refrained from open support of the new order? Or was their silence an indication of their opposition to—or, at least, lack of enthusiasm for—the revolutionary regime? Only indirect evidence exists to answer this question, but it all points in the same direction: there was little support for the Revolution to be found beyond that given by the fifty-four prorevolutionary barristers we can identify.[92]

The pattern of office holding lends credence to the view that the Toulousan bar provided only limited support to the Revolution. There were many desirable offices that would certainly have appealed to a barrister with some enthusiasm for the new order. But advocates did not fill many of these places—presumably because prorevolutionary advocates were in short supply in Toulouse. The Justices of the Peace were a case in point. Here was a position of respect and responsibility: these justices not only directed conciliations, essential pretrial procedures,[93] but they also judged disputes involving values up to 100 livres in the first instance. The office was a remunerative one, with an annual salary of 2400 livres—surely more than most barristers had earned at the Parlement.[94] In Paris, advocates dominated these offices and even took the gratuitous post of assessor, or assistant to the J.P.'s.[95] In

---

[92]I am using a rather loose definition of "revolutionary" at this point. Later in the chapter, I shall discuss the *quality* of the support these men gave to the Revolution. At this point I am interested in the fact that these fifty-four men separated themselves from their colleagues by working for the revolutionary regime. This is why I often employ the term "prorevolutionary" rather than "revolutionary."

[93]R. Legoux, *Recherches sur la procédure civile appliquée à l'époch révolutionnaire par le Tribunal du district de Toulouse* (Toulouse, 1933), p. 121.

[94]Richard M. Andrews, "The Justices of the Peace in Revolutionary Paris . . . ," *Past and Present*, no. 52 (August, 1971), pp. 58–60.

[95]*Ibid.*, p. 71.

Toulouse, however, barristers eschewed the position. The first elections of J.P.'s in 1791 placed only two barristers in the six positions in the city.[96] Over the next several years, the social composition of this group varied, but never were there more than three barristers at any one time; and there were periods when none served. Toulousan electors could find hardly any barristers to serve as assessors. Up to 1794, only one barrister held this post.[97] It does seem, then, that even with its superabundance of barristers, Toulouse had an insufficient number to staff its *bureaux de paix*.

Other office-holding patterns further support the claim that the fifty-four prorevolutionary barristers were exceptional in their support of the new order. If there had been a substantial number of respectable barristers who supported the Revolution, why was Meilhon, a mere advocate at the Municipal Court, chosen to teach at the Law Faculty? Moreover, holding several offices simultaneously was so common that one must wonder why more barristers did not share these responsible charges with their colleagues. And after the Terror, when representatives-on-mission filled the public offices by decree, the same barristers were again selected, apparently because there were not many others available.[98] Finally, the same barristers who held responsible positions in courts and administrative bodies were also the very ones who had to serve in minor public capacities: as jurors, for example, or as commissioners of the National Guard.[99] Were there no others with fewer burdensome duties available for these minor charges? The implication must be that prorevolutionary attitudes were confined to a minority not much larger than the fifty-four office-holding barristers.

Membership in the popular societies offers more evidence that the Toulousan bar was not heavily in favor of the Revolution. Barristers neither founded patriotic clubs nor joined them in large numbers. By the spring of 1790, Toulouse had three popular societies, the largest of which was the Literary and Patriotic Club, established in May. The founders of this society were ten artisans, two wholesale merchants, one shopkeeper, a rentier, and a *maître-d'hôtel*.[100] This club was open to all; within a year of its creation, passive citizens were eligible for admission as long as an active citizen nominated them.[101] A second

---

[96]*A.M.*, B–61, fol. 349. Also elected were a notary and two merchants. I have not been able to identify the sixth.

[97]This was François Double, during the Terror. See *A.D.*, L–2578.

[98]See *A.D.*, L–102–3, 107–8; L–45–54 for appointments made by representatives-on-mission Clauzel and Lawrence. This selection of the same barristers persisted beyond the early Thermidorian period, so it was not simply a matter of restoring the pre-Terror personnel.

[99]See, for example, the list of jurors in *A.D.*, L–2579–2580, and 202–U–176.

[100]*A.D.*, L–4542, fol. 3, register of popular society.

[101]*Ibid.*, fol. 53 (entry of 12 September, 1790).

society, the Friends of the Constitution at the Hôtel de Ville, was more select. When it merged with the Literary and Patriotic Club in September 1790, its membership was largely one of municipal officers and notables, usually rich merchants. Despite its more elite nature, there was only one barrister in it, Guillaume Augé of the Seneschal Court, incumbent judge of Villefranche.[102] The Society at the National Café included advocates Gary, Rouzet, and Malpel.[103] This society was short-lived, for the Literary and Patriotic Club became the only popular association by mid-1791. Altogether, only twenty-six advocates entered these popular societies between their founding and the Insurrection of 2 June 1793.[104] That is, only one in eleven barristers possessed enough revolutionary zeal to become a "Friend of the Constitution." There were at least seventy-nine *négociants* in the popular society and many more clegymen than barristers. The Toulousan bar in no way rallied to the support of the Revolution by joining patriotic clubs. Moreover, the Jacobins at the Toulousan bar were almost exclusively office-holders. Only two members of the popular society were not among the fifty-four participants in the new regime. This, again, indicates how few were the supporters of the Revolution outside the office-holding group.

It may be argued that membership in a popular society is too stringent a criterion for identifying prorevolutionary opinion. But in Toulouse the popular society was not composed of a small elite of patriots, each fervent in his devotion to the Revolution. By 2 June 1793, the popular society had no less than 630 members.[105] Those who belonged did not usually attend meetings on any regular basis. Moreover, the politics of the club were not especially radical until fairly late, and individual members were frequently more conservative than the majority.[106] Certainly, there was support for the Revolution outside the popular societies, but there was no reason why so few barristers should have been members—unless there were few who were prorevolutionary.

The most conclusive evidence for the absence of strong revolutionary support at the Toulousan bar can be derived from a study of the new judicial personnel. The legal reforms of the Constituent Assembly radically altered the barristers' profession. Its corporate, exclusive quality was eliminated; the profession was opened to everyone, even

---

[102]*Ibid.*, deliberations of 7 février, 1791.
[103]*Les Quatre Evangélistes*, no. 4 (nd.), pp. 42–45.
[104]*A.D.*, L–4542–4546, registers of the popular society.
[105]*A.D.*, L–4552–4553. Members were listed in these registers.
[106]See, for example, *A.D.*, L–4543, deliberations of 23 July to 10 September 1791. The club spent much time debating whether it should ally with Feuillants or Paris Jacobins. See also, L–4543 (entry of 18 July 1791), when a number of members opposed the closing of non-parochial churches.

those without a law degree; barristers were forbidden to wear distinctive costumes.[107] On the bench were not the high-born magistrates of the Old Regime, but rather the barristers' former colleagues. These changes stripped away much of the dignity of the occupation. Even the name *avocat* was dropped, and barristers used the titles "homme de loi" and "official defender" in criminal court. The barristers also suffered economically from the new judicial institutions. The Civil Tribunal of Toulouse had a jurisdiction only one fifth the size of the Parlement's.[108] The heavy loss and dispersal of clientele must have been bitterly resented by the barristers at the Parlement. The advocates of the suppressed courts of exceptional jurisdiction, like the Hôtel de Ville, *Bourse*, or *Officialité*, lost their sources of livelihood entirely. Rather than plead before judicial institutions that had so disrupted their lives and professions, many barristers seem to have retired from the bar. It became a sign of "patriotism" to plead before the new Civil Tribunal. As the revolutionary advocate Antoine Flottes declared, "Braving the aristocratic example of almost all the former barristers, I was one of the first to fill the functions of my profession before the different courts of the new regime."[109] In fact, the district court had only sixteen barristers ("hommes de loi") pleading in it during the first two years.[110] And these men were very different from the ones who had harangued the *fleur-de-lys* benches of the Old Regime. Instead of Bastoulh, Duroux, Mayniel, Viguier and the other leading pleaders of the Old Regime, the new barristers included a former Seneschal Court officer (Corail), a former notary (Viguié), three former attorneys (Saury, Carles, Caunes), three former advocates of the Seneschal Court (Flottes, Loubers, Bordes), and only eight former barristers at the Parlement.[111] Nine of the eleven former barristers were office holders—that is, they fall within our group of fifty-four revolutionary barristers. At the Criminal Tribunal, there were thirty-two "official defenders," including former barristers, attorneys, and notaries. All of the barristers pleading criminal cases were revolutionary officers.[112] None had been heard with any frequency in the criminal chamber (*Tournelle*) of the Parlement. The Revolution in Paris had unquestionably created a revolution at the Toulousan bar. Most barristers were "aristocrats" who preferred to desert the profession rather than support the new judicial order.

---

[107]*Réimpression de l'ancien Moniteur. . .* , V., pp. 543–44 (session of 2 Sept. 1790).
[108]This was the estimate of Bragouse, who became president of the court. See *A.D.*, L–2577.
[109]*A.D.*, L–310, dossier of Flottes.
[110]*A.D.*, 221 U–26–27, registers of sessions of the Civil Tribunal.
[111]These were Janole, Astre, Douyau, Clausolles, Double, Pons, Roques, and Druilhe.
[112]See the list in Jean-Marie Luc, "Le tribunel criminel de la Haute-Garonne, 1792–1799" (D.E.S., University of Toulouse, 1947), p. 63.

The negative stance of the Toulousan barristers was, in fact, typical of most of the personnel of the former Parlement. Like the barristers, the attorneys retired from their professions rather than serve the new courts. Only eight of the sixty-four former attorneys at the Parlement even took the oath to become *avoués* at the new tribunals.[113] And only eight attorneys held public charges during the Revolution.[114] Moreover, the minor clerks from the Sovereign Court sometimes served as militant counterrevolutionaries in the Second Legion of St. Barthélemy. Thus, the Revolution overrode those petty jealousies and vanities that had divided the personnel of the Parlement and reaffirmed their community of interest and identity after 1789.

By contrast, the personnel of the Seneschal Court actively supported the Revolution. Opponents of the Parlement in its struggles with the crown, the Seneschal Court magistrates remained opponents of the Parlement in its struggle with the National Assembly. Ten of the twenty-three judges were active particpants in the Revolution, some in important capacities.[115] The barristers at the Seneschal Court also supported the Revolution, in contrast to most of their colleagues at the Parlement. Nine of the fourteen—nearly two-thirds of them—were active participants in the revolutionary regime.[116] Less than a fifth of the Sovereign Court bar actively supported the new order. Underlying the Seneschal Court's revolutionary posture was its long-standing resentment of the Parlement.[117] In the end, the Revolution demonstrated the lasting importance of corporate divisions in Toulousan society. The cataclysm of 1789 created few new alignments or loyalties in the legal community of Toulouse; it transferred corporate tensions into a new framework and gave those conflicts new meaning.

DIVIDED LOYALTIES

The Revolution obviously ended the consensus that had existed at the bar of the Parlement on the eve of the cataclysm. The barristers,

---

[113]*A.D.*, L-2577, "Adresse à Monsieur le Ministre de l'Intérieur. . . ." *Avoué* was the new title for "attorney" (or *procureur*).

[114]They were Chauliac, Chirac, Caunes, Casseirol, I. Cames, Lagarrigue, Castaing, Souchon. Once again, because of incomplete or inaccurate documents, a few may have been overlooked.

[115]The ten were Carles, Compayre, Derry, Montané, Routte, Baric, Corail, Martin-Bergnac, Loubeau, and Mouysset. Derry (de Belbeze) was founder of a popular society and twice mayor of Toulouse. Montané (de la Roque) was a president of the Revolutionary Tribunal in Paris. These judges seemed to have been more radical than the average case recently described by Dawson in *Provincial Magistrates and Revolutionary Politics*, chap. 8.

[116]Most of the Seneschal Court attorneys took the oath to become *avoués* at the new courts, too. See *A.D.*, L-2577.

[117]See, for example, the jurisdictional dispute which the Parlement decided against the Seneschal Court in Jean-Marie Augustin, "Les capitouls, juges des causes criminelles

who sincerely desired reform, were soon faced with a Revolution that destroyed much that they valued. Profound, indeed, was their feeling of loss at the suppression of the Parlement. They, like the magistrates, derived status and identity from this august institution and their identification with it could be intense. Louis Joseph Faure, an older barrister, left Toulouse in the late summer of 1790 just to avoid witnessing the suppression of the court.[118] Then, too, the new courts could offer nothing like the prestige or the economic advantages of the Parlement. The Revolution took away a great deal, and the Toulousan barristers did not perceive it as offering them new and desired opportunities.

Though once in favor of reform and the suppression of privileges, barristers were now frightened by the rhetoric and social experimentation of the Revolution. It seemed to expose society to the viciousness of popular passions. On hearing that noble titles had been abolished, Faure wrote in a personal letter: "Equality of condition is desired. I don't know where it will end. I don't think it can result in anything good. Subordination is necessary, otherwise we will fall into anarchy."[119] The social philosophy of the *Quatre Evangélistes* echoed that of Faure: "In vain you [revolutionaries] repeat incessantly the praise of this chimerical equality which does not exist in nature and is impossible to establish in society."[120] The rhetorical appeals to the "people" made them anxious. As the editors of the journal wrote, ". . . the *gros peuple* resemble a tiger which allows itself to be fettered when it is satiated with blood and carnage."[121] Thus, many barristers retreated from any reforming ideals they may have had before the Revolution. Behaving like genuine aristocrats, they came to regard noble titles as the cornerstone of social stability. The rhetoric and ideals of the Revolution seemed to have no more appeal for those barristers than for parlementaires.

As men who valued the letter of the law, barristers had special difficulties in accepting many aspects of the Revolution. In the first year of the Revolution, the widespread rural disorders and urban riots were often perceived, as Faure saw them, as a series of frightening convulsions which the new government was unwilling to suppress.[122] Disorders, resistance, and scarcities sometimes forced authorities to

---

et de police à la fin de l'ancien régime," *Annales du midi* 84 (1972): 184. Of course, there was also the controversy over the edict of 1774, discussed in chapter 1.

[118]Pasquier, *Notes et réflections*, p. 41. Faure wrote in a personal letter, "Je ne voulais pas être en ville lors de la destruction du Parlement: je partis. . . ."

[119]*Ibid.*, p. 36.

[120]*Les Quatre Evangélistes*, no. 8 (n.d.), p. 86.

[121]*Ibid.*, no. 5 (n.d.), p. 51.

[122]Pasquier, *Notes et réflections*, pp. 29, 32–33. Faure believed that only the Parlement could restore order.

take unusual measures, and barristers could become outraged by these. The advocate François Beral was at first a supporter of the new order, but by 1791 he had become frightened by the lack of respect for lawful procedure. Bitterly resenting the imposition on his freedom when he was forced to sell grain for *assignats*, he wrote sarcastically in a letter, "This is what they call the reign of liberty!"[123] The arbitrary arrests of the Terror would undermine the revolutionary ardor of even leading republican barristers.

So far, we have adopted a rather loose definition of the "prorevolutionary" barrister, designating him as one who assumed public office at some point after 1789. Given the intransigent refusal of most barristers to participate in the revolutionary regime, this is a meaningful distinction. Yet it fails to tell us how much conviction there was behind their service to the new order and what they wanted the Revolution to achieve. The evidence we can bring to bear on these questions is limited, to be sure. There are indications, however, that the prorevolutionary barristers were generally quite moderate men with some traditional views and some grave reservations about many acts of the Parisian assemblies. Indeed, their social aims and attitudes hardly seem to have gone beyond the consensus on reform that had existed at the bar in the spring of 1789.

What type of society did the prorevolutionary barristers desire? Their words and, even more convincingly, their demeanor during the entire course of the Revolution indicated a negligible amount of radicalism at the Toulousan bar. The number of barristers who ceased to think in terms of a hierarchy, who wanted status to depend only on civic virtue and utility, who hoped for legislation that would gradually diffuse wealth, and who honestly accepted the sanctity of work and manual labor could not have been more than five or six.[124] All but these few desired social innovation of much more modest proportions. The barrister and academician Jacques Floret probably expressed the social aims of most of his prorevolutionary colleagues in his account of ancient Athenian law, written in 1789 or 1790.[125] Floret desired the suppression of all distinctions based on birth, but he still recognized the need for a ruling elite. The barrister lavishly praised Solon for making "wealth alone the distinction between citizens."[126] Floret

---

[123]*A.D.*, L-290, dossier of Beral.

[124]I have borrowed my definition of "radicalism" partly from Isser Woloch, *Jacobin Legacy: The Democratic Movement under the Directory* (Princeton, 1970), p. 13. See below for more information on these radical barristers.

[125]*Histoire et mémoires de l'Académie royale des sciences . . . de Toulouse*, 1790, pp. 129–48.

[126]*Ibid.*, p. 131.

believed that the wealthy should enjoy access to public offices and govern "those whose destiny is to acquire their subsistence by the work of their arms." His ideal was ancient Athens, where "there was no regard to birth . . . they left the charges, dignities, and magistracies in the hands of the rich."[127] Thus, Floret wished only to expand the Old Regime elite to include "that crowd of men which education, fortune, and talent raise above [the populace]."[128] Such, in effect, was the social order created by the Constitution of 1791.[129]

Though the revolutionary barristers rejected the restricted elite of the Old Regime, they still retained many loyalties and ties to the past. A special regard for the aristocratic magistrates was to be found even among those who led the Revolution in Toulouse. When the Constituent Assembly ordered the arrest of the parlementaires for their protest of September 1790, Gary, Bragouse, and Malpel, as municipal officers, refused to sign the order.[130] Later, the barrister Jean Castan de la Courtade tried to stall the efforts of the popular society to send denunciations of the magistrates to Paris. Failing at this, Castan undertook to write the denunciation himself. But he apparently blunted the attack, for the Parisian Jacobin Club criticized Castan's work. Castan retired from the popular society thereafter and was not heard from again.[131] Not even the heart of a leading Republican like Jean Joseph Janole was so filled with patriotic fervor that it abandoned all attachment to the Old Regime elite. Janole expressed great sympathy for Madame de Cassan, wife of a parlementaire, when she was guillotined, and he angered the Jacobin Club by his moderate interpretation of the law calling for the arrest of all nobles.[132] Nor did the Revolution entirely disrupt the barristers' social cohesiveness. Raymond Loubers, an important revolutionary barrister, remained the trusted friend of Pierre François Furgole, son of the famed jurisconsultant and a pronounced counterrevolutionary.[133] Thus, the Revolution did not cause even the barristers who supported it to break decisively with the past; it disrupted old loyalties, to be sure, but did not destroy them entirely.

[127]*Ibid.*, pp. 129, 132.

[128]*Ibid.*

[129]See Colin Lucas, "Nobles, Bourgeois," pp. 125–26. Floret expressed much the same social aims as Denis Richet discusses in his provocative article "Autour des origines idéologique lointaines de la Révolution française: élites et despotisme," *Annales: économie, société, civilisation* 24 (1969): 1–23.

[130]Jean Baptiste Dubédat, *Histoire du Parlement du Toulouse*, 2 vols. (Paris, 1885), 2: 689.

[131]*A.D.*, L–4542, fol. 64–65, 78.

[132]Damien Garrigues, *Jean Joseph Janole, magistrat toulousain* (Toulouse, 1930), pp. 28, 68.

[133]*A.D.*, J–929, letter of Furgole to Loubers, 23 Vendémiaire, an VII.

The Toulousan barristers were far too moderate, independent, and mindful of the past to be model revolutionaries. Michel Malpel, as head of the Department in 1792–93, neglected to close some convents and continued to have his daughter raised by the Black Dames of Levignac.[134] The president of the Civil Tribunal in 1790, Claude Bragouse, was denounced by the popular society for not enforcing the acceptance of *assignats*.[135] Loubers, as judge in the Year VIII, even referred to the Criminal Code of 1670—denounced so often by enlightened barristers of the Old Regime—as "these laws that are so wise."[136] Apparently, the revolutionaries at the Toulousan bar were ready neither to reject the past as a product of darkness nor to follow conscientiously the policies of the government in Paris.

Even Barère, whose radical notions were so outstanding before 1789, was slow to arrive at a democratic political and social outlook.[137] His former colleagues were even less interested in social innovation. They were moderates whose memories of the Old Regime were not all bad ones. The social revolution they desired was of very limited proportions: expansion of the existing elite to permit the full participation of propertied, educated men like themselves. They called for constitutional, legal, and humanitarian reforms, too; but they did not welcome civic equality or personal attacks on the Old Regime aristocracy. In the end, the rush of events since 1789 had not altered their social outlook very much.

For these men of moderation, trust in law, and lingering loyalty to the past, the continuing leftward drift of the Revolution was a disaster. At least twenty of the fifty-four prorevolutionary barristers had withdrawn from public life by the *journée* of 10 August 1792. The rest accepted the Republic, some eagerly, others reluctantly, until they sensed their loss of local leadership to socially inferior and outside elements. Then, every reason they had for supporting the Revolution—hope for moderate social change, opportunism, expediency—was threatened. The response of all but a few was federalist revolt.

During 1793, the prorevolutionary barristers received increasing pressure from the Jacobin Club and deputies-on-mission for absolute cooperation. It was this, more than their provincial jealousy of the capital, that precipitated the barrister's federalism. The club, domi-

---

[134]*A.D.*, L–49, fol. 1.
[135]*A.D.*, L–4542, fol. 101. It might be added that Rouzet defended Bragouse's "unpatriotic" behavior.
[136]*A.D.*, J–927, "Pages written in Year VIII."
[137]Gershoy, *Barère*, chaps. 5–8.

nated by artisans, shopkeepers, and wage-earners, was slipping from the control of barristers and their "respectable" associates.[138] From December of 1792 on, the popular society began to clash with the "constituted authorities" (that is, the courts and regular administrative bodies).[139] By March 1793, the barristers had stopped attending the sessions of the club, now fearing the society they once had led. The reason was not that all barristers refused to countenance a policy of repression in the name of the Republic. Indeed, future federalist leaders like Janole, Arbanere, and Loubet had participated in surveillance committees, suggested arbitrary arrests, and removed elected officials from their posts.[140] Arbanere himself had recommended the purging of the judiciary in August of 1792.[141] But then the repression had been in *their* control, and they saw themselves as using power responsibly. The barristers would not trust the popular elements in the Jacobin Club or their "demagogic" leaders to do the same.

In mid-May, the Jacobins and the representative-on-mission precipitated a crisis by suspending Malpel from the departmental administration. From then on, the constituted bodies united to face the threat to their authority. They declared illegal all denunciations made before "improper" bodies. But this attempt to contain the popular forces turned into open rebellion with the news of the Insurrection in Paris on 2 June.[142] Once again, barristers played a leading role in the movement. With a declaration written by the former barrister Arbanere, the Municipality called for a meeting of the Toulousan sectional assemblies. Barristers led five of the fifteen sections, and Gary penned their remonstrance.[143] Aware of the impending revolt, the National Convention summoned Loubet, Arbanere, Janole, and other leaders to Paris, where the guillotine awaited those who would not flee. Ultimately the federalist revolt failed, partly because of the vigorous action of the Jacobins, but also because the federalist leaders lacked the will to oppose Paris. Their federalism had been very much a response to the loss of power to the Jacobin Club and deputy-on-mission in addition to the threat of social revolution at home.

[138]For a complete study of this movement, see Madeleine Albert, *Le fédéralisme dans la Haute-Garonne* (Paris, 1932). I have been able to identify the occupations of 203 of 541 "purified" members of the Jacobin Club in the Year II. Over a third (89) were artisans; a fourth (52) were *marchands*. See *A.D.*, L-4552-4553. Many of the others were wage-earners.

[139]Paule Maury, *Le loyalisme révolutionnaire des autorités toulousaines* (Toulouse, 1939), p. 16.

[140]See *A.M.*, 1 D-1, deliberations of the Municipality.

[141]*A.D.*, L-4544, deliberations of 11 August 1792.

[142]*A.D.*, L-49, and Albert, *Le fédéralisme*.

[143]*Dénonce contre François Chabot*, in the *B.M.T.* pamphlet collection. The barristers who signed this were Bragouze, Janole, Loubet, Lafage, Flottes, and Arbanere.

Not since the establishment of the Parlement in the fifteenth century had barristers played such a reduced role in local affairs. Only about a dozen barristers remained in office and these positions were minor ones.[144] Power passed to the deputy-on-mission and to the merchants, artisans, surgeons, and others in the Municipality, a development that barristers undoubtedly perceived as a social revolution of sorts.[145] The new mayor, Groussac, was a former shopkeeper who possessed a fortune of only 5200 livres.[146] The number of barristers who supported this Jacobin regime with conviction could not have been more than a handful. The "purified" popular society of the Year II had only four advocates, and a principal journal of the Thermidorian Reaction named only four barristers as "Terroristes, Buveurs de Sang."[147] And only a few barristers associated themselves with the Jacobins under the Directory.[148] In the end, arbitrary acts by the deputy-on-mission and power held by socially inferior elements were insupportable to nearly every barrister.

As a result, the Year II was a time of suffering for many Toulousan barristers. Fifty-eight of them—a fifth of the bar—were incarcerated.[149] This included both prominent federalists like Romiguières and Lafage and the counterrevolutionaries of 1790, who had to pay for their reputations as "aristocrats, enemies of liberty" in still larger numbers. How many Toulousan barristers, in or out of prison, longed to return to those halcyon days when noble magistrates presided over an orderly society that assured them peace and respect!

[144]Those in office were Guion, Clausolles, Londois, Gratian, Gleizes, Dubernard, Dupuy, Mathieu, Double, Corail and, perhaps, Loubers, Valette, and Pouderoux. The records are particularly confused for this period.

[145]The Municipality under the Terror consisted of nineteen shopkeepers, seventeen artisans, three surgeons, four *agriculteurs*, and twelve others. See *A.M.*, L-4327. As M.T. Lagasquié as pointed out in "Etude sur les terroristes toulousains" (D.E.S., University of Toulouse, 1962), not all supporters of the Terror were of modest means. But this did not alleviate the situation as far as the barristers were concerned, for the richer men were considered "demagogues."

[146]Jean Sentou, *Fortunes et groupes sociaux à Toulouse sous la Révolution* (Toulouse, 1969), p. 265. Groussac had replaced the Seneschal Court magistrate Derry, whose family had purchased an estate worth 550,000 livres. See Jean Bastier, "La féodalité au siècle des lumières dans la région de Toulouse," 2 vols. (thesis, University of Toulouse, 1970), 1: 38.

[147]*L'Anti-Terroriste, ou Journal des principes*, no. 83 (8 Pluviôse, an V), "Table des Terroristes." The four were Maynard, Meilhon, Double, and Corail.

[148]Verieu, Tissinier, Maynard, and Double were active supporters of the Jacobin regime. See Jean Beyssi, "Le parti Jacobin à Toulouse sous le Directoire," (D.E.S., University of Toulouse, 1946), pp. 64–72, 175, 193, 211. But note that Beyssi was clearly mistaken in thinking Bragouse and Romiguières were Jacobins (p. 79). In addition, there were a few barristers who seemed to be republicans without being Jacobins: Guion, Londois, Gratian, and perhaps Loubers.

[149]*A.D.*, L-283–344, lists and dossiers of suspects and detained.

THE REVOLUTIONARY BARRISTERS

Who were the barristers who broke with the majority of their colleagues and supported, even led, the Revolution? And what motivated them to do so? If it were possible to identify these barristers with a particular socioeconomic or ideological category, their backgrounds would indicate the kinds of tensions that engendered revolutionary activity. However, the prorevolutionary barristers had not been a group of malcontents, with special social or ideological grievances, prior to 1789. In fact, they constituted a fair cross-section of the bar in 1789 and their profile differed only marginally from that of their colleagues. The revolutionary movement reflected the diversity of the bar itself—as did the counterrevolutionary movement.

Despite the slander of the *Quatre Evangélistes*, the fifty-four barristers who participated in the Revolution had been well-established, respectable professionals before 1789. Their mean age was surely above 40, for they had been practicing for an average of 19.4 years.[150] As table VI-1 indicates, their age profile was similar to that of the bar as a whole. Though older barristers were more likely to be actively counterrevolutionary, senior pleaders were by no means absent from the other side.[151] By all other measures, the prorevolutionary group seemed well-integrated into the legal world. They lived in the legal quarter of Toulouse, and 72 percent of them were natives of the city. Nearly 40 percent were sons of men who had been attached by profession to the courts of Toulouse. It appears that these barristers revolted against a world in which they had been entrenched, like their counterrevolutionary colleagues, by long practice, residence, and family ties.

In level of wealth, too, the supporters of the Revolution hardly differed from their colleagues. Their average fortune of 41,200 livres was slightly above the mean for the entire bar. And, as table VI-2 demonstrates, the revolutionary advocates came nearly proportionately from all economic levels.[152] The actively counterrevolutionary advocates were not quite so representative, for they did not include the more

---

[150]They were, thus, about the same average age as the men in the National Convention. See Patrick, *Men of First Republic*, p. 248.

[151]Using the chi-square test, the probability of there being no significant difference between all barristers and the prorevolutionary ones was quite high (50 percent). There was, however, a statistically significant difference (at the .05 level) between all barristers and the counterrevolutionary ones.

[152]The chi-square test demonstrates a strong fit between all barristers and the prorevolutionary ones (.80 percent probability of no significant difference). The counterrevolutionary group was less representative of the entire bar, but the difference was not statistically significant.

TABLE VI-1.   Duration of Careers and Attitudes toward the Revolution

Year Entered Profession	All Barristers[a]		Prerevolutionary		Counter-revolutionary	
	No.	%	No.	%	No.	%
Before 1760	39	17.0	6	12.5	22	35.0
1760-1779	140	60.8	32	66.5	31	49.1
1780-1789	50	22.2	10	21.0	10	15.9
Total	229	100.0	48	100.0	63	100.0

Source: *Almanach historique de la province de Languedoc* (1789), list of barristers with year of inscription on *matricule*.

[a] The barristers at the minor courts had to be excluded since the dates they entered the bar were unknown.

TABLE VI-2.   Level of Fortune and Attitude toward the Revolution

Wealth (thousands of livres)	All Barristers		Prerevolutionary		Counter-revolutionary	
	No.	%	No.	%	No.	%
0-15	35	15.2	8	22.8	1	2.3
15-30	78	33.9	12	34.3	13	29.5
30-50	52	22.6	8	22.8	13	29.5
50-75	39	17.5	4	11.4	11	25.0
75+	25	10.8	3	8.7	6	13.7
Total	229	100.0	35	100.0	44	100.0

Sources: See Table II-4 for sources.

humble barristers at the minor courts. The counterrevolutionary agitation of 1790 was the work of the Parlement personnel, and support was apparently not sought beyond their legal community.

In regard to professional status and career prospects, the prorevolutionary barristers had been a decidedly favored group before 1789. Table VI-3 demonstrates that many supporters of the Revolution had had at least respectable practices, and several had been true masters of the bar. The claim that marginal members of the profession were dangerous malcontents, advanced by commentators on the Revolution since Edmund Burke, seems disproved here.[153] The caseless barristers at the Parlement were frequently men from well-to-do families who had been more concerned with preserving their status than with pursuing successful careers; they probably perceived the Revolution as a disrup-

[153]Edmund Burke, *Reflections on the Revolution in France* (New York: Doubleday, 1961), pp. 54-57. Note, too, the remarks of a deputy, Adrien Duquesnoy, about so many of his fellow deputies enjoying "a small reputation as members of the small bars of their small towns" in his *Journal sur l'Assemblée Constituante, 3 mai, 1789-3 avril, 1790*, ed. Robert de Crevecoeur, 2 vols. (Paris, 1894), 1: 57.

TABLE VI-3.   Professional Status and Attitude toward the Revolution

Status	All Barristers		Prorevolutionary		Counter-revolutionary	
	No.	%	No.	%	No.	%
Obscure	115	40.0	5	10.9	8	13.5
Respectable	65	22.6	13	27.8	24	41.4
Potential Leaders	12	4.2	9	19.8	3	4.5
Leaders	23	8.0	5	10.9	15	26.2
Non-inscribed	11	4.0	3	6.2	6	10.2
Non-Parlement	61	21.2	11	24.4	2	4.2
Total	287	100.0	46	100.0	58	100.0

Source: A.D., B–registers of audiences of the Parlement.

tive force that destroyed their way of life. The few caseless barristers of the Parlement who supported the Revolution were the poor ones, like François Double and Jean Marie Theule, both of whom had private fortunes of less than 20,000 livres. The Revolution even failed to rally the advocates who formed the lower branch of the profession, those at the minor tribunals. The Constituent Assembly suppressed their courts and their livelihoods. These barristers apparently did not see the Revolution as offering new opportunities; or perhaps the more respected barristers from the other courts used their superior reputations, contacts, and new public functions to monopolize the reduced volume of legal business in the city.[154] In any case, obscure barristers may have identified themselves as the victims, not the beneficiaries, of the new order.

The Revolution appealed much more to the successful advocates, especially those who were young and rising. Masters of the bar were at least proportionately represented in the prorevolutionary group. Their younger colleagues who had been on the verge of important careers were the most revolutionary group among the Toulousan barristers. Some of these (Mailhe, Roques, Janole, Rouzet) had risen from modest backgrounds to successful professional situations, with eventual ennoblement a distinct possibility for them. So, far from being a movement supported by "failures," the Revolution strongly attracted the most upwardly mobile element among the barristers.

The cleavage at the Toulousan bar did not even cut neatly across the barrier that motivated so much revolutionary rhetoric, the noble-commoner divide. The percentage of noble barristers who supported the Revolution was slightly higher than the percentage of prorevolutionary men at the bar as a whole. There were thirty-six noble

---

[154]I have found only two barristers of the minor courts out of forty-seven who actively supported the Revolution.

barristers in 1789, and nine served the new order.[155] This is probably a reflection of the fact that *anoblis* were as thoroughly excluded from the aristocracy as their *roturier* colleagues. It demonstrates, too, how the rhetoric of the Revolution failed to fit social relations in Toulouse.

The prorevolutionary advocates were, thus, fairly representative of the entire bar in their socioeconomic background; and, far from having suffered under the Old Regime, they had enjoyed solidly respectable careers. Some had even experienced enviable success. Furthermore, we cannot identify the prorevolutionary barristers as those who were "enlightened" or ideologically disaffected prior to 1789. The advocates with the widest intellectual horizons, contacts, and achievements were on both sides of the revolutionary cleavage. Six of the twelve barrister-academicians were active in the counterrevolution. Indeed, Jamme and Gez were leading conspirators against the Republic after 1794.[156] Their colleagues Gouazé and Labroguières of the scientific academy renounced chairs at the Law Faculty rather than swear allegiance to the Revolution. On the other hand, Mailhe and Barère were both important revolutionaries, while their colleagues in the Academy, Verny, Castillon, and Floret gave support to at least the first stages of the Revolution.[157]

The Revolution failed to win the support of many who had called for enlightened humanitarian or economic reforms, even though the revolutionary assemblies promised and effected these changes. Criminal law reformers and proponents of physiocratic legislation seem to have been much more numerous at the Toulousan bar than supporters of the Revolution. Three advocates who had publicly urged legal change—Gez, Besaucelle, and Jamme—opted for tradition in the most pronounced manner after 1789. Even Théodore Sudre, the barrister whom Voltaire praised for his skillful defense of Jean Calas and a man who was a leader of the Conference of Charity (with Duroux and Barère), opposed the revolutionary movement. Moreover, membership in Masonic lodges or religious fraternities did not in any way forecast the political choice a barrister made in 1789. The revolutionary barristers had supported the same reforms, read the same books, and

[155]These were Dupuy, Gary, Laviguerie, Maynard, Taverne, Desazars, Gary (junior), Turle-Labrepin, and Clausolles. Dubernard was either the son or a nephew of a capitoul. Several other prorevolutionary barristers, like Purpan and Rigaud, had claimed noble status.

[156]Louis de Santi, "Notes et documents sur les intrigues royalistes dans le midi de la France de 1792 à 1815," *Mémoires de l'Académie des sciences . . . de Toulouse* 4, ser. 2 (1916), p. 68.

[157]On Verney, see Philippe Poitevin, *Mémoires pour servir à l'histoire des Jeux Floraux*, 2 vols. (Toulouse, 1815), 2: 376-83. Castillon served as librarian of the Royal (later, National) *Collège* until 1793. One more academician, Martel, was an old, blind man by 1789.

joined the same associations as had their counterrevolutionary colleagues.

Perhaps it should not be surprising that the prorevolutionary advocates were typical of the bar as a whole and had no special reasons to deplore the established order. This conforms with what we know about their engagement in revolutionary politics: they were carried along by the tide of events to support an upheaval they had not anticipated, with consequences they had not desired. And the cleavage at the Toulousan bar did not separate reactionary from radical or the supporters of noble privilege from the social levelers. Rather, the great cataclysm split a group of men with a fairly uniform social and cultural outlook. The major issue dividing the barristers concerned the tactics and immediate consequences of revolution. For many barristers shortsightedness, personal loyalty to the magistrates, fear of social disorder, or mistaken notions about the meaning and direction of events determined their opposition to the revolutionary movement. The barristers at the Seneschal Court were provided with a firmer sense of direction, because the Revolution reinforced a conflict that had long engaged them. But only a minority of their colleagues at the other courts possessed the grasp of events, opportunistic drive, or political acumen to break with their past.

Personal factors, then, matters of individual situation and temperament, determined how barristers faced the choices which the Revolution thrust upon them. To identify the individual contingencies and traits that brought the fifty-four barristers to the support of the new order is impossible, for the documents rarely reveal personal nuances, and barristers with remarkably similar background characteristics took opposing stances in 1789.[158] It is important to note, too, that their break with the Old Regime was not always a sudden or spontaneous one. Barristers did not emerge in numbers as leading patriots until November 1789, and their support of the upheaval was frequently a result of careful deliberation, not an immediate identification with revolutionary goals. The distinguished consultant Laviguerie, for example, weighed matters for several days before declining an invitation to serve the parlementaires as their special deputy at Versailles and giving his support to the new order.[159] Some took much longer to choose a side. Janole, who became a leading republican in 1792, was involved with counterrevolutionary activity until quite late. In April of 1790 he

[158]To illustrate this, consider the cases of Jean Laviguerie and Théodore Delort. Both were wealthy, distinguished consultants and sons of capitouls. They had both been admitted to the Maupeou Parlement and were both expelled in 1775. Yet Delort supported the counterrevolution and Laviguerie became a revolutionary officer in 1790.

[159]Auguste Albert, *Eloge de Laviguerie* (Toulouse, 1844), pp. 27–30.

attended the public assembly supporting Duroux. Noting this association, the Jacobin Club denied him membership for over a year.[160] And Janole was not the only prorevolutionary to have supported Duroux in 1790; so had Arbanere and Chas.[161] Calculated self-interest may have been one basis of their conversions, but this did not preclude a sincere adoption of revolutionary goals and a commitment to serve the new order.[162] It seems clear that many barristers pondered two alternatives, both of which seemed viable: to move back to a defense of the Parlement or forward to an undefined future, fraught with possible dangers and rewards. The first months of the Revolution threw the bar into confusion, and the emergence of a sizeable group of patriots was by no means inevitable.

Most barristers thought that the correct decision was to oppose or withdraw from the new political and institutional order. The Revolution threatened to destroy a valued way of life, creating intense fear and social dislocation. Barristers soon abandoned the reforms they had considered briefly in that hopeful spring of 1789, but they lamented the passing of the Old Regime for generations thereafter.[163]

[160]Garrigues, *Janole*, pp. 9-13.

[161]*Délibérations des citoyens actifs de Toulouse assemblés au nombre de plus de 150.*

[162]Despite appearances, Janole seems to have been a sincere if vehemently anti-Jacobin republican. (See Beyssi, "Parti Jacobin," pp. 211-41). Accused of having taken part in the royalist insurrection of the Year VIII, he was apparently cleared of the charge. See *A.D.*, L-2285, petition of Janole.

[163]David Higgs, *Ultraroyalism in Toulouse from Its Origins to the Revolution of 1830* (Baltimore, 1973), p. 84. Most barristers were ultraroyalists during the Bourbon Restoration.

VII

CONCLUDING REMARKS

To the chagrin of nearly all Toulousan barristers, revolutionary or counterrevolutionary, theirs was one of the very few important cities to remain under Jacobin domination during the Directory. Former federalists like Janole and Gary reappeared in public life and combatted the Jacobin municipality with such vehemence that they were easily taken for royalist sympathizers. The whole Toulousan bar undoubtedly took heart when Napoleon came to power and ended the "anarchy" of Jacobinism. The barristers showed their appreciation by rallying to the Napoleonic regime. Even pronounced counterrevolutionaries concluded that Bonapartist law and order deserved support, at least until the Bourbons could be restored. Jamme emerged from hiding to become rector of the University of Toulouse. Furgole and Duroux *fils* accepted magistracies at the civil court.[1]

Although a few counterrevolutionaries did return to honorable positions, most passed into obscurity, unrewarded for their fidelity to the parlementaires. In the end, the beneficiaries of the Revolution proved to be the moderate revolutionaries, those who had accepted the Republic but had dissociated themselves from Jacobinism. Such barristers—Desazars, Flottes, Mousinat, and others—were placed in honorable public positions by the succeeding regimes, Napoleonic and Bourbon alike.[2] Gary's son became a baron of the Empire, and Loubers, once a modest advocate at the Seneschal Court, presided over the Civil Tribunal after the Restoration.[3] Those who had refused to anchor themselves to any one regime did well, for in the revolutionary period flexibility was rewarded above all else.

---

[1]For Furgole and Duroux, see *Calendrier de Toulouse pour l'an X de la République française* (Toulouse, 1802); p. 59; for Jamme, see Armand Pratviel, "La réorganisation des Jeux Floraux en 1806," *Revue des pyrénées* 18 (1906): 208-9.

[2]David Higgs, *Ultraroyalism in Toulouse from Its Origins to the Revolution of 1830* (Baltimore, 1973), p. 131 and *passim*.

[3]Jules Villain, *La France moderne. Grand dictionnaire généalogique, historique, et biographique (Haute-Garonne et Ariège)*, 4 vols. (Montpellier, 1911), 2: 554-5; *A.D.*, J-926, papers of Loubers family.

183

It seems strange that there was so much shortsightedness and so little flexibility at the Toulousan bar after 1789. Why did the barristers perceive the Revolution as a threat, a source of dislocation? Was this not a Revolution made by men like themselves in Paris in the name of "commoners"? It was, to be sure, but Toulousan society (and, probably, much of French society) was not structured in such a way that broad appeals to "the Third Estate" could evoke a uniform response—even within the narrow stratum of the well-to-do. Frenchmen in the same general legal and economic categories, like Seneschal Court officers and barristers, had very different interests, loyalties, and political traditions; these differences were significant in 1789.

The men we have studied had stronger identities as "barristers" than as "commoners." They confronted the revolutionary events not as autonomous individuals but as a group whose responses, leadership, frames of reference, and loyalties were shaped by its particular interests and by past experiences. The barristers' ties to the aristocracy of magistrates were strong and were reinforced by shared interests (both material and psychological) in preserving the integrity of the Parlement. Furthermore, the barristers' social isolation strengthened their professional *esprit* and inhibited a consideration of other interest alignments. It was as such a group that the Toulousan advocates faced the events of 1789. The result was that they were particularly sensitive to the destructive elements of the Revolution, remained oblivious to its long-term advantages for themselves as individuals, and retreated to a defense of the Old Regime. A more realistic political response would have required wider loyalties, greater individualism, and more self-assertiveness than the barristers' social habits permitted. The minority who did possess independence of judgment and the capacity to identify with "commoners" supported the new order and joined the "revolutionary bourgeoisie," which was just emerging as a political entity.

Most barristers at the Parlement probably wished to forget that they had lent their support to commoners in that "war between the Third Estate and the other two orders" about which Mallet du Pan wrote in January of 1789. By attacking privileges and by advocating a stronger voice for the Third Estate at Versailles, the barristers had cooperated in the destruction of the Old Regime. Their action had not arisen from a sense of social oppression, though; nor was it a response to career frustrations or to resentments caused by blocked channels of social advancement.[4] Instead, most of these barristers were guided by new

---

[4]There are several reasons for believing that changing rates of social mobility were unimportant in explaining the barristers' role in the initial stages of the Revolution. On the one hand, their high level of mobility into the *noblesse* did not inhibit the barristers from attacking privileges. Conversely, complete exclusion from the Parlement failed to

attitudes concerning privilege and merit and by the fear that France could not be properly reformed without a commanding role for the Third Estate in the Estates-General.[5] This political stance did not preclude a continued attachment to Old Regime elites and institutions.[6] The barristers followed the revolutionary movement only so far as it suited their interests as *avocats au Parlement*; beyond this point, most withdrew their support.

The legal men who were most animated by a sense of social antagonism and who led the attack on the local aristocracy were the personnel of the Seneschal Court. Their long-standing conflict with the Parlement was, evidently, an important impetus for revolt. Before 1789, this discord corresponded only imperfectly to "noble-commoner" divisions, and it was hardly a matter of opposing privilege on abstract or philosophical grounds. But it did create a tradition of contention with the aristocracy, and in 1789 this corporate conflict fused with the nationwide attack on the "privileged orders." Ultimately, it proved a more potent force for revolutionary mobilization than did enlightened attitudes or exclusion from the Parlement.[7]

The social and political cleavages within the Toulousan legal community—both before and after 1789—belie attempts to generalize about the barristers on a national level.[8] The many deputies in the Constituent Assembly who came from the bars of provincial France must have reflected the multiplicity of interests, opinions, and loyalties within this professional category. Jean Baptiste Viguier could not have been the only advocate to leave the assembly in disgust with its work. On the other hand, the very process by which deputies were selected ensured the presence of a disproportionately large number of outspoken barristers like Barère or Robespierre, men who had long been conspicuous on the local level for their talents, ambition, and

---

attenuate the attachment of many barristers to this court and to the magistrates. And as we have observed, the Revolution most readily attracted the successful, rising advocates. Demands for careers open to talent, as expressed in the cahiers, seemed to reflect rising expectations, not frustrated ones.

[5]Thus, this case study supports George V. Taylor's argument that the origins of the Revolution were essentially political. See his article "Noncapitalist Wealth and the Origins of the French Revolution," *American Historical Review* 72 (1967): 469–96.

[6]As late as the end of November, 1789, Duroux addressed "Nosseigneurs of the National Assembly," requesting them to preserve a Parlement in Toulouse. See his petition in *A.M.*, AA-95.

[7]John McManners has written of a similar kind of corporate tension in his brilliant *French Ecclesiastical Society under the Ancien Régime: A Study of Angers in the Eighteenth Century* (Manchester, 1960), chap. 8. I have borrowed from his model of conflict between canons and *curés*.

[8]A collective biography of the men in the National Assembly would be an important contribution to the study of the French Revolution. Hopefully, this work provides an understanding of the socioprofessional context from which at least a fourth of the deputies were drawn.

bold speculation. Advocates in the left wing of the Constituent Assembly had often practiced before nonsovereign courts outside the provincial capitals.[9] Moreover, all these barristers, as deputies, were removed from local influences and placed in contact with new men and ideas in the capital, where their political preferences and options appeared in a new light. By deciding to settle the struggle against privilege and absolutism outside the framework of traditional institutions and legal relations, the deputies rejected their professional identities along with their loyalties to their provinces and to their courts. For many, pleading became a defunct occupation to which they would never return.[10] The new France they were about to create had no place for those black-robed men who claimed mastery of an obscure and labyrinthine law.

[9]According to Philip Dawson, *Provincial Magistrates and Revolutionary Politics in France, 1789-1795* (Cambridge, Mass., 1972), p. 238, there were seventy-seven former *avocats* in the "patriot" minority of deputies in 1791 (totaling 287 altogether). Sixty-five came from outside the *villes parlementaires*, twenty-seven of them from cities without *bailliage* courts.

[10]See Alison Patrick, *The Men of the First French Republic* (Baltimore, 1972), p. 268.

APPENDIX
Barristers in Public Office during the Revolution

The following list of revolutionary officials has been constructed from a wide variety of manuscript and printed sources (see the note below). Though every effort has been made to double-check the sources for mistakes or omissions, they inevitably occurred. Key documents were often incomplete or missing, and homonyms sometimes imposed insuperable problems. Nevertheless, this list can be regarded as a reasonably complete one that accurately reflects the office-holding patterns of the Toulousan barristers during the Revolution.

I JUDICIAL OFFICES
    A.   Civil Tribunal of the District of Toulouse
        1790:   Verieu, Bragouse, Arbanere, Romiguières, Taverne, Boubée, Gary (Alternates: Loubers, Guion, Faure, Roques)
        1791:   Bragouse, Guion, Loubers, Boubée, Loubet, Janole, Gary
        1792:   Loubers, Roques, Gary, Janole (later Romiguières, Clausolles)
        1793:   Loubers, Guion, Janole, Roques, Clausolles
        Year II: Guion, Clausolles, Londois, Gratian, Gleizes
        Year III: Guion, Londois, Janole, Loubers, Romiguières, Valette
        Year IV: Gratian, Janole, Dupuy, Guion, Loubers, Londois, Clausolles (alternate: Double)
        Year V: Guion, Loubers, Dupuy, Tissinier, Roques
        Year VI: Guion, Loubers, Londois, Clausolles, Roques

    B.   Criminal Tribunal–Department of the Haute-Garonne
        1791:   Arbanere, Dubernard, Loubet
        1792:   Arbanere, Dubernard, Loubet
        1793:   Unknown
        Year II: No barristers of Toulouse (Hugueny, from Beaumont; Capelle, from Faget)
        Year III: Bragouse, Flottes
        Year IV: Bragouse, Flottes (alternate: Valette)
        Year V: Gratian, Janole, Londois
        Year VI: Gratian, Tissinier, Malpel *fils*, Janole

    C.   Justices of the Peace
        1791:   Loubet, Tissinier, Faure (later, Gleizes)
        1792:   Tissinier, Gleizes
        1793:   Tissinier, Gleizes, Faure

Year II: Corail, Mathieu (Assessor-Double)
Year III: Dupuy, Faure, Tissinier, Dubernard
Year IV: Tissinier, Faure, Maynard
Year V: No barristers
Year VI: No barristers

   D.   Law School
      Professors: Rouzet, Bec, Loubers, Clausolles, Turle-Labrepin (later, Maynard)
      Agrégés: Janole, Soulié, Corail, Meilhon

   E.   Bureau of Conciliation
      1791:   Rouzet, Desazars, Clausolles
      1792:   Loubers, Rouzet, Clausolles
      1793:   Gleizes, Gratian
      Year II: Dubernard, Londois
      Year III: Gary, Laviguerie, Gratian

II   MUNICIPAL OFFICES
      1790:   Mayor–Rigaud
           Councilmen–Bragouse, Gary, Romiguières, Malpel, Dupuy
           Notables–Rouzet, Laviguerie, Cassagnere
           Attorney–Dupuy
      1791:   Mayor–Rigaud
           Councilmen–Rouzet, Theule
           Notables–Unknown
           Attorney–Dupuy
      1792:   Mayor–Not a barrister (Derrey, former Seneschal Court officer)
           Councilmen–Desazars, Baras *fils*
           Notables–Loubeau, Tissinier, Loubet, Janole, Arbanere
           Attorney–Dupuy (substitute: Corail)
      1793:   Mayor–Not a barrister (Derrey)
           Councilmen–No barristers
           Notables–Loubeau, Tissinier, Loubet, Janole, Arbanere, Rouzet, Gleizes
           Attorney–Dupuy (substitute: Corail)
      Year II: Mayor–Not a barrister (Groussac, retail merchant)
           Councilmen–Dupuy
           Notables–Corail, Mathieu (?), Dorliac *fils* (?)
           Attorney–Londois
      Year III: Mayor–Not a barrister (I. Cames, attorney)
           Councilmen–Lafage, Bellomaire
           Notables–Laviguerie, Londois, Guion
           Attorney–Gary *fils*
      Year IV: Mayor–Not a barrister (Roussillon, merchant)
           Councilmen–Bellomaire, Roques
           Notables–Laviguerie, Guion
           Attorney–Gary *fils* (later, Verieu)

III   ADMINISTRATION OF THE DEPARTMENT
    1790:   Attorney-General Syndic: Mailhe
                 Councilmen-Romiguières, Pelleport, Dorliac, Purpan
    1791:   Attorney-General-Syndic: Malpel
                 Councilmen-Pelleport, Rouzet
    1792:   Attorney-General-Syndic: Malpel
                 Councilmen-Pelleport
    1793:   Unknown
    Year II: Attorney-General-Syndic: Not a barrister (Descombels)
                 Councilmen-No barristers
    Year III: Attorney-General-Syndic: Gratian (later, Gary *fils*)
                 Councilmen-Lafage, Pons de Vié, Gary, Clausolles,
                 Bragouse

IV   ADMINISTRATION OF DISTRICT
    1790:   Attorney-Syndic: Malpel
                 Councilmen-No barristers
    1791:   Attorney-Syndic: Rouzet
                 Councilmen-Roques
    1792:   Attorney-Syndic: Rouzet
                 Councilmen-No barristers
    1793:   Attorney-Syndic-Not a barrister (Lespinasse, former noble)
                 Councilmen-Baras
    Year II: Unknown
    Year III: Attorney-Syndic-Not a barrister (Lespinasse)
                 Councilmen-Ruotte, Tissinier, Loubers

V   DEPUTIES TO NATIONAL ASSEMBLIES
    Constituent: Viguier, Mousinat, Barère (for Bigorre), Hebrard (as
                 alternate)
    Legislative: Dorlac, Mailhe, Theule
    Convention: Mailhe, Pérès, Rouzet, Barère, Solomiac (for Tarn?)
    Council of 500:   Pérès, Mailhe, Verieu

Sources: *A.D.*, L-39, -45, -51, -77, -80, -102, -103, -205, -2578, -4244, -4553; 208 U-1 -2, 208 U-26 -27; *A.M.*, 2 I-14; BB-61; 1 D-1 -2; *Journal universel et affiches de Toulouse* (1790-1792); *L'Anti-Terroriste* (Year III-Year V); works by Connac, Luc, Madoul, Beyssi, and Lagasquié, as cited in bibliography.

BIBLIOGRAPHY

I. MANUSCRIPTS

A. Departmental Archives of the Haute-Garonne

Series B—Registers of *audiences* of the Chambers of Parlement (1740-90); registers of *audiences* of the Seneschal Court; registers of the *Cour des Monnaies*; registers of the *officialité*; seigneurial justice; registers of the royal letters of provision; registers of civil decrees; remonstrances of Parlement

Series C—Administrative correspondence; tax rolls (*vingtième* of 1750); *dénombrements*

   2C—Registers of control (*insinuation, centième dernier*)

Series E—Deliberations of the Community of Attorneys (*Procureurs*); papers of the brotherhoods of Penitents (Black, White, Grey, Blue)

   3E—Notarial registers; arbitration papers; separated testaments; inventories-after-death

Series J—Loubers family papers; Clavière family papers

   3J—Papers of family d'Hautpoul

   4J—Papers of family Riquet de Bonrepos

   7J—Papers of family Barbot

Series L—Administrative correspondence; papers concerning justice, elections, police, royalist insurrection, personnel; dossiers of those suspected and detained; deliberations of popular society; deliberations of administrative bodies; certificates of *civisme*

Series M—Personnel of Consulate; justice

Series U—Registers of *audiences* of the Civil Tribunal of the district of Toulouse; registers of Civil Tribunal of the department; registers of criminal tribunal

B. Municipal Archives of Toulouse

Series AA—Papers relating to the election of deputies to the Estates-General

Series BB—Deliberations of municipal councils (until 1790)

Series CC—Tax rolls (*capitation*)

Series D—Deliberations of municipal councils (after 1790)

Series G—Declarations of the Forced Loan; rolls of the *Quart* tax; real-estate tax rolls (*contribution foncière*)

Series I—Registers of denunciations; registers of oaths by public functionaries

Series K—Tax roll for St. Etienne (1 K-6); papers relating to the elections

Series S—Inventories of property of *émigrés*

191

C. Departmental Archives of the Hautes-Pyrénées
    Fonds Barère-Laisse 31

D. Bibliothèque Nationale
    Fonds maçonnique—Lodges of Toulouse, XVIIIe Century

E. Municipal Library of Toulouse
    MSS 1182-1185—documents relating to Toulousan Freemasonry
    MS 1324—Notes of Louis de Santi on Rouzet
    MS 1026—Legal notes of Jamme (1806)
    MSS 704-706—"Heures perdues" of Pierre Barthès

II. PRINTED SOURCES

A. Almanacs
    Almanach historique de la province de Languedoc. 1780-1790.
    Almanach historique de la ville de Toulouse. 1780-1785.
    Almanach historique et chronologique de Languedoc et des provinces du ressort du Parlement de Toulouse. 1752.
    Calendrier de la Cour de Parlement pour l'année 1739.
    Calendrier de Toulouse. 1750-1790.
    Calendrier de Toulouse pour l'an X de la République.

B. Newspapers
    Affiches, annonces, et avis divers de Toulouse et du Haut Languedoc. 1789.
    Affiches, annonces et avis divers, ou Feuille hebdomadaire de Toulouse. 1775-1776.
    L'Anti-Terrorist, ou Journal des principes. 21 février, 1795—8 septembre, 1797.
    Journal de Toulouse, l'Observateur républicain, ou l'Anti-royaliste. 21 Thermidor, an II—23 Thermidor, an VIII.
    Journal révolutionnaire de Toulouse, ou le Surveillant du midi. 13 octobre, 1793—4 août, 1794.
    Journal universel et affiches de Toulouse et du Languedoc. 6 janvier, 1790—10 juillet, 1793.
    Les Quatre Evangélistes, ou Supplément aux actes des apôtres. Nos. 4-12, n.p., n.d.

C. Works by Toulousan Barristers
    Aguier. *Recueil d'arrêts notables, ou Supplément au journal du Palais de Toulouse.* 2 vols. Nîmes, 1782.
    Barère, Bertrand. *Eloge de Jean-Baptiste Furgole, avocat au Parlement de Toulouse.* n.p., n.d.
    Discours prononcé par M. Duroux, avocat au Parlement, et Capitoul, dans l'Assemblée tenue pour le Tiers Etat de la ville de Toulouse le 10 mars, 1789. n.p., n.d.
    Dorliac, Guillaume Louis. *Opinion sur les droits féodaux.* Paris, 1792.
    Duroux fils, Joseph Marie. *Observations pour le sieur Jean Calas.* n.p., 1762.
    Furgole, Jean Baptiste. *Traité de la seigneurie féodale universelle et du franc-alleu naturel.* Paris, 1767.

——. *Traité des testamens, codicilles, donations à cause de mort et autres dispositions de dernière volonté.* . . . 4 vols. Paris, 1745–1748.

Gez, Jean Joseph. *Discours adressé (le 9 mars, 1783) à une société d'avocats au Parlement de Toulouse sur son projet d'une Conférence de Charité.* n.p., 1783.

Histoire et mémoires de l'Académie royale des sciences, inscriptions, et belles lettres de Toulouse. Toulouse, 1782–1790.

Jamme, Alexandre Augustin. *Aux maire, et officiers municipaux, aux autorités constitués, aux comités de surveillance.* n.p., n.d.

——. *Lettre des avocats au Parlement de Toulouse à Monseigneur le Garde des Sceaux, sur les nouveaux édits transcrits . . . dans les registres du Parlement, le 8 mai, 1788.* n.p., n.d.

Lacroix, Pierre Fermin. *Lettres d'un philosophe sensible.* Paris, 1769.

Lavaysse, David. *Mémoire de M. David Lavaysse . . . pour le sieur Lavaysse, son troisième fils.* Toulouse, n.d.

Laviguerie, Jean Baptiste. *Arrêts inédits du Parlement de Toulouse.* 2 vols. Toulouse, 1831.

Lettre d'un avocat au Parlement de Toulouse à un avocat au Parlement de Paris au sujet de l'arrêt par lequel le Parlement a prorogé sa séance. n.p., n.d.

Mailhe, Jean Baptiste. *Avis aux français.* Paris, an VII.

Pasquier, Félix, ed. *Notes et réflections d'un bourgeois de Toulouse au début de la Révolution d'après des lettres intimes.* Toulouse, 1917.

Poitevin-Peitari, Philippe. *Mémoires pour servir à l'histoire des Jeux Floraux.* 2 vols. Toulouse, 1815.

Raynal, Jean. *Histoire de la ville de Toulouse.* Toulouse, 1759.

Recueil de plusieurs pièces d'éloquence et de poésie présentées à l'Académie des Jeux Floraux. Toulouse, 1760–1790.

Rodier, Marc-Antoine. *Questions sur l'ordonnance de Louis XIV du mois d'avril, 1667 relatives aux usages des cours de Parlement et principalement de celui de Toulouse.* Toulouse, 1769.

Rouzet, Jacques Marie. *Lettre de M. Rouzet, avocat, à un de ses amis.* n.p., 1790.

——. *Projet de Constitution française.* Paris, 1793.

——. *Opinion concernante le judgement de Louis XVI.* Paris, 1792.

Soulatges, Jean Antoine. *Coutumes de la ville, gardiage, et viguerie de Toulouse.* Toulouse, 1770.

——. *Observations sur les questions notables du droit décidées par divers arrêts du Parlement de Toulouse.* Toulouse, 1784.

——. *Traité des crimes.* 2 vols. Toulouse, 1762.

Sudre, Théodore. *Mémoire pour le sieur Jean Calas.* Toulouse, n.d.

——. *Traité des droits seigneuriaux de Boutaric.* Toulouse, 1757.

D. Published correspondence, memoirs, official documents, contemporary tracts

Adher, J., ed. *Recueil de documents sur l'assistance publique dans le district de Toulouse de 1789 à 1800.* Toulouse, 1918.

Aldeguier, J.-B.-A. d'. *Histoire de la ville de Toulouse depuis la conquête des romains jusqu'à nos jours.* 4 vols. Paris, 1835.

Alembert, Jean d'. "Essai sur la société des gens de lettres et des grands."
    In *Mélanges de littérature, d'histoire, et de philosophie,* vol. 1. Amster-
    dam, 1760.
Barbier, E. J. F. *Journal historique et anecdotique du règne de Louis XV.*
    4 vols. Paris, 1847-1856.
Berryer, Pierre Nicolas. *Souvenirs de M. Berryer.* 2 vols. Paris, 1839.
Boucher d'Argis, Antoine-Gaspard. *Règles pour former un avocat.* Paris,
    1778.
Brette, Armand, ed. *Recueil de documents relatifs à la convocation des
    Etats Généraux de 1789.* 4 vols. Paris, 1894-1915.
Brissot, Jean Pierre. *Un indépendant à l'ordre des avocats sur la déca-
    dence du barreau en France.* Berlin, 1781.
Camus, Armand-Gaston. *Lettre sur la profession d'avocat, sur les études
    relatives à cette profession, et sur la manière de l'exercer.* Paris, 1777.
*Délibérations des citoyens actifs de Toulouse assemblés au nombre de
    plus de 150 . . . (le 12 avril 1790).* n.p., n.d.
Despeisses, Antoine. *Oeuvres . . . où toutes les plus importantes matières
    du droit romain sont méthodiquement expliquées et accommodées au
    droit français.* 3 vols. Toulouse, 1778.
Duquesnoy, Adrien. *Journal sur l'Assemblée Constituante, 3 mai 1789-
    3 avril 1790,* edited by R. de Crevocoeur. 2 vols. Paris, 1894.
Ferrière, Claude. *Dictionnaire de droit et de pratique.* 2 vols. Toulouse,
    1779.
Gauret, Jaques. *Stile universel de toutes les cours et jurisdictions du
    royaume pour l'instruction des matières civiles.* Paris, 1716.
Gayot de Pitaval, François. *Causes célèbres et intéressantes.* Amsterdam,
    1775.
*Journal de ce qui s'est passé à l'occasion du rétablissement du Parlement
    de Toulouse dans ses fonctions.* n.p., n.d.
*Journal du Palais, ou Recueil de plusieurs arrêts remarquables du Parle-
    ment de Toulouse.* 2 vols. Toulouse, 1758.
*Lettre d'un habitant de Toulouse à un habitant de Rabastens, du 30 mars,
    1789.* n.p., n.d.
Ligou, Daniel, ed. *Cahiers de doléances du Tiers Etat du pays et jugerie de
    Rivière-Verdun.* Paris, 1961.
Linguet, Simon Henri. *Nécessité d'une réforme dans l'administration de la
    justice et dans les loix civiles en France.* Amsterdam, 1764.
Marais, Mathieu. *Journal et mémoires sur la régence et la règne de Louis
    XV.* 4 vols. Paris, 1864.
Marmontel, Jean-François. *Oeuvres complètes, I-II: Mémoires.* Paris,
    1818-1820.
Martin, Henri, ed. *Documents relatifs à la vente des biens nationaux.*
    Toulouse, 1916.
Michon, Georges, ed. *Correspondance de Maximilien et Augustin
    Robespierre.* Paris, 1926.
Pasquier, Félix, and Galabert, F., eds. *Cahiers paroissiaux des séné-
    chausée de Toulouse et de Comminges en 1789.* Toulouse, 1928.
*Procès-verbal de l'assemblée des citoyens actifs de la ville de Toulouse
    (18-20 avril 1790).* n.p., n.d.

Procès-verbal de l'assemblée générale de tous les ordres et corporations formant le Tiers Etat de la ville et banlieu de Toulouse, le 19 janvier 1789. n.p., n.d.

Puis, Augustin ed. *Une famille de parlementaires toulousains à la fin de l'Ancien Régime. Correspondance du Conseiller d'Albis de Belbèze.* Paris, 1913.

Recueil de toutes les pièces qui constatent ce qui s'est passé au Parlement de Toulouse le 3 mai jusqu'au 20 octobre, 1788. n.p., 1789.

Table par lettre alphabétique, des citoyens . . . qui ont signé dans Toulouse l'adhésion aux protestations de la minorité des représentants . . . sur le décret du 13 avril, et à la fanatique et incendiaire délibération des soi-disant Catholiques de Nîmes. n.p., n.d.

Le Toulousain à Versailles, chargé de présenter au roi . . . doléances de ses concitoyens. n.p., n.d.

Tournier, Clément, ed. *Le Mesmérisme à Toulouse, suivi de lettres inédites sur le XVIIIe siècle d'après les archives de l'Hôtel du Bourg.* Toulouse, 1911.

Voltaire (François-Marie Arouet). *Correspondence.* Edited by Theodore Besterman, 107 vols. Geneva, 1953–1965.

E. Genealogies

Bremond, Alphonse. *Nobiliaire toulousaine.* 2 vols. Toulouse, 1863.

Roton, Robert de. *Les arrêts du Grand Conseil portant dispense du marc d'or de noblesse.* Paris, 1951.

Villain, Jules. *La France moderne. Grand dictionnaire généalogique, historique, et biographique (Haute-Garonne et Ariège).* 4 vols. Montpellier, 1911.

III. SECONDARY WORKS

A. Works on law and legal institutions

Bar, Carl Ludwig. *A History of Continental Criminal Law.* Boston, 1916.

Bastard-d'Estang, Vicomte d'. *Les Parlements de France. Essai historique.* 2 vols. Paris, 1857.

Bastier, Jean. "L'affaire Sirven devant la justice seigneuriale de Mazamet." *Revue historique de droit français et étranger* 49 (1971): 601–11.

Bouwsma, William J. "Lawyers and Early Modern Culture." *American Historical Review* 78 (1973): 303–27.

Brissaud, Jean. *A History of French Private Law.* Boston, 1912.

Cauvière, Henri. *L'idée de codification en France avant la rédaction du code civil.* Paris, 1910.

Chenon, Emile. *Les anciennes facultés des droits de Rennes (1735–1792).* Rennes, 1890.

Church, William F. "The Decline of the French Jurists as Political Theorists." *French Historical Studies* 5 (1967): 1–40.

Curzon, Alfred de. *L'enseignement du droit français dans les universités de France aux XVIIe et XVIIIe siècles.* Paris, 1920.

Delbèke, Baron Francis. *L'action politique et sociale des avocats au XVIIIe siècle.* Paris and Louvain, 1927.

Esmein, Adhémar. *Histoire de la procédure criminelle en France et spécialement de la procédure inquisitoire depuis le XIIe siècle jusqu'à nos jours.* Paris, 1882.

Forsyth, William. *Hortensius, an Historical Essay on the Office and Duties of an Advocate.* London, 1879.

Fouchier, Charles de. *Règles de la profession d'avocat à Rome et dans l'ancienne législation française.* Paris, 1895.

Fournel, Jean. *Histoire des avocats au Parlement et du barreau de Paris.* 2 vols. Paris, 1813.

Imbert, Jean. *Histoire du droit privé.* Paris, 1966.

Kelly, Donald. "Fides Historiae: Charles Dumoulin and the Gallican View of History." *Traditio* 22 (1966): 347–402.

Lefebvre, Charles. *Cours de doctorat sur l'histoire du droit civil français. L'ancien droit des successions.* 2 vols. Paris, 1918.

Lepaulle, Pierre. "Law Practice in France." *Columbia Law Review* 50 (1950): 945–58.

Levy-Bruhl, Henri. *Sociologie du droit.* Paris, 1971.

Mackrell, John. "Criticism of Seigneurial Justice in Eighteenth-Century France." In *French Government and Society, 1500–1850.* Edited by J. F. Bosher. London, 1973.

Maillet, J. "De l'exclusion coutumière des filles dotées à la rénunciation à succession future dans les coutumes de Toulouse et Bordeaux." *Revue d'histoire de droit français et étranger* 30 (1952): 514–45.

Merryman, John Henry. *The Civil Law Tradition.* Stanford, 1969.

Moore, Wilbert E. *The Professions: Roles and Rules.* New York, 1970.

Ourliac, Paul, and Malafosse, J. *Histoire du droit privé,* 3 vols. Paris, 1968.

Paquin, Pierre. *Essai sur la profession d'avocat dans les duchés de Lorraine et de Bar au XVIIIe siècle.* Paris, 1961.

Parsons, Talcott. "A Sociologist's View of the Legal Profession." *Conference on the Profession of Law and Legal Education,* pp. 49–64. Chicago, 1952.

Regnault, Henri. *Les ordonnances du Chancelier D'Aguesseau.* Paris, 1938.

Rodière, Animé. *Les grands jurisconsultes.* Toulouse, 1874.

Sagnac, Philippe. *La législation civile de la Révolution française.* Paris, 1898.

Timbal, Pierre. *Droit romain et ancien droit français.* Paris, 1960.

——. "La succession testamentaire dans la coutume de Toulouse." *Annales de la Faculté de droit d'Aix* 43 (1950): 283–306.

——. "La dévolution successorale 'ab intestat' dans la coutume de Toulouse." *Revue d'histoire de droit français et étranger* 33 (1955): 51–82.

——. "L'esprit du droit privé au XVIIe siècle." *Dix-septième siècle,* nos. 58–59 (1963), 30–39.

Viollet, Paul. *Histoire du droit civil français.* Paris, 1893.

B. General works on the Old Regime and studies of regions other than Toulouse

Acomb, Francis. *Anglophobia in France, 1763–1789.* Durham, 1950.

Agulhon, Maurice. *Pénitents et francs-maçons de l'ancienne Provence (essai sur la sociabilité méridionale)*. Paris, 1968.

———. *La vie sociale en Provence intérieure au lendemain de la Révolution*. Paris, 1970.

Ariès, Philippe. *Centuries of Childhood: A Social History of Family Life*. Translated by Robert Baldick. New York, 1962.

Babeau, Albert. *Les bourgeois d'autrefois*. Paris, 1886.

Barber, Elinor. *The Bourgeoisie in 18th Century France*. Princeton, 1955.

Barral, Pierre. "Un siècle de maçonnerie grenobloise (1750-1830)." *Cahiers d'histoire* 2 (1957): 373-94.

Bien, David D. "La réaction aristocratique avant 1789: l'example de l'armée." *Annales: économie, société, civilisation* 29 (1974): 23-48, 505-34.

Bluche, François. *Les magistrats du Parlement de Paris au XVIIIe siècle*. Paris, 1960.

Bouchard, Marcel. *De l'humanisme à l'Encyclopédie: essai sur l'évolution des esprits dans la bourgeoisie bourguignonne*. Paris, 1929.

Carrière, Charles. "Le recrutement de la Cour des comptes, aides, et finances d'Aix-en-Provence à la fin de l'ancien régime." In *Actes du 81e congrès national des sociétés savantes. Rouen-Caen*, pp. 141-59. Paris, 1956.

Cocatre-Ziligien, André. "Les doctrines politiques des milieux parlementaires dans la seconde moitié du XVIIIe siècle." *Annales de la Faculté de droit de Lille*, 1963, pp. 33-155.

———. "Un génie méconnu du XVIIIe siècle: l'avocat Linguet," *Annales africaines de la Faculté de droit de Dakar*, 1960, pp. 83-122.

Darnton, Robert. "Reading, Writing, and Publishing in Eighteenth-Century France," *Daedalus* 100 (Winter 1971): 214-256.

———. "The *Encyclopédie* Wars of Prerevolutionary France." *American Historical Review* 78 (1973): 1331-52.

Daumard, Adeline. *La bourgeoisie parisienne de 1815 à 1848*. Paris, 1963.

——— and Furet, François. *Structures et relations sociales à Paris au milieu du XVIIIe siècle*. Paris, 1961.

Deyon, Pierre. *Amiens, capitale provinciale*. Paris, 1967.

Doyle, William. "The Parlements of France and the Breakdown of the Old Regime." *French Historical Studies* 6 (1970): 415-57.

———. "Was There an Aristocratic Reaction in Pre-Revolutionary France?" *Past and Present*, no. 57 (1972), pp. 97-122.

Echeverria, Durand. "The Pre-Revolutionary Influence of Rousseau's *Contrat Social.*" *Journal of the History of Ideas* 33 (1972): 543-60.

Egret, Jean. *Le Parlement de Dauphiné et les affaires publiques dans la deuxième moitié du XVIIIe siècle*. 2 vols. Grenoble, 1942.

———. *Louis XV et l'opposition parlementaire, 1715-1774*. Paris, 1970.

Flammermont, Jules. *Le Chancelier Maupeou et les Parlements*. Paris, 1883.

Ford, Franklin L. *Robe and Sword. The Regrouping of the French Aristocracy after Louis XIV*. Cambridge, Mass., 1953.

Ghestin, J. "L'action des Parlements contre les mésalliances au XVIIe et XVIIIe siècles." *Revue historique de droit français et étranger* 34 (1956): 74-110, 196-224.

Goblot, Edmond. *La barrière et le niveau. Etude sociologique sur la bourgeoisie française moderne.* Paris, 1925.

Gossman, Lionel. *Medievalism and the Ideologies of the Enlightenment: The World and Work of LaCurne de Sainte-Palaye.* Baltimore, 1968.

Henry, Louis. "The Population of France in the Eighteenth Century." In *Population in History,* edited by D. V. Glass and D. E. C. Everley, pp. 434-56. London, 1965.

———. *Anciennes familles genèvoises.* Paris, 1956.

Hufton, Olwen. *Bayeux in the Late Eighteenth Century.* Oxford, 1967.

Julia, Dominique. "Le clergé paroissial dans le diocèse de Reims à la fin du XVIIIe siècle," *Revue d'histoire moderne et contemporaine* 13 (1966): 195-216.

Kafker, Frank. "A List of Contributors to Diderot's *Encyclopédie.*" *French Historical Studies* 3 (1963): 106-22.

Katz, Wallace. "Le Rousseauisme avant la Révolution." *Dix-huitième siècle* 3 (1971): 205-22.

Labrousse, Camille Ernest. *La crise de l'économie française à la fin de l'ancien régime.* Paris, 1943.

———. *Esquisse du mouvement des prix et des revenus en France au XVIIIe siècle.* 2 vols. Paris, 1933.

Lefebvre, Georges. *Etudes orléanaises.* 2 vols. Paris, 1962.

Léonard, Emile G. *L'armée et ses problèmes au XVIIIe siècle.* Paris, 1958.

Ligou, Daniel. "Etude fonctionnelle de la population de Montauban à la fin de l'ancien régime." In *Actes du 86e congrès national des sociétés savantes. Montpellier,* pp. 579-89. Paris, 1962.

———. "La Franc-maçonnerie française au XVIIIe siècle." *L'information historique* 1964, mai-juin, pp. 98-110.

McManners, John. *French Ecclesiastical Society under the Ancien Régime. A Study of Angers in the Eighteenth Century.* Manchester, 1960.

Mornet, Daniel. *Les origines intellectuelles de la Révolution française.* Paris, 1933.

———. "Les enseignments des bibliothèques privées (1750-1780)." *Revue d'histoire littéraire de la France* 17 (1910): 449-97.

Mousnier, Roland. "D'Aguesseau et le tournant des ordres aux classes sociales," *Revue d'histoire économique et sociale* 49 (1971): 449-64.

Muller, Dominique. "Les magistrats et la peine de mort au 18e siècle." *Dix-huitième siècle* 4 (1972): 79-107.

Proust, Jacques. *L'Encyclopédisme dans le Bas-Languedoc au XVIIIe siècle.* Montpellier, 1968.

Reinhard, Marcel. "Elite et noblesse dans la seconde moitié du XVIIIe siècle." *Revue d'histoire moderne et contemporaine* 3 (1956): 4-37.

Robin-Aizertin, Régime. "Franc-maçonnerie et lumières à Semur-en-Aurois en 1789." *Revue d'histoire économique et sociale* 43 (1965): 234-41.

——. "La loge 'Concorde' á l'orient de Dijon." *Annales historiques de la Révolution française* 41 (1969): 433–46.

——. *La société française en 1789: Semur-en-Auroix.* Paris, 1970.

Trénard, Louis. *Lyon, le l'Encyclopédie au préromantisme.* 2 vols. Grenoble, 1958.

Vovelle, Michel. "Bourgeois, rentier, propriétaire: éléments pour la définition d'une catégorie sociale à la fin du XVIIIe siècle." In *Actes du 84e congrès national des sociétés savantes. Dijon,* pp. 419-52. Paris, 1959.

Weulersse, Georges. *Les Physiocrates.* Paris, 1931.

C. Works on Toulousan society and institutions in the Old Regime

Adher, J. *Les confréries de Pénitents de Toulouse avant 1789.* Toulouse, 1897.

Albert, Auguste. *Eloge de Laviguerie.* Toulouse, 1844.

Amilhau, Henry. *Nos premiers présidents du Parlement de Toulouse.* Toulouse, 1882.

Astre, Florentin. *Les procureurs près le Parlement de Toulouse.* Toulouse, 1858.

——. *Les arrêtistes du Parlement de Toulouse.* Toulouse, 1856.

Augustin, Jean-Marie. "Les capitouls, juge des causes criminelles et de police à la fin de l'ancien régime." *Annales du midi* 84 (1972): 183-211.

Barada, J. "Toulouse et la vie toulousaine de 1786 à 1822 d'après des correspondances contemporaines." *Annales du midi* 44 (1932): 41-78.

Barranguet, P. "Les confréries dans le diocèse de Toulouse au milieu et à la fin du XVIIIe siècle." In *Dixième congrès d'études de la Fédération des sociétés académiques et savantes, Languedoc-Pyrénées-Gascogne.* Toulouse, 1956, pp. 293-302.

Bastier, Jean. "La féodalité au siècle des lumières dans la région de Toulouse." 2 vols. Thesis, University of Toulouse, 1970.

Benech, Raymond. *De l'enseignement du droit français dans l'ancienne Université de Toulouse.* Toulouse, 1847.

Bien, David D. *The Calas Affair: Persecution, Toleration, and Heresy in Eighteenth-Century Toulouse.* Princeton, 1960.

Biographie toulousaine, ou Dictionnaire historique. 2 vols. Paris, 1823.

Bordeur, André. "Les magistrats toulousains non-parlementaires à la fin de l'ancien régime." D.E.S., University of Toulouse, 1967.

Calas, F. P. *Histoire de la loge L'Encyclopédique de Toulouse depuis sa création en 1787 jusqu'à ce jour.* Toulouse, 1887.

Castan, Yves. "Mentalité rurale et urbaine à la fin de l'ancien régime dans le ressort du Parlement de Toulouse d'après les sacs à procès criminels (1730-1790)." Thesis, University of Toulouse, 1961.

Casteras, Paul de. *La société toulousaine à la fin du XVIIIe siècle.* Toulouse, 1891.

Chalande, Jules. *Histoire des rues de Toulouse.* 3 vols. Toulouse, 1913.

Chaussinaud-Nogaret, Guy. *Les financiers de Languedoc au XVIIIe siècle.* Paris, 1970.

Coppolani, Jean. *Toulouse, étude de géographie urbaine.* Toulouse, 1954.

Crebassol, G. "Le Parlement Maupeou à Toulouse." D.E.S., University of Toulouse, 1949.

Degert, Antoine. "La Jansénisme au Parlement de Toulouse." *Bulletin de littérature ecclésiastique* 25 (1924): 260-334, 338-52.

Douais, Célestin. *L'Académie des sciences, inscriptions, et belles-lettres de Toulouse au dix-huitième siècle.* Toulouse, 1896.

Dubédat. Jean-Baptiste. *Histoire du Parlement de Toulouse.* 2 vols. Paris, 1885.

Duboul, Axel. *Les deux siècles de l'Académie des Jeux Floraux.* 2 vols. Toulouse, 1901.

Dutil, Léon. *L'état économique du Languedoc à la fin de l'ancien régime.* Paris, 1911.

―――. "La réforme du capitoul toulousain." *Annales du midi* 19 (1907): 305-63.

Engelmann, Gérard. "Etude démographique d'un village de la commune de Toulouse: Pourvoirville (1756-1798)." *Annales du midi* 77 (1965): 427-33.

Forster, Robert. *The Nobility of Toulouse in the Eighteenth Century.* Baltimore, 1960.

Frêche, Georges. "Dénombrement de feux et d'habitants de 2973 communautés de la région toulousaine." *Annales de démographie historique,* 1968, pp. 389-421; 1969, pp. 393-471.

Gadave, René. *Les documents sur l'histoire de l'Université de Toulouse.* Toulouse, 1910.

Godechot, Jacques, and Moncassin, Suzanne. "Structures et relations sociales à Toulouse en 1749 et en 1785." *Annales historiques de la Révolution française* 37 (1965): 129-67.

Gros, J. "Les loges maçonniques à Toulouse (de 1740 à 1870)," *La Révolution française* 40 (1901): 234-70.

Jourdain, Charles. "L'Université de Toulouse au dix-septième siècle." *Revue des sociétés savantes des départements* 8 (1862): 314-35, 406-35.

Lacroix, M. de. "Pierre Fermin de Lacroix, avocat au Parlement de Toulouse." *Revue des pyrénées* 20 (1908): 528-48; 21 (1909): 97-123.

Lamouzèle, Edmond. *Essai sur l'administration de la ville de Toulouse à la fin de l'ancien régime.* Paris, 1910.

―――. *Toulouse au XVIIIe siècle d'après les "Heures perdues" de Pierre Barthès.* Toulouse, 1914.

―――. "Le Parlement Maupeou à Toulouse et l'exile de l'ancien Parlement." *Revue des pyrénées* 19 (1907): 231-43.

Lapierre, Eugène. *Le Parlement de Toulouse, son ressort, ses attributions, et ses archives.* Toulouse, 1869.

―――. *Histoire de l'Académie.* Toulouse, 1905.

Larboust, Philippe de Peguilhan de. "Les magistrats du Parlement de Toulouse à la fin de l'Ancien Régime (1775-1790)." D.E.S., University of Toulouse, 1965.

Larnaudie, M.-L. "L'immigration à Toulouse de 1750 à 1775." D.E.S., University of Toulouse, 1969.

Lavergne, Géraud. "Un périgourdin capitoul de Toulouse: Jean-Léonard Gaillard." *Annales du midi* 49 (1937): 261-86.

Madrange, Alain. "Les avocats au Parlement de Toulouse de 1610 à 1715." D.E.S., Faculty of Law of Toulouse, 1966.

Marinière, G. "Les marchands d'étoffes de Toulouse à la fin du XVIIIᵉ siècle." *Annales du midi* 70 (1958): 251-308.

Mesple, Paul. *Vieux hôtels de Toulouse.* Toulouse, 1948.

Monbrun, Pierre-Joseph. "La lutte philosophique en province: les Jeux Floraux de Toulouse." *Bulletin de littérature ecclésiastique* 19 (1918): 135-47, 197-217, 265-82; 20 (1919): 266-84; 22 (1921): 285-307; 23 (1922): 161-81, 280-95; 24 (1923): 115-32.

———. "Les Jeux Floraux et Jean Jacques Rousseau." *Bulletin de littérature ecclésiastique* 4 (1912): 311-25.

Muller, Dominique. "Médecins et chirurgiens à Toulouse de 1740 à 1830." D.E.S., University of Toulouse, 1961.

Ousset, P. E. *La confrérie des Pénitents bleus de Toulouse.* Toulouse, 1927.

Rives, Jean. "L'évolution démographique de Toulouse au XVIIIᵉ siècle." *Bulletin d'histoire économique et sociale de la Révolution française* (1968): 85-146.

Rodière, Animé. "L'enseignement du droit à·la Faculté de droit de Toulouse." *Recueil de législation de Toulouse* 15 (1866): 210-41.

Rozy, Henri. "Un conflit en 1782 entre le capitoulat de Toulouse et le Parlement." *Mémoires de l'Académie des sciences . . . de Toulouse* 7 (1875): 479-98.

Sentou, Jean. *Fortunes et groupes sociaux à Toulouse sous la Révolution.* Toulouse, 1969.

———. "Impôts et citoyens actifs à Toulouse au début de la Révolution," *Annales du midi* 61 (1948): 152-79.

Sicard, Germain. "Société et comportement juridique: une enquête sur les contrats de mariages au XIXᵉ siècle." *Annales de la Faculté de droit de Toulouse* 18 (1970): 245-52.

Sicard, Roger. *L'administration capitulaire sous l'ancien régime.* Toulouse, 1952.

Soulié, Joseph. *Le coup d'état judiciaire du Chancelier Maupeou et le barreau toulousain de XVIIIᵉ siècle.* Toulouse, 1896.

Thore, Pierre-Henri. "Essai de classification des catégories sociales à l'intérieur du Tiers Etat de Toulouse." *Actes du 71ᵉ congrès national des sociétés savantes. Toulouse, 1953,* pp. 149-65. Paris, 1954.

Thoumas-Schapira, Micheline. "La bourgeoisie toulousaine à la fin du XVIIIᵉ siècle." *Annales du midi* 67 (1955): 313-29.

Tragans. "Eloge de M. Jamme," *Recueil de l'Académie des Jeux Floraux,* 1819, pp. 27-40.

Vives de Regie, Roger de. *Les femmes et la société de nos derniers parlementaires toulousains.* Toulouse, 1901.

Wolff, Philippe. *Histoire de Toulouse.* Toulouse, 1961.

D.   General works on the Revolution

Andrews, Richard M. "The Justices of the Peace of Revolutionary Paris, September 1792-November 1794 (Frimaire Year III)." *Past and Present,* no. 52 (August 1971), 56-105.

Bouton, André. *Les francs-maçons Manceaux et la Révolution française.* Le Mans, 1958.

Brinton, Crane. *The Anatomy of Revolution*. New York, 1952.
———. *The Jacobins*. New York, 1930.
Carré, Henri. *La fin des Parlements (1788–1790)*. Paris, 1912.
Cavanaugh, Gerald J. "The Present State of French Revolutionary Historiography: Alfred Cobban and Beyond." *French Historical Studies* 7 (1971): 587–606.
Cobban, Alfred. *The Myth of the French Revolution*. London, 1955.
———. *The Social Interpretation of the French Revolution*. Cambridge, 1965.
Dawson, Philip. *Provincial Magistrates and Revolutionary Politics in France, 1789–1795*. Cambridge, Mass., 1972.
Egret, Jean. *La Pré-Révolution française*. Paris, 1962.
———. "Les origines de la Révolution en Bretagne." *Revue historique* 213 (1955): 189–215.
———. "La Pré-Révolution en Provence." *Annales historiques de la Révolution française* 26 (1954): 97–126.
———. "La révolution aristocratique en Franche-Comté et son échec," *Revue d'histoire moderne et contemporaine* 1 (1954): 245–71.
Furet, François. "Le catéchisme révolutionnaire." *Annales: économie, société, civilisation* 26 (1971): 255–86.
Gershoy, Leo. *Bertrand Barère, A Reluctant Terrorist*. Princeton, 1962.
Giraud, Emile. *L'oeuvre d'organisation judiciaire de l'Assemblée nationale constituante*. Paris, 1921.
Godechot, Jacques. *Les institutions de la France sous la Révolution et l'Empire*. Paris, 1951.
———. *La contre-révolution, doctrine et action, 1789–1804*. Paris, 1961.
Grivel, Albert. *La justice civile dans le District de Montpellier en 1790–91*. Montpellier, 1928.
Hampson, Norman. *A Social History of the French Revolution*. London, 1963.
Lefebvre, Georges. *The Coming of the French Revolution*. Translated by R. R. Palmer. Princeton, 1947.
Ligou, Daniel. "A propos de la révolution municipale." *Revue d'histoire économique et sociale* 38 (1960): 146–77.
Lucas, Colin. "Nobles, Bourgeois, and the Origins of the French Revolution." *Past and Present*, no. 60 (Aug., 1973), 84–126.
McDonald, Joan. *Rousseau and the French Revolution*. London, 1964.
Martin, Gaston. *La Franc-Maçonnerie française et la préparation de la Révolution*. Paris, n.d.
Palmer, Robert R. "Polémique américaine sur le rôle de la bourgeoisie dans la Révolution française," *Annales historiques de la Révolution française* 39 (1967): 369–80.
Patrick, Alison. *The Men of the First French Republic*. Baltimore, 1972.
Richet, Denis. "Autour des origines idéologiques lointaines de la Révolution française: élites et despotisme." *Annales: économie, société, civilisation* 24 (1969): 1–23.
Schafer, Boyd. "Quelques jugements de pamphlétaires sur le clergé à la veille de la Révolution." *Annales historiques de la Révolution française* 16 (1939): 110–22.

Shulim, Joseph I. "The Youthful Robespierre and his Ambivalence toward the Ancien Régime." *Eighteenth-Century Studies* 5 (1972): 398–420.

Taylor, George V. "Revolutionary and Non-Revolutionary Content in the Cahiers of 1789." *French Historical Studies* 7 (1972): 479–502.

——. "Non-Capitalist Wealth and the Origins of the French Revolution." *American Historical Review* 72 (1967): 469–96.

Tocqueville, Alexis de. *The Old Regime and the French Revolution.* Translated by S. Gilbert. New York, 1955.

Woloch, Isser. *Jacobin Legacy. The Democratic Movement under the Directory.* Princeton, 1970.

E.   Works on the Revolution in Toulouse

Adher, J. "Lettres de Barère à Mailhe." *La Révolution française* 68 (1904): 78–80.

Albert, Madeleine. *Le fédéralisme dans la Haute-Garonne.* Paris, 1932.

Archès, Pierre. "Les origines du conventionnel toulousain Jacques-Marie Rouzet." *Annales du midi* 83 (1971): 431–39.

Baudens, G. "Les brochures et l'état des esprits à la veille de la Révolution." *Recueil de législation de Toulouse* 6 (1910): 283–379; 7 (1911): 323–411; 9 (1913): 297–393.

Beyssi, Jean. "Le Parti Jacobin à Toulouse sous le Directoire." D.E.S., University of Toulouse, 1946.

Bouglon, Baron R. de. *Les reclus de Toulouse sous la Terreur.* 3 vols. Toulouse, 1912.

Bouyoux, Pierre. "Les 'six cents plus imposés' du département de la Haute Garonne en l'an X." *Annales du midi* 70 (1958): 317–27.

Connac, Emile. *Histoire de la Révolution à Toulouse et dans le département de la Haute-Garonne.* Toulouse, 1902.

Delpa, Claude. "Etude du niveau intellectuel des émigrés toulousains (d'après les inventaires de bibliothèques)." D.E.S., University of Toulouse, 1959.

Donat, J. "L'Université de Toulouse et les Etats Généraux de 1789." *Annales du midi* 49 (1937): 286–304.

Duboul, Axel. *La fin du Parlement de Toulouse.* Toulouse, 1890.

——. *Le tribunal révolutionnaire de Toulouse.* Toulouse, 1894.

Garrigues, Damien. *Jean Joseph Janole, magistrat toulousain.* Toulouse, 1930.

Higgs, David. *Ultraroyalism in Toulouse from Its Origins to the Revolution of 1830.* Baltimore, 1973.

Lacouture, Joseph. *Le mouvement royaliste dans le Sud-Ouest, 1797–1800.* Toulouse, 1932.

Lagasquié, Marie-Thérèse. "Etude sur les terroristes toulousains." D.E.S., University of Toulouse, 1962.

Legoux, R. *Recherches sur la procédure civile appliqué à l'époque révolutionnaire par le Tribunal de District de Toulouse.* Toulouse, 1933.

Luc, Jean-Marie. "Le tribunal criminel de la Haute-Garonne, 1792–1799." D.E.S., University of Toulouse, 1947.

Madoul, J. "Les municipalités de Toulouse pendant la Révolution." *Recueil de législation de Toulouse* 59 (1906): 348–409.

Maury, Paule. *Le loyalisme révolutionnaire des autorités toulousaines.* Toulouse, 1939.

Pratviel, Armand. "La réorganisation des Jeux Floraux en 1806." *Revue des pyrénées* 18 (1906): 204-30.

Santi, Louis de. "Notes et documents sur les intrigues royalistes dans le midi de la France de 1792 à 1815." *Mémoires de l'Académie des sciences . . . de Toulouse* 4, ser. 2 (1916).

Sentou, Jean. *Les fortunes immobilières des toulousains et la Révolution française.* Paris, 1970.

Thore, Pierre-Henri. "L'union dans la lutte contre les Etats de Languedoc." *Actes du congrès regional des fédérations historiques de Languedoc,* pp. 225-42. Toulouse, 1952.

———. "Fédérations et projets de fédérations dans la région toulousaine." *Annales historiques de la Révolution française* 21 (1949): 346-68.

———. "Le Tiers Etat de Toulouse à la veille des élections de 1789." *Annales du midi* 65 (1953): 181-91.

Thoumas, Geneviève. "La jeunesse de Mailhe." *Annales historiques de la Révolution française* 43 (1971): 221-47.

Vié, Louis. *L'Université de Toulouse pendant la Révolution.* Toulouse, 1905.

INDEX

205

Library of Congress Cataloging in Publication Data

Berlanstein, Lenard R
    The barristers of Toulouse in the eighteenth century
(1740-1793)

    (Johns Hopkins University studies in historical and
political science; 93d ser., 1)
    Bibliography: pp. 191-204
    Includes index.
    1. Lawyers—Toulouse. 2. Toulouse—History.
I. Title. II. Series: Johns Hopkins University.
Studies in historical and political science ; 93d ser., 1.
Law   340'.094486   75-9784
ISBN   0-8018-1582-7